OCR Media Studies

for **A2**

Third Edition

Julian McDougall

HODDER
EDUCATION
ART OF HACHETTE UK

Author's acknowledgements

For Mike McDougall (Old Labour proper socialist), Lydia, Ned and Alex.

Special thanks in relation to this book go to Cathal Tierney, Steve Dixon, Stephen Bromberg, Georgia Sell, Pete Fraser, Keith Pearsall, Sophie Hughes, Ben Andrews, Paul Dodd, Jason Mazzocchi, Donna Cooper-Cliftlands, Clive Edwards, Wayne O'Brien, James Baker, Graham Stephenson, Hilary Dunphy and Lynda Howell.

More general recognition for inspiration and support is due to David Buckingham, David Gauntlett, Roy Stafford, Jenny Grahame, Andrew Burn, John Atkinson, Nick Lacey, Barney Oram, Matt Hills, the mysterious Dr Nick, Dave Trotman, John Wardle, Yahya Nakeeb, Richard Berger and Stan Tucker.

Orders: please contact Bookpoint Ltd, 130 Milton Park, Abingdon, Oxon OX14 4SB. Telephone: (44) 01235 827720. Fax: (44) 01235 400454. Lines are open from 9.00–5.00, Monday to Saturday, with a 24-hour message answering service. You can also order through our website www.hoddereducation.co.uk.

British Library Cataloguing in Publication Data
A catalogue record for this title is available from the British Library

ISBN: 978 0 340 958 711

First Published 2009
Impression number   10 9 8 7 6 5 4 3 2 1
Year   2015 2014 2013 2012 2011 2010 2009

Hachette UK's policy is to use papers that are natural, renewable and recyclable products and made from wood grown in sustainable forests. The logging and manufacturing processes are expected to conform to the environmental regulations of the country of origin.

Cover photo © Stockbyte/GettyImages
Typeset by Phoenix Photosetting, Chatham, Kent
Printed in Italy for Hodder Education, part of Hachette UK, 338 Euston Road, London NW1 3BH

Contents

Figures

Foreword

There has been a dramatic change in media in recent years. The rise of the Web and all manner of digital technology has shifted the ways in which media texts are produced and consumed almost beyond recognition. When I was taking my A-levels in the late 1970s, my school had just one video player, which took about 20 minutes to warm up! We listened to music in the common room on cassette tapes. My family had only recently acquired a house phone; previously, to call relatives, we had to go round the corner to a red phone box. When I started teaching in the mid-1980s, only half of my students had access to video at home, and the UK had only recently introduced a fourth TV channel. We had only one video camera and we had to carry around a big portable VHS player to plug it into whenever we wanted to film.

Fast forward a decade, and when I surveyed my classes in 1996, no-one had the Internet at home and only 1 per cent of students had even been on it. We had video cameras costing approximately £1000 each, and to edit we had to shuttle back and forth between two VHS machines. By then, we had Sky and cable TV, so we had much more choice of channels to watch. Most households had acquired a games console; the PS1 had just been released, taking graphics to a new level—but the first DVD player we bought in the late 1990s cost us over £300.

Now, almost 100 per cent of students at our college have a computer at home; only slightly fewer have broadband internet access; almost every student has a presence on the Web in the form of Facebook, MySpace or Bebo, and a significant proportion actually upload video to YouTube. I don't know anyone who doesn't have a mobile phone, most of which are equipped with cameras and MP3 players that hold several hundred songs, and that even play back videos and access the Internet.

For media teachers, the changes in media over the past few years have led to a radical re-think of the subject that you are studying. Much of what we used to watch on TV, we would be unlikely to have repeated. Now it is increasingly to be found online, breaking copyright on sites like YouTube or broadcast legitimately via programs like BBC iPlayer. DVD box sets mean that we can consume TV series like we used to read a book—in our own time, at a pace we choose. Everything we want to know about is, potentially, there at our fingertips via Google and Wikipedia, and now we can add our own thoughts for the world to read via blogging and our own creativity can be up there seen by thousands, even millions, of people.

A2 Media is about exploring all this. One part involves the creation of your own material for the coursework, gaining a more sophisticated sense of conventions, institutions, technologies and audiences. The other part is for the exam, where you reflect on your own experiences as a media producer and then look at the live debates about the media that characterise our times. From issues around the representation of social groups in collective identity to regulation of the media—censorship and control and grappling with debates like postmodernism—you will be considering the impact that all this change has had, is still having, and will continue to have for the future. We are in the Online Age, the global era of the media and, in some ways, we are becoming the producers of the media. All six topics that Julian considers in this book provide a framework for looking at how the media impacts upon our lives and how we engage with it.

This book is not about providing you with the answers: it is about raising the questions. The media texts that Julian uses should be seen as the starting point; when he wrote the book, they were fresh in the mind as texts that help to raise the issues of the time. By the time you read the book, there will be others with which you should be engaging, to test out the ideas and the issues raised by the A-level and by this book. Everything is relevant, everything can be questioned. That is your task as a media student.

Pete Fraser
September 2008

How to use this book

If you used the *OCR Media Studies for AS* book, you will be familiar with the structure used here. The majority of the book is devoted to Critical Perspectives in Media, the examined A2 unit. This is because the material covered in that unit is the most theoretical and the most varied. As well as a substantial chapter on each of the six **themes** (from which you may be studying more than one), there is a range of guidance and exemplary material to support your own critical reflections on production work, which forms the first part of the examination for Critical Perspectives.

There is a section on each of the Advanced Portfolio production briefs, with the emphasis on creative process and **media literacy**, rather than technical skill, as much of this was covered in the AS book, and the expectation is that A2 production work starts from those learned 'competences'.

The final section offers guidance for those of you who are considering making the step up to a media degree. As the author of this book is a Principal Examiner for OCR Media and also teaches in a university context, this should give you a clear and realistic sense of how undergraduate study will be different, and how your A2 studies will prepare you for this. While this part of the book is clearly optional, the introductory chapter on media literacy must not be ignored, as it is written with the intention of providing you with a '**metalanguage**' about media studies. Put simply, it will give you a good idea of what the 'point' of media studies is in the broadband era, and that can only help you study the subject and perform well at the assessment stage.

Throughout the book there are a range of images to illustrate both theoretical and practical elements of the subject. Where clear developmental work from the AS course is needed, **Synoptic link** boxes are included to flag up these links. **Case study** boxes offer specific **micro** examples for you to connect to the macro themes, theories and perspectives. **Activity** boxes give you ideas about how to take each theme area further, beyond the detail possible in a textbook like this, with so many areas to cover. And **Production tip** boxes will help you integrate theory and practice throughout your course, as it is crucial that you do not think of these as being isolated from each another. Each subsection of the book ends with a **Practice task**. For the Critical Perspectives exam, these are straightforward practice exam questions. For the Advanced Portfolio briefs, these are to help you with the evaluation of your outcomes.

The **Study resources** section should equip you with all the books, articles and websites you could possibly need to add value to your work and take each theme to another level. And the **Glossary** is there as a reference tool to support you with the more academic language and technical jargon that you will encounter on the journey.

Acknowledgements

The author and publishers would like to thank the following for allowing use of copyright materials:

1.2	AP/KABC-TV/PA Photos
2.1.1	Science Photolibrary
2.2.2	© Photos 12/Alamy
2.2.4	Author
3.3.1	Waseem Akbar
3.3.2	Sophie Hughes
4.1.1	© BBC
4.2.1	© Alex Tehrani/Corbis
4.2.2	Courtesy of Birmingham City Council
4.3.1 (a)	Courtesy of Cooking Vinyl
4.3.2	*Wikinomics* cover courtesy of Atlantic Books, printed with permission
4.3.3	© The Guardian, printed with permission
4.4.1	*We the Media* by Dan Gilmore. Copyright © 2004 O'Reilly Media, Inc. All rights reserved. Used with permission. See http://oreilly.com/catalog/9780596/02272
4.4.2	© Ken McKay/Rex Features
4.4.3	© 2005 Roger-Viollet/Topfoto
4.5.3	Courtesy of Henry Moltke
4.6.3	akg-images
4.6.4	© The Kobal Collection/Jet Tone
4.6.5	© HBO/Everett/Rex Features
4.6.6	The Ronald Grant Archive
4.6.7	Courtesy of Kudos Film and TV Ltd

1

Media literacy for A2

Media literacy is a relatively new term, but it is now widely used by educators, policymakers, regulators and media producers. Some people see it as a competence (you are media-literate or media-illiterate); others see it as a social practice (how we read and make media); and others see it as an entitlement (to protect us from potential danger associated with new media in particular). To get us started, here are the definitions of media literacy provided for this book by senior examiners from the OCR A level qualification. As these are the people who will ultimately assess your work, these contributions will be enlightening and will go some way towards equipping you with a metalanguage about media studies and what it is for.

The ability to create, use, analyse and understand media products, within the context of their audiences and institutions.

(Donna Cooper-Cliftlands)

A broader version of conventional **literacy**, which includes all visual, aural and **digital forms**, seeking to enable people to become more thoughtful producers and interpreters of media.

(Pete Fraser)

Media literacy can be defined as the ability to read a media **text**, in understanding the process of communication through the construction of an artefact and its sets of **representations**. The ability to read a media text, in its visual or audio form, is itself paramount to understanding the meaning that a text may convey, which is dependent upon the individual, **psychological** and **sociocultural** context of the reader.

(Jason Mazzochi)

Media literacy is the ability to understand how any media text constructs its meaning as much through its form as its content.

(James Baker)

Media literacy is being able to engage not just with the immediate content of a media text, but also to be able to apply knowledge and understanding of the institutional factors that have an impact on shaping the text itself and on the messages and values embedded within the text. Media literacy also involves knowledge and understanding of how different audiences in different times and places may interpret the text in different ways. Crucially, the media-literate reader of the text is able to see that his/her own reading of the text may well be at odds with that applied by some or all of the target audience.

(Wayne O'Brien)

Activity

Read the definitions of media literacy from the examiners above.

• What ideas about media literacy do they all seem to share?
• What ideas about media literacy are unique to particular examiners?
• How much agreement is there overall?
• Where does there seem to be disagreement?

Now produce your own three-sentence definition of media literacy to summarise the examiners' contributions.

Read through the assessment objectives for the OCR A2 Media Studies course reproduced here, and map the various aspects of your three-sentence definition against these printed objectives.

• *Use appropriate investigative and critical techniques to independently research and analyse a media theme and present the findings.*
• *Develop critical arguments about media issues and debates, evaluating contemporary ideas and applying knowledge of them to texts in order to illustrate the arguments.*
• *Originate and construct a media text, demonstrating technical skills, the ability to be creative and communicate meaning, and showing under-standing of concepts such as audience, genre, representation and form.*
• *Critically evaluate the process and outcome of their own media pro-duction, drawing on knowledge of media institutions, audiences and critical theories.*

How well does your definition match up overall against these assessment objectives?

In a book I wrote for teachers of media (called, without enigma, *The Media Teacher's Book*), I began with this quote from Steven Johnson (2005: xi), which I called an 'establishing shot' for media studies in the digital age.

> I see a progressive story: mass culture growing more sophisticated, demanding more cognitive engagement with each passing year. Think of it as a kind of positive brainwashing: the popular media steadily, but almost imperceptibly, making our minds sharper, as we soak in entertainment usually dismissed as so much lowbrow fluff.

This idea is the opposite of the way many people think about young people and digital culture. People often 'demonise' young people and their use of text language, digital television, MySpace and video games. Sometimes this is just because they are a bit jealous of youth and because it is a natural part of the ageing process that we believe that music, television, films and culture in general were somehow 'better' when we were teenagers. Nick Barham describes the 'disconnect' between games players and those who make assumptions about how the games are influencing them in this way.

> Modern entertainment fans have little respect or time for people who don't understand something, making comments about the effect that it has on the people who do understand it.

(Barham 2004: 284)

But there are also more serious concerns about the way that modern culture is 'saturated' by media and entertainment, and there are associated anxieties about losing control – of what people are doing, where they 'are' (**virtually**), how they are communicating (think of the POS code when a parent appears at the computer) and whether they are missing out on more 'enriching' culture – novels, plays, news and art. Johnson believes the opposite: that people are becoming more intelligent, 'sharper' and that we should not be worried. In his book, he celebrates the rich, multilayered nature of streamed television drama, the participatory nature of blogging and the intense motivational energy demonstrated by gamers.

Media studies is with Johnson on this one. The whole idea of the subject is to do with *you* creating digital media and developing a theoretical understanding of media in society – including your own media. The subject is relativist, which means there are no judgements to be made about which media texts and products are of more value than others, unlike English, which has a canon – a list of books which are labelled 'classic literature', seen as distinct from mere 'fiction'.

But as you move from AS to A2, it is essential that you understand the difference between just using and making media and being media-literate enough to qualify with an A level in the subject. To put it bluntly, your friends who are not 'doing media' might post **remix** or 'sweding' material on YouTube, watch *The Wire* and DJ, and they might have interesting things to say about these digital activities. But you, as an A2 Media Studies student, will be able to create media material that observes a set of **conventions** and has an informed, research-based **mode of address** for your **audience**; and you will be able to theorise your own media creativity and a range of existing commercial media texts and products, using such **academic** ideas as **postmodernism**, **democracy**, representation and **discourse**.

In the corresponding section in the AS book, we spent some time exploring the relationship between media literacy and more general forms of literacy, and distinguishing between a media-literate student and a member of the general public – in other words, the difference it makes doing media studies. For A2, we need a more developed theoretical understanding of how literacy is being 'reframed' by digital culture, so that you not only demonstrate – in your production work and theoretical research for Critical Perspectives – your own high levels of media literacy, but also offer an intellectual, academic and informed understanding of media literacy when you are reflecting on your creative outcomes and processes, and when you are answering questions about how the contemporary media and culture are 'read' in new ways.

You will be aware that, traditionally, literacy has been associated with reading and writing, and has usually been discussed in relation to deficit – people were seen to be literate or not. Those who were illiterate were a target group for educational programmes seeking to equip them with literacy. There was little discussion of levels of literacy or different types of literacy. You will find throughout this book that we return again and again to the idea that **web 2.0** – the second phase of the internet, defined as a new stage by the rapid increase of content and ideas being shared by ordinary people online – has made a big difference to how the media are distributed and exchanged. In relation to literacy, experts see web 2.0 as a profound historical shift in how people communicate, how they read and write, and what these things now mean. So web 2.0 leads to the concept of 'new literacies' (see Lankshear and Knobel 2006).

New literacies

In between the old-school idea of literacy as something you either have or do not have, and this new web 2.0 world, came a range of theories and strategies based on literacy as a social and **political** practice. Freire (1972) described how people are excluded from literacy and thus disempowered in relation to the social structure – in simple terms, if you cannot read and write, there are many things you cannot conceptualise, understand or participate in. Crucially, according to Freire, exclusion from literacy makes it very difficult for a person to develop a critical view of the world, so we can see from this that somebody who lacks literacy can be kept in place, oppressed, even controlled. So literacy is placed centre stage in the desire to promote social justice – to make the world a better place.

> Within Freire's approach to literacy, the process of learning to read and write words was an integral part of learning to understand how the world operates socially and culturally in ways that promote unequal opportunities and outcomes for different groups of people. Ultimately this was a starting point for participants to take action on the world in an attempt to change it in ways that would create social processes and relations that were more just. Groups would undertake cultural action for change in the world in the light of their understanding of their circumstances.
>
> (Lankshear and Knobel 2006: 9–10)

In terms of power, access and control, we can see in current debates about immigration and citizenship a range of ideas and tensions that Freire's contribution can help us to make sense of. The current government (Gordon Brown's Labour, at the time of writing) believes that people making a living or claiming benefit in the UK should learn to read, write and speak English in order to integrate into the host society. This understanding of literacy as inclusion places responsibility on the individual citizen: if you do not 'make the effort', you are excluding yourself from the 'values' of the country you have chosen to move to. This is articulated in relation to concerns about national security and threats of terrorism, the assumption being that people who do not 'join in' with the spoken language of the country are more likely to see themselves as outsiders, and those who do participate in language are less likely to see the host nation as an enemy, regardless of foreign policy or religious differences. So Freire and the current UK government share the belief that literacy is linked to social change, but the difference is that one side of this discussion sees literacy as a way out of social control – as empowering in a critical sense – while the other seems to see the 'obligation' of literacy as a form of social control, or at least as an aspect of social cohesion.

The same 'duality' can be seen at work in the recent attention given to media literacy, which is, of course, what interests us. Media literacy is seen as an empowering critical attribute, in Freire's sense – people can understand how the media are constructed, and then be more critical and strive for change or at least resist media influence. And it is also seen, by **Ofcom** – the regulatory body for the media in the UK – as a tool for creating more 'responsible' media consumers, as an alternative to **censorship**. The idea here is that media-literate citizens will self-regulate their use of media, so the chances of people being negatively affected by violent video games or urban rap music, for example, are reduced if the audience has the critical skills to 'decode' what they are seeing/hearing/reading/playing. Again, we have empowerment and social justice and social control all mixed up together in this discussion.

It gets more complicated when we start to consider James Gee's idea (2007) that people need to operate within several literacies to be successful in society, and that a higher level of literacy is achieved by those who understand how to use different literacies at different times – the development of a 'meta-understanding' of literacies as discourses. This skill he calls 'powerful literacy'. It is really a simple idea: discourse. If you listen to a football commentary, you will either immediately understand and respond to terms like 'keeping it tight', 'losing the shape' and 'stopping them playing', or you won't. So at this stage you are either included in or excluded by the discourse of football. But if you can switch from that discourse to another one – for example, a formal meeting at work – without thinking about it, then you are working with more than one literacy. And if you can reflect on one of those discourses by using the other, like we are doing here, then you have 'powerful literacy' – the ability to work between and to step outside of each literacy, to understand how it works as well as being able to use it. This is no different to the way a plumber is not only able to use a shower like everyone else, but also knows how the water pressure works; or how some of us know what to do when a computer crashes and some of us do not.

Language and literacy, then, are both tools for us to use and systems for us to understand. But one problem with this is that, in recent years, the word 'literacy' has been bolted on to virtually every area of human activity, and this is often done without much attention to these more complex aspects, as described by Gee. So we get emotional literacy, computer literacy, physical literacy and functional literacy. It is important when discussing any of these to keep in mind the range of ways of being literate that we have explored here, and not to go back to thinking of these literacies as things you have, need or can 'get' quickly. In a nutshell, literacy is social and it is practised in contexts – it cannot be learned or measured in isolation from social life and interaction.

So far we have thought about literacy as a **commodity** – you have it or you do not have it – as an aspect of integration into society, as a critical tool that leads to freedom, and as an element of social control. We have agreed as a fundamental point that literacy is social and that 'powerful literacy' is the ability to step outside of discourses and be critical about them. Now let us return to the idea that web 2.0 has changed everything.

Digital literacy

The internet generally, YouTube, social networking sites, on-demand media, video games, virtual worlds and MP3 are all cultural developments arising from technological change, and, it is argued, the cultural part of this relates to the new ways in which we communicate and participate now that were not possible before web 2.0. Going back to the political nature of literacy, in terms of inclusion and exclusion, digital literacy can be seen as a tool for reducing the 'digital divide', and thus as a social justice agenda. Some of these areas of activity have spawned their own literacy, so we can read about 'web literacy' and 'game literacy', but there tends to be a lack of clarity about what these digital literacies are all about. Is it just the ability to find information on websites quickly and accurately, or is it about protecting yourself from internet fraud or suspicious 'lurkers'? Is it about completing a video game by knowing how to 'read' the rules and the conditionality of the programming, or is it about protecting yourself from the dubious morality of *Grand Theft Auto IV*? Is it just about critically reading and understanding Facebook, YouTube and *Second Life*, or is it about creating material and sharing it? And how do these notions of new literacy relate to another broad area – creativity?

Memes and remix

There are very general ways in which people are communicating in new ways as an outcome of web 2.0, and there are highly specific examples, of which one is memes. A **meme** is 'a popular term for describing the rapid uptake and spread of a particular idea presented as a written text, image, language "move" or some other unit of cultural "stuff"' (Lankshear and Knobel 2006: 217).

There are new examples every day, but just one is the satirical remix video 'Read my lips Bush/Blair love song' posted on YouTube, viewed by a huge audience and then, crucially, disseminated across a range of more traditional media. A meme will communicate a particular idea, signified in an interesting and 'novel' way; it will assume a shared response from a cultural group and thus relate to a particular discourse about the world; and it will be exchanged widely through forms of social action and engagement – in simple terms, when people 'pass on' the meme, they will be reinforcing their own sense of the world. In the seminal book, *The Selfish Gene* (2006), Dawkins used the term 'meme' in relation to Darwinian principles of evolution, arguing that it is an aspect of human nature, related to survival instincts, that we will pass on ideas in various cultural contexts, just as a gene is circulated in biological terms. So it is no surprise that the term for online word-of-mouth **promotion**, intended or otherwise, is '**viral** marketing' – ideas spread through culture, like a virus spreads through a population.

Production Tip

Read the above, research some internet memes and then start your own. And to make it more interesting, talk to your teachers about how you might use a meme as part of your A2 Media Studies production work.

In the same vein, Dixon (2008: 14) explains how this seemingly (post)modern form of cultural practice is actually a new product of a much more established communication principle.

> In common usage, the neologism 'internet meme' refers to the propagation of a (often humorous) digital file from one person to others, much in the same way jokes and cartoons were photocopied in offices in the 70s and 80s. What is crucially different now is the means of propagation, allowing the meme to evolve through informal networks, even often engendering imitations or parodies of itself.

This, then, resonates again with our idea of literacies as social practices in contexts. Memes are just one example, along with sweded videos and fan montages, of people working within a remix culture, where media texts are constantly reworked and exchanged by consumers who instantly become producers.

Case study: The Rick Roll

There are countless memes created every day, so apologies if this one is out of date by the time this book is published. The Rick Roll was a meme that led innocent internet users to click on a link to a URL that they thought was of interest but which actually led to a video of Rick Astley performing 'Never gonna give you up' in the 1980s. More information about this meme can be found at www.urbandictionary.com/define.php?term=rickroll%27d (accessed August 2008) – but be careful not to get rickroll'd yourself in the research process!

Activity

In the web 2.0 spirit of this section, it is more illuminating for you to do this bit yourself, even though in a way this constitutes you doing the author's research for him!

- Enter 'remix culture' into Wikipedia and see where it takes you.
- Enter 'remix literacy' into Google and spend one hour of your life reading what you find and following the links. You should find some ideas by people like Henry Jenkins and James Gee along the way.
- Enter 'remix video' into YouTube and spend another hour watching what is there.
- Go back to Wikipedia and enter 'media literacy and remix culture'. If there is still no page there (there wasn't in May 2008 when this was written), create one. If you are not the first reader of this book to do so, then there will, of course, be a new page which will have been set up by a fellow media student, so you can add to it. Over the course of 2009 and 2010, the readers of this book can develop a rich and mutually helpful **wiki** on this theme, all starting from this activity.

If you find this helpful, there is nothing to stop you developing a page in Wikipedia for all of the Critical Perspectives themes we will come to later in this book – as they all relate to each other, they are perfect subject matter for a wiki.

Ofcom and media literacy

In May 2008, the regulatory body Ofcom held a Media Literacy Research Forum in London, and a group of media experts developed a framework for media literacy. Or rather they tried to, but ended up with loads of different versions. Here are some of the main issues that were discussed.

- Media literacy is framed by the need to educate and develop people so they can *access*, *analyse*, *evaluate* and *create* media.
- Changing media behaviour does not happen just because technology becomes available, but because people's domestic situations change.
- People find it difficult to evaluate internet content, to know what to trust and what to believe. Generally, people tend to be too trusting and to assume that websites which have been visited by the most people will be the most trustworthy. At the same time, people are losing their trust in television because of rigged phone votes and awards, and the exposé of distorting documentaries. So, generally, trust of media content is a problem and people lack literacy in this regard.
- A 'self-help' culture is emerging in relation to technology. People who know what they are doing help out their friends and family, so official guidance and manuals are rarely accessed.
- Ofcom is seeking to outsource the responsibility for **regulation** to us, so we can self-regulate, and taking media studies is seen as one way of doing this, so by doing this course and reading this book you are helping the government. Well done!
- There is confusion about the relationship between 'DIY' media production and media literacy. If you make videos and put them on YouTube, does that make you media-literate, or do you need extra education? If you are a media student who also uploads and gets playback, you will know the answer to this better than the Ofcom 'experts'.
- It is really important not to assume that young people are all 'digital natives'. Because everyone assumes they are, a real social problem is emerging where young people who are not media-savvy feel too embarrassed to admit it, so they suffer in silence. To be media-illiterate, then, carries as much stigma for teenagers as being unable to read and write the printed word.
- It is another mistake to assume that there is something worthwhile in itself in blogging or uploading content. Actually, people who do this want to be heard and for their contributions to lead to actions of some kind. Just making something without an audience or a response does not in itself constitute literacy.
- Perhaps most importantly, literacy should never be thought of as an individual capability. Literacy is embedded in social experiences, so we must think of media literacy as being to do with communities and distribution.

Figure 1.1 Inside Plato's Cave: A Canadian online media literacy project

While Robin Blake of Ofcom says that 'media literacy is just the literacy of our times', that cannot mean that we take it for granted or assume it develops naturally just because we are exposed to so much media. That would be like surrounding a child with books and expecting her to learn to read on her own. In fact, as Sonia Livingstone pointed out, the modern media world can be illegible, hard to understand and very hard to trust compared to analogue culture. So we need to work harder as a society to develop literacy capabilities.

Media literacy is now a wide-ranging and very popular idea. The Ofcom conference in 2008 brought together international teachers, regulators and industry people, with the idea of coming up with a common framework. But what does all this mean for you, the A2 Media Studies student in the UK?

Media literacy for A2

We have covered a range of theoretical ideas about how literacy is changing in broad and often quite challenging terms. What difference does all this make for a media student taking the A2 Media Studies course? Taking web 2.0 as the basis for a new kind of media studies, David Gauntlett (2007b) suggested that it might be a good time to think about **media studies 2.0**, which would be defined in this way.

> The view of the internet and new digital media as an 'optional extra' is replaced with recognition that they have fundamentally changed the ways in which we engage with all media.

Questions that arise for our study of the media are: Do people 'watch television' in the traditional sense anymore? Are there any distinct 'media institutions' in the era of **convergence**? If you can share music on Facebook with your 'friends', and they can purchase it at the click of a mouse and then access the video almost immediately on YouTube, how does this change the music industry? And is there such a thing as 'the audience' in this day and age? There is still priority given on the OCR course to your learning about media power, influence, access and issues of representation – these are tremendously important aspects of contemporary citizenship. But the way in which these cultural practices are circulated and disseminated is changing fundamentally.

Gauntlett suggests that people do not just get represented *by* the media any more. Instead, they use web 2.0 platforms to make their own media, share it with the world and thus represent themselves. So media studies now needs to engage with the ways in which people make sense of their identities and then creatively, through the media, express this. This means that media students need to move away from the 'media 1.0' way of doing things by 'questioning the traditional approach to people who "produce" media and people who "use" media', and by exploring people's contemporary media experiences by encouraging creative responses (Gauntlett 2007b).

Why are you being told this at the start of this course textbook? Is this not just extracurricular extension material? Surely what you need here is material that is going to help you with each unit and theme, not a philosophical debate about the subject itself? Actually, there is a really good reason for spending some time on this here: the OCR Media Studies A level, and particularly the A2 units, were designed with media 2.0 in mind. The examiners who created the specification wanted to embrace these changes and create a course of study that would reflect the changing nature of the media. So by understanding this context, you acquire some of the 'metaliteracy' we explored earlier on in this section.

Media 2.0, then, is more about people and less about 'the media' in isolation. Another version of this theme comes from Dan Gillmor's book, *We, the Media* (2004). Looking specifically at 'citizen journalism' in the form of blogs, Gillmor offers a similar assertion to Gauntlett, arguing that web 2.0 enables ordinary people to participate in **politics** and news, by producing their own accounts of real events and commenting immediately (and loudly) on 'official' journalism. Another media academic, John Hartley (2007), describes the shift from a demand-led market of creative industries to a social network market. Describing the **long tail** of media distribution, he suggests that the liberating potential of web 2.0 might be equal not only to the emergence of 'mass literacy', but beyond that, to the introduction of mass public schooling. We look at all of these new concepts in detail in the Critical Perspectives section, but for now, taking these ideas together, we end up thinking of the media more as a range of networks via which the public can decide to participate more or less in creative, communicative, collaborative and democratic activities, and less as a group of powerful organisations influencing us.

Let us consider two examples of how these changes make a difference to media studies in more straightforward ways.

Britney 2.0

The plight of Britney Spears in 2007 offers us another way of thinking about all this. A fairly 'traditional' issue for media studies at A level might be for you to evaluate the claim made by Alastair Campbell (previously Tony Blair's press officer and spin doctor) in 2008 that Britney has ceased to be considered a human being by the public and is now understood primarily as a news commodity. Taking the media 2.0 idea further to explore this, how might we distinguish 'old' and 'new' approaches to this question?

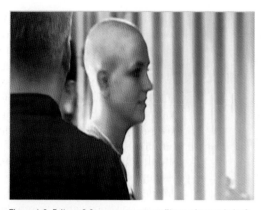

Figure 1.2 Britney 2.0 – a news commodity or a human being?

Britney 1.0	Britney 2.0
News values	Online news
Infotainment	Rolling news
Celebrity culture	Blogs
Gender	YouTube
Ideology	Lack of regulation
Media regulation	Notions of truth
Deregulation	People responding
News agendas	People creating

We are not thinking here that the Britney 1.0 list is replaced by Britney 2.0. Instead, the right-hand list is added to the first column. But it is not an optional extra – you cannot make sense of what Alastair Campbell is saying about the 'fallen icon' without debating the extent to which her commodification is amplified and accelerated by the online dispersal of her as a 'sign'.

Fan culture

Hills (2002) analyses fandom as a form of cultural expression. While many of his examples have nothing to do with web 2.0 – Trekkies and Elvis impersonators, for example – it is clear that **broadband** internet can accelerate fan interpretations and reimaginings of media products. Check out the enormous range of 'mash up' and 'sweded' video material on YouTube. From Harry Potter fans sharing fan literature online, to the many commentary edits of *The Sopranos* finale that you can find online, media producers now have to accept that fans can and will upload their own versions of material within hours of the official broadcast.

So how can *you* become a media 2.0 student? Gauntlett argues that the media play a role in the construction of **identity**, but not

Practice Task

When you have completed all your production work, draw a diagram that visually represents the kinds of media literacy that you have demonstrated in your creative processes (in one colour), and the kinds of media literacy that people will need to engage with the media products you have made (in another colour).

that big a role in relation to other aspects of social experience; and it is this finding that leads him to suggest that media studies has, until now, been too interested in *just* the media, especially the notion of the self-contained media text, and insufficiently attentive to people and how they give meaning to culture. But we must tread carefully. Taking the Britney analysis as a template, you need to approach media products in an academic (when looking at existing media) and creative (when making your own) way that combines tried and tested concepts, such as representation, with an understanding of *how people make sense of media* in the online age. You will be making your own media products in the Advanced Portfolio, and using web 2.0 to research, plan and evaluate these projects in progress. And you will be theorising this creative work in the first part of your Critical Perspectives exam. Then you will answer a question on a theme, from a choice of six, all of which are very much to do with the changes we have explored here. Your mission, should you choose to accept it, is to make sense of this changing landscape by *creating* media, *accessing* content and information through research, *analysing* cultural products and *evaluating* theories. All of this adds up to media literacy, which is what you are about.

2.1

Advanced Portfolio: the step up from AS

It is a good idea to map out the increases in the level of demand at A2 compared to AS when it comes to production work. The process is similar. You produce a main outcome, with other elements alongside it. You demonstrate – alone or in a group – how your creative media work is the result of research and planning. And you evaluate your work, reflecting on process and outcomes. But there are two clear, tangible differences at A2, and a range of more synoptic expectations.

The physical distinctions are these: instead of a preliminary task that is not really marked in terms of quality, but is rather a development 'stepping stone', at A2 it is expected that your creative skills are now advanced enough for you to be in charge of your own experimentation. So you are required to produce a main task and two other media outcomes that are equal in quality. You will be working across media areas and you need to develop skills in each of them. If your music video is accomplished, but the website for the band is shoddy, the mark comes down. The other clear change is that you have to keep in your head a **synoptic** range of memories – an experiential 'bank' to draw from in the Critical Perspectives exam. In this book, we devote a whole section to the art of **reflective**, theoretical writing about production work. You should make use of this, because you will be assessed not only on your creative skills, but equally on your ability to **theorise** your work formally in an exam context. So the electronic evaluation and work-in-progress blogging and wiki-building will build up to a more traditional written outcome.

Often, people in education use words that students do not understand to describe the ways we choose to mark your work. Developing a metalanguage to describe assessment is really helpful. Simply, it is easier to do well if you know what you are being tested on, and this is too often a mystery to learners. So let's spend a bit of time looking at *synoptic assessment*.

When you get to the end of your Advanced Portfolio work, you will have produced at least five media products. Alongside these, you may have produced media-related material in other subjects and outside of formal education. These creative activities must *not* be thought of as separate from your work on institutions and audiences, TV or radio drama and the Critical Perspectives theme(s) you have researched.

The OCR website states: 'Synoptic Assessment explores connections between different areas and levels of a given subject' (www.ocr.org.uk – accessed August 2008).

A synoptic weather chart, like the BBC one in Figure 2.1.1, shows a range of meteorological factors all coming together to produce one easy(ish) to understand visual representation of how the weather will be at any one time.

The book and film *The Perfect Storm* told the story of a small fishing boat caught up in a freak meteorological 'coming-together' of elements – tides, storms and pressure – making being in a boat on the sea a perilous situation.

Figure 2.1.1 A synoptic weather chart brings everything together at a glance

Practice Task

When you have completed all your production work, draw a mind-map to visually represent five synoptic links that you can make between some of the following areas (each link must connect at least two areas together).

- Production outcomes
- TV or radio drama
- Media institutions and audiences
- Genre
- Narrative
- Representation
- Media language
- Audience
- Media literacy
- Global media
- Media regulation
- Online media
- Identity
- Postmodern media
- Democracy

So we get the idea! Synoptic means bringing everything together, and the OCR specification is distinct from other media courses because the examiners believe that creative media production is where all the learning is demonstrated, not just technical skills. Bear this in mind.

2.2

Advanced Portfolio: responding to a set brief

In this section, you are provided with a sample assignment, responding to six of the OCR A2 main tasks, and a 'real media' starting point for each of them. In addition, a range of production tips are offered. With a few exceptions, the emphasis here is on creative ideas and research, rather than technical skills, as the expectation at A2 is that the technical skills were acquired at AS. Here, your task is to develop further your creative application of those skills.

Website for TV channel

The OCR brief asks you to produce:

Three hyperlinked web pages and two from these three:

- Newspaper advertisement
- Listings magazine double-page spread
- Ident sequence.

Sample response

Develop a website for a new 'First News' TV channel for children, taking the weekly newspaper First News *as the starting point and template.*

Existing media starting point

First News is a weekly newspaper produced in collaboration with the National Literacy Trust. At the time of writing, it has been running for over two years. The paper is supported by a website (www.firstnews.co.uk – accessed August 2008), which will, in the conception of your project, link to another site for the new TV channel. Your job is to work out the **scheduling** hours for the target audience, research the way that contracts are secured with Freeview, and then develop a website that adds to but does not undermine the TV channel. You will need online, **interactive** elements that link to the programmes and bulletins offered by the TV service.

Production resources

These two websites offer a range of materials and tutorials for image production which will help with still and moving image briefs alike:

- www.ehow.com (accessed August 2008) – photography tutorials
- www.videojug.com (accessed August 2008) – another range of tutorials aimed at the web 2.0 DIY end of the market.

Music promotion

The OCR brief asks you to produce:

A **music video** and two from these three:

- Home page for the band
- DVD cover
- Magazine ad for the DVD.

Sample response

Produce a music video for a band, artist or DJ on a music course at your school or college. The intellectual property must be owned by the musician(s) you produce the video for. At the start of the project, you will pitch three different ideas for the video to the musician(s), and they will select the idea they want to develop.

Figure 2.2.1 *First News*: the template for your new TV channel

Existing media starting point

Many of the most notable pop videos are the least conventional. This example is highly unlikely to be an influence on your work, but it might offer you some broader creative inspiration. Can you imagine anything less marketable than an old country and western singer? Music producer and promoter Rick Rubin, one of the pioneers of the Def Jam label, teamed up with Johnny Cash in the later years of his life, to produce several albums of stripped-down cover versions, or to put it in more theoretical terms, postmodern reworkings of Cash as a text. One of the songs that worked the best was his cover of *Hurt* by Nine Inch Nails, the video for which (at www.youtube.com/watch?v=SmVAWKfJ4Go – accessed August 2008) has taken on a cult status beyond the song itself. View the video and consider the relationship between original song, cover version, singer, his legendary status and his state of health at the time of production. Look at the montage of images you see put together with his performance, the *mise-en-scène*, pace and cultural reference points – footage of his own career alongside present-tense imagery relating to his demise. As you will be producing a video for an unknown artist or band, you will be at the polar opposite to this in terms of the cultural references you can draw on, but it is still a helpful starting point as a pop video which 'remixes' the song visually. The video was directed by Mark

Production Tip

Here are three key tips from Pete Fraser, whose students at Long Road in Cambridge have been producing high-quality music videos for a long time.

- First, organisation – plan for everything and make sure performers have rehearsed and learnt the lyrics.
- Second, set up a blog for work in progress and use it to upload YouTube videos of examples that inform your work, post photos and plans from your recces and an animatic of the storyboard, by simply filming each drawing and then adding the music in iMovie® or a similar programme.
- Third, pay most attention to the pace of your video – it must be dynamic and feature lots of cuts.

From his perspective as Chief Examiner, this is good advice – 'it's rare that shots feel too short but common to see videos where shots drag on' (Fraser 2007b: 30).

Another tip is a resource – have a look at www.emusu.com (accessed August 2008), a promotion and digital distribution resource from the West Midlands. Attention to this portal will help you to consider your music promotion work in relation to the online media age.

And an industry perspective is presented here from Suzy Davis (interview in Fraser 2007a: 20), previously an A-level media student, now working as an editor, offering specific advice for media students editing music videos.

Keep it simple, without any complicated narrative. Think about how you can use your lighting to create simple effects in camera. If your shots don't look as good as you'd hoped, there are tricks you can use which professional editors do have to resort to, the colour grading tool can be applied to every shot, you can drop in 'flash frames' for effect, or even to link two boring-looking shots more interestingly by flipping one upside down or creating some kind of interesting movement. Sometimes you have to use the motion tool to create in-camera moves that aren't really there.

Romanek (www.markromanek.com/index.html – accessed August 2008). You might choose to take another route and go for a more faithful visual 'application' or pure performance video, but in your research and planning you should consider a range of approaches.

Production Tip

Light and depth of field

For all photography and moving-image production work, it is essential to get to grips with some basic artistic principles. Here are two basic tips for making your images carry more meaning.

- Get your backlight right – use the backlight control on the camera to adjust the lighting, and make sure that the camera is not facing the main light source. Then think about the **symbolic** effect you want to achieve and make sure your lighting set-up reflects that. If you have shadow in the shot, it should only be because you want it to connote mystery or guilt or threat.
- Depth of field – this is really complicated, but at a simple level it is about how much you want in focus. The larger the aperture (which you set on the camera), the more 'shallow' the depth of field (i.e. not much will be in focus beyond what is at the front of the image), so you use a shallow depth of field to draw attention to a specific part of an image. But just to make it hard to remember, the bigger the aperture number, the shallower the depth of field. So choose a larger aperture for more detail at the 'front' of the image, and a smaller aperture for an image where everything will be in focus, but the eye will not be drawn to any one detail in particular.

Film promotion

The OCR brief asks you to produce:

A **trailer** and two from these three:

- Home page for the film
- Poster
- Magazine cover featuring the film.

Sample response

Produce a viral marketing campaign for a new film, aiming to attract an audience primarily through social networking sites and YouTube. The trailer and the website will be the primary marketing tools to be disseminated via the internet. The poster and magazine cover will be the secondary phase, adopting mainstream 'above- and below-the-line' marketing techniques after the viral marketing campaign has secured media interest.

Existing media starting point

Cloverfield is a prototype for this approach. The film was produced on a low budget, but recouped large dividends, and viral marketing is credited with this positive input/output equation. Given the tag 'monster movie for the YouTube generation', the film is shot as an 'eyewitness video', making the conventions of the text fit the target audience. But equally important was the way the film was promoted through the ultimate in teaser trailers – a promo that did not name the film. This led to a great deal of blog discussion, as the producer's name (which did appear on the trailer) led to associations with *Lost* and *Alias*, both of which are the subject of a great deal of online fan activity. After this initial interest was sparked, a more traditional trailer was released, with an accompanying film website leading to the lead characters' social networking pages, an important element in building up a (postmodern) sense of the reality of the 'user-generated' fiction. A widget was offered to web visitors that embedded the opening of the film into the user's own social networking page. If that wasn't enough, a range of 'extratextual' games and video-blogs appeared that are related to the characters, offering an enhanced, hyperdiegetic extension of the meanings of the film itself. All these distribution methods are entirely based on a savvy use of

Figure 2.2.2 *Cloverfield* – promoted by 'hypertextual' viral marketing

web 2.0 platforms, and how they offer word-of-mouth opportunities which, after a small outlay, are free. Hence the viral marketing success. Hendry (2008: 37) offers this description of what she calls the creation of a '*Cloverfield* Universe' for a target audience that is increasingly hard to reach through traditional promotional tools.

> Alternative advertising methods were needed if *Cloverfield* was going to attract the attention of the group of people who could be used to make this film a success in the cinema. A specialised online and computer-savvy audience was specifically targeted as their interaction with the marketing was vital in the film generating interest from another valuable audience group, the mainstream movie-goer. The story of *Cloverfield*'s marketing shows how the online audience was used to create a buzz about the film to support a more traditional marketing campaign.

Production Tip

Photo composition

Despite the fact that image-editing software such as Adobe Photoshop® allows a great deal of licence in post-production, professional photographers encourage us to think more seriously about the moment of capture and not to rely on editing. In the AS book, Huw Meredith reminded us of the simple fact that the quality of our final images will depend on the printer we are using; so at one end of the operation we have to remember that photos will eventually be printed, and the fact that they appear on screen in one form may not translate into hard copy as well. At the other end of the operation, consider this piece of advice from awarding-winning photographer Magoli Delporte (interview in Card and Herd 2007: 36).

> Compose your photos as you shoot, not afterwards (by cropping). You'll find natural framing devices everywhere: a window, a door frame, even patterns and textures can enhance your composition.

Advertising

The OCR brief asks you to produce:

Two TV ads and two from these three:

- Radio ad
- TV sponsorship sequence
- Web pop-up.

Sample response

Produce two TV ads for a new handheld device to rival the iPod®/iPhone®, using the same 360-degree branding strategy as

*Apple® have used, where the functionality of the product is important, but design **aesthetics** and the attempt to 'badge' the zeitgeist (the iPod generation) is more important.*

Existing media starting point

The TV advertising campaign for the iPod was considered by many to be advertising as an art form. While the product itself was of great value to the consumer – the first and ever since 'standard' MP3 player, the Apple design and the use of a single dancer (and later celebrity dancing), with the **iconic** white lead and headphones, became a **semiotic** moment that arguably transcended commerce and became a signifier for a cultural shift. How can your adverts for a new handheld device challenge the 'Apple hegemony'?

Production resource

The English and Media Centre's *Doing Ads* resource is something your media teachers may well have at their disposal, but if not, it is worth asking them about it. The material contained in the study pack and DVD will be very useful for the research and planning element of the campaign, as the pack considers the various approaches advertisers take in the media-saturated twenty-first-century world to the simple but difficult job of getting the message across.

Local newspaper

The OCR brief asks you to produce:

Two pages and two from these three:

- Poster
- Radio ad
- Two web pages.

Sample response

Produce a local newspaper that is free, linked to online services and takes an 'ultralocal' strategy.

Existing media starting point: *Craven Herald & Pioneer*

This is a cynical and unethical starting point, but a realistic one. The *Craven Herald & Pioneer* (www.cravenherald.co.uk – accessed August 2008), the local paper of Skipton in Yorkshire, owned by Newsquest, is just one example of a paid-for local paper which has ridden the storm of the internet and free rival papers by 'going ultralocal'. Described by the local rector as 'like a good pub landlord', the paper focuses on the **micropolitics** of community life, rather than adopting more **macro news values**. But if a free version came along doing the same thing, the situation really would be grave. This is hypothetical, and it is unlikely that a free paper would sustain itself with such a narrow local focus, but your task here is to develop a free 'ultralocal' paper, with online elements, that you think would do well in the market in your community.

Production resources: online material for video

There are hundreds of websites that are useful for moving-image production. Here are five to bookmark (all accessed August 2008):

- www.firstlightmovies.com/how_to_make_a_film – this is self-explanatory content from First Light Movies, an organisation which may fund your film if you are 19 or under, so well worth a browse
- www.mediacollege.com/video/camera/tutorial – focus on camera techniques
- www.bbc.co.uk/films/oneminutemovies/howto – editing, sound and lighting are covered here
- www.apple.com/ilife/tutorials – essential for Mac® video work
- http://community.filmbirmingham.co.uk – excellent 'knowledge transfer' resource. If you are not from Birmingham, use this as a template to find your own regional equivalent.

Short film

The OCR brief asks you to produce:

Short film and two from these three:

- Poster
- Radio trailer
- Film magazine review page.

Sample response

Produce a short film with the title The Man Next Door. *The film should be designed for digital distribution and should deal with issues pertinent to contemporary British culture.*

Existing media starting points

The UK Film Council's Digital Shorts project (www.ukfilmcouncil.org.uk/shortfilms – accessed August 2008) has led to the production of a range of short films which will give you some ideas and inspiration. And to view the work of a now well-known director working in the medium of short film, visit the Channel 4 website to see Shane Meadows' collection of short films, *Shane's World* (www.channel4.com/film/ makingmovies/microsites/S/shanes_world/shaneWorld_main.jsp – accessed August 2008).

Video game level

The OCR brief asks you to produce:

Game level and two from these three:

- Cover for the game
- Magazine ad
- Radio ad.

Production Tip

Simon Quy, a teacher trainer who specialises in short film within media education, offers the following good advice and 'ways in' to working in this medium. Short films are often a 'laboratory for experimentation and innovation' (Quy 2008: 39) rather than just a shorter version of conventional feature film-making.

Short films are now a booming medium because of digital technology, which means you can find an audience through web-streaming. For example, see www.depict.org (accessed August 2008), a project challenging the public to make films that are 90 seconds or under.

Short films go very well with converging technologies. See the Arts Council-funded www.onedotzero.com (accessed August 2008) for examples of computer-generated short films.

Here is Quy's (2008: 39) summary of the importance of the medium.

If the feature film has parallels with the novel, then the short film might be considered as the literary equivalent of the poem or short story. The best short films are crystalline creations of precise, prismatic intensity, offering the careful 'refinement' of the director's idea, the distilled essences of his/her imagination.

Quy also offers advice on distributing your short film, suggesting that you enter competitions (Media Magazine run one – www.mediamagazine.org.uk – accessed August 2008), submit your work for film festivals (e.g. Bristol's Brief Encounters – www.brief-encounters.org.uk – accessed August 2008) and make use of bespoke short film distributors (e.g. www.bigfilmshorts.com – accessed August 2008). But it is crucial to know that if you want to take your work further than the requirements of the OCR specification, in order to share it through these networks, it must be legally compliant (Quy 2006: 54).

You'll only be able to distribute and screen your film in public if it is 'cleared'. This means that you have written permission to use everything and everyone that appears in your film. This includes script, music, locations, actors, contributors, products, company logos. Companies and broadcasters are particularly hot on this area as they are likely to be sued if they show something that has not been approved by all 'parties' with an 'interest' in the film.

Sample response

Produce the first level of a new video game, to be marketed at females aged 8 to 12 years. Either use software to develop a game within existing conventions that expands the market for a new audience – for example, you might develop a new strategy game with MissionMaker that relates to an already successful media product, which you can invent also; or produce a 'standalone' game that will appeal to this age range, relating to a hobby or activity which you know to be in favour with the target audience.

Existing media starting point

The Mario™ franchise is synonymous with Nintendo® consoles, but the development of the Wii™ platform led to the convergence of the female, arguably more social, collaborative gaming audience, with the technology to take this beyond wireless social gaming on the Nintendo DS™. Commercial exploitation, as always, followed with the roll-out of a range of essential peripherals, like the steering wheel in Figure 2.2.4, which is necessary for *Super Mario Kart*. When media academics try to fit existing concepts like **narrative** and representation to video games, it works well with games like *Harry Potter* or *Charlotte's Web*, but you might wish, in your production work, to produce a more 'ludic' game, where character and story are less important than immersion and action that is physically experienced. This will depend, of course, on the software available for this new area of media production.

Figure 2.2.4 *Mario Kart*: innovative, next-generation design and marketing brought gaming to Lydia, Hazel and Jen – members of a previously under-represented audience

Production resource: MissionMaker

MissionMaker is a piece of software that is being purchased by schools and colleges for students to use to design video games. By the time this book is published, there may be a range of alternatives, and your media teachers may be using a different 'solution' for games design, but in 2008, this resource is the market leader for education, as it is designed for school use (as opposed to a more complex programming tool).

Information about the software can be read and viewed at www.immersiveeducation.com/MissionMaker (accessed August 2008).

MissionMaker is an easy-to-use software tool that enables us to develop our understanding of the key gaming principles of rules, economies and conditionality, and to apply these practically – the programming of if…then conditions into a game. An alternative software is 3D Game Maker, but as stated already, there will be more on the market by the time you read this.

Production case study: Games in the West Midlands

Media students are increasingly interested in a career in the games industry, and compared to other media areas that have been around a lot longer, there is less careers advice that media teachers can provide. There are now a range of games-related degrees that you will find via the UCAS website (www.ucas.com – accessed August 2008), but alongside research for a degree course, you are well advised to look for work experience. The West Midlands is one region where games development is seen as a major part of the 'skills economy', and these details should give you some idea of the range of roles you could play in a games-related career.

Gaming is now such a **multimedia** business that Achanak and Tigerstyle, musicians from Smethwick, Birmingham, recently produced the first Bhangra soundtrack for a video game. At the other end of the spectrum, Codemasters is a games publishing company based in Leamington Spa, employing 400 people. And the Serious Games Institute in Coventry is a regional employment incubator, supported by Advantage West Midlands, which helps businesses to use virtual worlds, such as *Second Life*, and games engines and software templates, to their commercial advantage. The head of Codemasters, Rod Cousens, offers an idea of the potential jobs market around gaming (in Carson 2008: 11).

> I don't know of any other industry that offers the same level of dynamic growth. It can test all your skills, and for me it's absolutely the area to be in. Videogames are at the silent pictures stage of movies: there's a lot more to open up.

Practice Task

When you have completed your electronic research, planning and evaluation, use this considerably less exciting, but nonetheless vital exercise to prepare for the exam element of this work.

Spend 30 minutes reviewing your electronic materials, then shut down your computer and spend 10 minutes completing this writing frame:

- I used online networking to develop my ideas and gain feedback. Here are some examples of how I did this …
- Three micro creative decisions I made were …
- To pick out one macro media skill I have developed, I would have to select …

3.1

Critical Perspectives: writing about production

If you were asked to produce a 'job description' for an A2 Media Studies student, listing all the crucial skills and areas of knowledge required to succeed, you would be forgiven for leaving out **critical reflection**. This is a highly specialist skill, and it is quite different from analysing media texts, creating media products, debating media in society or researching media institutions. Reflective practice is a skill that is much sought after and is highly regarded by universities and employers. So we need to devote some time here to developing this skill – the ability to take a step away from your own practice (in this case the production of media, but the skill is transferable to any complex process), to analyse from a critical point of view what you did. This is beyond mere evaluation of the outcomes; we are not only thinking about strengths and weaknesses. Here we need to develop the 'instinct' to theorise our own practice, to form a dialogue between the media theories we have utilised to deconstruct 'real media' and our own creative practice. This is probably the most difficult part of the A2 course.

Below are ten key elements of reflective writing, which will be followed by an example of student work – the CD cover for the first album by *Woman Clone*, and a sustained 'exemplar' of how the producer of *Woman Clone* might go about the process of critical reflection, from the perspective of an OCR examiner, so you can see at a glance how the metalanguage of assessment works in relation to these examples of student writing. Your job is to use this as a benchmark for your own work.

The Ten Commandments for reflective writing

1. **Focus on creative decisions informed by institutional knowledge** (you did what you did partly because of what you had learned about how the media produce, distribute and share material).
2. **Focus on creative decisions informed by theoretical understanding** (you know that you did what you did because of having a point of view in relation to media and meaning, and you can describe that in relation to cultural media theories).
3. **Evaluate the process – don't just describe it** (why some things worked well and others not so well).
4. **Relate your media to 'real media' at the micro level** (give clear, specific examples of how you used techniques and strategies to create **intertextual** references to media you have been influenced by).
5. **Try to deconstruct yourself** (don't ever think of your own tastes, decisions, preferences, behaviour as just being 'the ways things are'; instead, try to analyse the reasons for these things – it is tough to do this, but worth the effort).
6. **Choose clearly relevant micro examples to relate to macro reflective themes** (you can't write about everything you did, so be prepared with a 'menu' of examples to adapt to the needs of the reflective task).
7. **Avoid binary oppositions** (your media products will not either follow or challenge existing conventions; they will probably do a bit of both).
8. **Try to write about your broader media culture** (don't just limit your writing to your OCR production pieces, but try to extend your response to include other creative work or other media-related activities you have been engaged in).
9. **Adopt a metadiscourse** (step outside of just describing your activities as a media studies student to reflect, if possible, on

the 'conditions of possibility' for the subject and your role within it – what kind of an activity is making a video for media studies, compared to making a video as a self-employed media producer?)

10. **Quote, paraphrase, reference** (reflective writing about production is still academic writing, so remain within this mode of address).

Woman Clone by Sophie Hughes

Woman Clone is a postmodern punk band with all female members, and the image we will be discussing is the CD cover for the first, eponymous album. The CD cover is not the main task, but it is crucial that you produce all of your media products to the same standard. So we focus here on an ancillary task for two reasons. First, we cannot reproduce the whole video in a textbook for you to refer to; and second, it gives us more of a 'steer' for theorising the whole brief and the **synergy** between the products. Had we only reflected on the main task, the other materials would be marginalised, and this would reinforce a common failing of student production work – one excellent outcome and then a few vague afterthoughts, with no consistency. For Sophie, the whole package is very well conceived. The members of the band, like Gorillaz, appear to the audience in computer-generated form, but that side of the postmodernist aesthetic at work here is more relevant to the other materials produced for the A2 portfolio – the music video in particular. For this section of the book, we are going to put just one production outcome under the theoretical microscope, to give you a sustained example of how to theorise your creative practice. The element we are deconstructing is a CD cover (see Figure 3.1.2). While the CD is a media form with a limited shelf life, music **downloaders** make liberal use of cover art, so music being 'packaged' in this way still has relevance. Cultural meaning is made for music through commercial images and aesthetics, even in the online age – and perhaps more so.

Sophie was taking media studies alongside art and graphics at A2, and took a highly synoptic approach to her creative work, not only linking a range of theoretical and institutional aspects from her media work in *Woman Clone*, but also making an explicit link with her other subjects. This is to be encouraged, as long as strategic and theoretical reasons can be given in the reflective writing. If all Sophie had done were to duplicate her work, this would be a problem. But if she explains that she is taking an abstract piece of her artwork, situated in a theoretical context, and then adapting it for a specific set of institutional and commercial practices (the selling, through images, of music), then this is a **theorised** activity which shows an astute understanding of the

Figure 3.1.1 Sophie Hughes

Figure 3.1.2 *Woman Clone* by Sophie Hughes – media art in commercial context

boundaries between different kinds of cultural practice – producing art work, compared to mass media.

Creativity in context

For Critical Perspectives in Media, Sophie might write about *Woman Clone* in a number of ways. For the part of the unit that demands a reflective analysis of the creative process and skills development, she can situate this CD cover alongside other still and moving-image production work and write specifically about the use of Photoshop for filtering, resizing and toning, and set this against the more 'traditional' montage techniques used for a standalone piece of artwork. She might compare the work of image manipulation to post-production for video, and reflect on the fact that some aspects are common to both. She would do well to conceptualise *Woman Clone* as a synoptic 'meeting point' of a range of developed skills and creative approaches, writing about the AS preparatory task, AS final outcome and other A2 production work as leading up to this work; and she might write about the process by which the CD and other material for the band was developed through 'work in progress' blog postings and feedback, making use of Blogger and Flickr. Crucially, she will need to write about the personal investment in *Woman Clone* as a piece of personal artwork which takes a position on the representation of women alongside the commercial status of this piece as an album/CD cover. And the 'conditions of possibility for this' are the long-standing tradition of music being promoted through the use of artwork – see The Beatles, Joy Division, The Smiths, The Stone Roses and, more recently, Coldplay, for just a few examples.

'Theorised' creativity

To respond to the part of Critical Perspectives in Media that looks at one production outcome in relation to a particular theoretical concept, Sophie would need to be prepared to adapt her writing to the particular concept that presents itself. But it is important to state clearly that you will need to prepare to write about several production pieces, as each one will 'fit' most readily with a different range of concepts. Here are some suggestions for how she might do this.

Media language

Sophie can write a lot about the cover image for *Woman Clone* by using a semiotic approach in dialogue with theoretical ideas from **feminism** and postmodernism. She can make lots of synoptic links with her research for the theme areas of Critical Perspectives. The image features a 'flattened' montage of signs which are, in the main, iconic and indexical, but the overall effect is symbolic. In other words, we can pull out any one of the micro images that make up the cover and analyse it in isolation. For example, the text 'That's what happens when women design a cooker' is taken from somewhere else, and the audience will not know where it comes from. This could be taken as a positive representation of women – perhaps the producer of this statement is bearing witness to women's design skills compared to their male counterparts. Or it could be negative – a kind of 'woman driver' discourse. But actually it could be both – positive in the first sense, but negative in that it reinforces the representation of women as being concerned primarily with the domestic sphere. So we can do a 'commutation test' to substitute cooker with engine, and this will fundamentally change everything in the statement.

Another micro element is the couple in formal dress. On one level, this is purely a straightforward representation of a particular social activity, and is thus recognisable to the audience without controversy. But placed in this frame, alongside the rest of the images and the anchoring name of the band/album, the sign is motivated towards a cynical response – all the images are suggesting a 'cloning' of women in relation to dominant ideas about gender. At this point, Sophie might usefully quote and **paraphrase** a range of theoretical writers – Barthes on how images reinforce cultural **myth**, Althusser on **interpellation**, Winship on gender complicity and

Foucault on self-regulation. The section on Media and Collective Identity covers these theories. Here, suffice to say, they are all to do with the ways in which our ideas about gender are formed and reinforced. If Sophie has studied Media and Collective Identity, she will have links to make with regard to the representation of women in media, and she might juxtapose Winship's feminist perspective with Gauntlett's work on the 'pick-and-mix' reader and Kendall's work on the 'knowing' nature of female magazine reading. So we can see how easy it is to go from the micro description of an aspect of just one of your media production outcomes, to a full and applied theoretical analysis of how meaning is made in sociocultural contexts. The theory helps us do this.

Genre

This is the concept that Sophie is least likely to select *Woman Clone* to deal with, as genre is not a terribly useful theoretical tool with which to tackle the representation of music in CD cover design. That said, in a Taschen *1000 Record Covers* collection, it is possible to locate different styles of covers in subgenre categories, so Sophie might consider how her abstract, symbolic approach to *Woman Clone* would sit alongside other genres – covers that depict the artist or band being the obvious contrasting style. More interesting would be an articulation by Sophie of how *Woman Clone* defies genre as a concept. You should remember at all times that the examiner will give you credit (maybe even more credit) for taking issue with theories and explaining how you think your work does not fit with these orthodox, handed-down ways of thinking theoretically about media. Why is it, Sophie might muse, that genre is applied bluntly to media texts, but not applied in the same reductive fashion to works of art? Does her CD cover **transgress** these boundaries? She might paraphrase Mark Reid's (2001) wise words on genre at this point. Reid asks the critical question of whether we read genre as noun or adjective. He offers tomato purée as an example, suggesting that we ask a philosophical question: what would happen to this item if it were shelved in another part of the shop? Would the 'thing itself' be any different? Then she might quote Reid directly – for example: 'How something is categorised is determined by who does it, for whom, where, and when. The same is true for films' (Reid 2001: 1). And then she might extend this to all media texts (or products), and then return to *Woman Clone*. So the more interesting and, ultimately, more useful approach for Sophie to take here in relation to her own work and why it does not fit the theory neatly is not to avoid writing about genre, but to ask two metadiscourse questions: *how does genre work?* and *why does genre happen?*

Narrative

What is the narrative structure of this image? The narrative meaning of the CD cover is entirely grounded in cultural knowledge of what a CD cover is, which sounds rather obvious, but is actually an important point. We are socialised in our media culture to expect a relationship between texts and the ways they are packaged. While we are told not to judge a book by its cover, we prefer it if the cover of the book pleases us, or at least fits with the idea of the type of book it is – the same goes for music packaging. Woman Clone is a female band, with things to say about gender and postmodern ways of 'being a band'. The decision not to depict the members of the band as iconic, but to create a range of commodifying images for the musicians and, in this image, for women as a whole, is a storytelling technique. Sophie might well relate this to the 'story' of Gorillaz, the punk movement, the creative practice of idea and pastiche, and how music and image come together to make statements about music as product, art, commodity, rebellion and text. All these are questions of narrative.

In relation to the cover image specifically, Sophie would write about the logo of the band, and how that serves to anchor the selection of images and thus construct a coherent narrative out of the various parts, and the displacement of text. There are a range of extracted textual statements, all of which served another narrative originally and have here been removed and remixed. And she might explain how the image was constructed in relation to how the human eye reads a page and how she expects the reader to map the various signifiers – how the reader of the text will construct a narrative. To further discuss the relevance of narrative theory for commercial and/or artistic images, as opposed to fiction, Sophie might comment on John Berger's *Ways of Seeing*, in which he argues that human beings are preconditioned to make narrative in preference to the alternative of shapeless, eventless existence; and Nick Lacey's work (2000: 6), from which the following extract would be useful in quotation.

> Narrative is such a powerful analytical tool that it is, arguably, an even more important key concept than genre. Narrative has probably existed as long as human beings; it is likely that the stone age artists who drew the 18,000 year old cave paintings in the Ardeche, France, expected narratives to be woven around their images.

Crucially, Sophie's job here will be to test out Lacey's assertion that narrative (and genre) are fundamental to human existence. Where she is most likely to agree with Lacey is in relation to his suggestion that narratives are 'woven around' texts, as opposed to being embedded in them in a fixed way. How will the music-buying audience weave a narrative around *Woman Clone*?

Representation

This is the 'big one' for *Woman Clone*. Sophie's reflective writing here will be a fluid interplay between the personal (as a woman) and the academic (as a student analysing her own creative outcomes in theoretical contexts). The CD cover, in semiotic terms, presents the band as a text and connotes the 'world of the text' in ways that are both straightforwardly feminist – dealing with the representation of women as clones, as commodities and as objects – and at the same time postmodern and post-feminist. This means that the audience is not expected to be exposed here to the idea that women are represented in traditional ways for the first time, but that this representation of a media reality is actually a return to a feminist perspective in the context of a backlash (see Faludi 2003) against feminism. In this post-feminist environment, women are seen as complicit. The 1990s 'girl power' culture was a manifestation of this, through which females were represented as seeking equality, but at the same time dressing and appearing in ways which were in keeping with the **male gaze**. But the 'return' to feminism can only be understood with this cultural knowledge – this is a multilayered representation, as the computer-generated band members are themselves mythic representations of various female 'types', as constructed in media imagery. So the blending of the CD cover with these band member images, and the punk aesthetic of the music itself, deliberately complicates the meaning of *Woman Clone* and plays with gender representation to displace the audience. Here are two academic perspectives which Sophie can make use of in relation to her work.

> Striptease is based on a contradiction. Woman is desexualised at the very moment when she is stripped naked. We may therefore say that we are dealing here with a spectacle based on fear.

(Barthes 1972: 91)

Roland Barthes, the French **structuralist** writer, is here giving an example of mythologies – a seminal theory outlining the way that media representations relate to broader cultural myths and belief systems. He is suggesting that it is clothes that sexualise women more than the naked body itself, which is why the female stripper leaves the stage at the point of removing the last garment. We can see evidence of this in all media, and especially in women's magazines and in the appearance of female pop artists. *Woman Clone* seeks to subvert this by adhering to these mythic representations of women in the computer-generated form of each band member, while challenging this in the name of the band, the CD cover art and the lyrics of the songs.

> In a world ordered by sexual imbalance, pleasure in looking has been split between active/male and passive/female. The

determining male gaze projects its phantasy on to the female figure which is styled accordingly.

(Mulvey in Humm 1992: 348)

Laura Mulvey's hugely influential theory is actually quite a simple idea. Men look at women and the media reinforce this by filming or photographing women from a male point of view – so the norm for media representation is that the camera is male. Sophie can easily relate this to *Woman Clone* and how this also connects to her postmodern approach. The male gaze is reinforced through the computer-generated images of the band members, but challenged in the cover art, although this is multilayered because the CD cover also 'remixes' traditional male gaze representations – of a woman with make-up, of a pair of lips, of a male dancer taking the lead with a female counterpart.

Finally, Sophie will need to address the question of feminism itself, a much misunderstood and derided political project, often undermined by the very people it seeks to liberate – women. The following quote from Humm (1992: 403) is important.

Historically people and movements have been called feminist when they recognised the connections between social inequalities, deprivations and oppressions and gender differences. Currently feminists are pursuing questions about the consequences for women and for men when gender oppressions intersect with other forms of oppression, with homophobia, classism, ageism, disability and racism.

Almost twenty years on from this quote, we might come to the sad conclusion that there is more symbolic oppression in the media than at the time of Humm's description, as we add the xenophobic reaction to Islam in the post 9/11 context to the list, and the gradual erosion of civil liberties which is partly facilitated by media representations of 'the threat'. Sometimes media studies *has* to be political, and Sophie's work is a great example. On the one hand, she is imitating commercial practice – selling music as a commodity through media art. On the other hand, she is embedded in political cultural practices that make a difference to how we treat each other in daily social life.

Audience

While it is getting harder in the online age to conceive of a media audience as a stable, identifiable group, a key question for media studies remains this: how do people make sense of and give meaning to cultural products? During the production process, Sophie will have used blogs and social networking tools more generally to share images and gain feedback, and this can be described reflectively in the Critical Perspectives response. She will

Practice Task

Write a 300-word theoretical comparison of the *Woman Clone* CD cover and any one of your production outcomes, relating your comparison to any two of the following areas:

- Genre
- Representation
- Narrative
- Audience
- Media language.

relate the music of *Woman Clone* to other bands and artists, making intertextual connections to justify her commercial decisions in relation to an existing audience for this music, and then she can go on to describe how the postmodern images were constructed to appeal to this group of people. But she will also need to complicate matters by reflecting on the difference between artwork – which is arguably originated on a more personal level and then sold commercially – and CD cover art – which is perceived as being 'always-already' commercial in orientation and desired outcome. And in relation to her attempts to produce a knowing, reflexive, postmodern return to feminism in her CD cover, she might usefully relate her creativity to the following theoretical intervention from Paul Willis (1990: 57).

Pop stars are, to some extent, symbolic vehicles with which young women understand themselves more fully, even if, by doing so, they partly shape their personalities to fit the stars' alleged preferences.

Woman Clone arrives at a time when the interplay between pop idol, female fan and media is already knowing and ironic, but nevertheless the symbolic exchange of gendered meanings around music is still powerful. Sophie can write at length about how she is deliberately displacing the relations between band, cover art and fan, to expose and subvert the conditions of possibility for a female listener to 'understand herself' in relation to *Woman Clone*. This displacement and mixing of meaning is what allows her to theorise her work in relation to the postmodern turn.

3.2
Critical Perspectives: themes

This part of the A2 Media Studies course asks you to consider some key academic debates. These debates are concerned with the media in social and cultural contexts. Put simply, this means: how important is the media in society, and what different roles do the media play in people's lives? But as the nature of 'the media' changes to the point where it is increasingly difficult to conceive of it as a singular entity, we have to pay attention instead to all the complex and unique formulations of media practice in people's lives. So we might need to think about a person **uploading** a music playlist to a social network page alongside them watching a film at the cinema. There are no obvious 'right answers' here, but you will need to engage with a range of theoretical perspectives on how people use media; know about a variety of research that people have carried out in order to discover specific audience practices and habits; and, most importantly, demonstrate a personal position on the issues. But this personal position must always be informed by academic understanding.

Which theme you study, whether you focus on just one, two or a few, and which media you look at within each theme, will be determined by a range of factors – your teachers' specialist knowledge, your own interests, how this unit will be linked to the rest of your media studies course, resources, perhaps even the local area. And the choice is vast – you can literally study any aspect of the media that fits in with the theme heading and the specified areas of learning, which are set out for you here in a box at the start of each section. For each theme, it is mandatory to focus on three areas within your exam answer:

- **Historical**: you do not need to write a great deal here, but you must at some point in your response show that you understand how relevant aspects of the contemporary media can be compared to the past.
- **Contemporary**: most of your time will be spent demonstrating an up-to-date, accurate, theoretical and academic analysis of today's media.
- **Future**: again, this will not be the main focus, but to gain the higher marks you will need to have some ideas about where the media are going next.

Synoptic Link

Throughout this section, a range of examples of how your AS studies offer you important 'scaffolding' for A2 will be provided. To start with, here are some general points about how you are already prepared for this unit.

Your AS production work will have included a main task, and this will have been produced with a particular set of representations, either intentional or accidental. This activity relates to **Media and Collective Identity** – how did you portray groups of people in society through your production work?

In critically reflecting on your production work and in evaluating the outcomes, you will have discussed yourself as a media producer, but you are also a consumer. When we use technology to reach audiences without needing the support of media industries, this can be called **We Media**. If you designed your media product for broadband exchange, you will have been thinking about **Media in the Online Age**.

In researching and writing about an area of the contemporary media in relation to institutions and audiences, you may have been preparing for any of the Critical Perspectives themes, but here are just two examples from a potentially much longer list. You may have looked at music downloading, which is relevant to several themes – **We Media, Media in the Online Age, Postmodern Media** and **Contemporary Media Regulation**. Or maybe you researched the British film industry, which will have given you a good grounding for **Media and Collective Identity, Media in the Online Age** and perhaps **Global Media**.

And your analysis of television or radio drama will have given you a basic training in linking micro (small, specific details) to macro (broader theories and concepts, such as representation) analysis – a skill you will need for Critical Perspectives. Furthermore, in considering how gender, ethnicity, age, sexuality and other **demographic** qualities are portrayed in drama texts, you will have been developing an understanding of **Media and Collective Identity**.

It is misleading to keep mentioning 'the media' here as the focus of study. Really we are interested in how people, in cultural contexts, use the media at the end of the first decade of the twenty-first century.

Media studies is a subject which is concerned with **popular culture** – the media that ordinary people access in large numbers. While some people think this makes it easier than other subjects (after all, you already know about popular music, film and video games, and the physics student has less familiarity with, say, the speed of light), you will find that there are a number of quite difficult academic theories of popular culture to get to grips with. For example, one of the themes you can choose from is Postmodern Media, and this theme really illustrates this easy/difficult balance well. On the one hand, you might analyse *Big Brother* for this theme – hardly the most 'scholarly' text in the world, you might think. But to do so, you will have to explore the extent to which reality TV demonstrates a 'fetishised **hyperreality**', in which **simulation** has defeated any notion of the objective 'real'. Strinati (1995: 224) offers a useful description.

Postmodernism is said to describe the emergence of a social order in which the importance and power of the mass media and popular culture means that they govern and shape all other forms of social relationships. The idea is that popular cultural signs and media images increasingly dominate our sense of reality, and the way we define ourselves and the world around us. It tries to come to terms with, and understand, a media-saturated society. The mass media, for example, were once thought of as holding up a mirror to, and thereby reflecting, a wider social reality. Now reality can only be defined by the surface reflections of this mirror. Society has become subsumed within the mass media. It is no longer even a question of distortion, since the term implies that there is a reality, outside the surface simulation of the media, which can be distorted, and this is precisely what is at issue according to postmodern theory.

But don't panic. This section of the book will guide you through each theme in a way that will scaffold your understanding, from what you already know from your AS studies, to the more complex aspects of each theme, like Strinati's offering above in relation to Postmodern Media.

There are a number of different subjects or approaches that inform media studies. There are parts of the subject – TV or radio drama, for example – that are similar to English, as we are studying texts and considering their conventions. There are parts which are more like art or performing arts or IT – production work, most clearly. And there are themes which require an understanding of how people make sense of and use media products as part of their lives. This part of your course is to do with an approach called cultural studies, and it is important that you know this because it will help you remember that we are not just looking at texts and what they 'mean' or how they are 'consumed'. Instead, we are looking at people and what they do with media. This description from Toby Miller (2006: 1) will help get us started.

> By looking at how culture is used and transformed by social groups, cultural studies sees people not simply as consumers, but as potential producers of new social values and cultural languages.

We need to break this down, to look in detail at the elements Miller works with here.

Culture

A recent BBC promotional campaign for *The Culture Show* provided a wide range of definitions of culture from famous people. Indeed, the point was to show how hard it is to define it, which does not help much here. A common way of thinking about culture is to say that it is everything that is not nature. In other words, culture is made by humans. But perhaps it makes more sense to say that culture describes all the various forms of belief, communication, ritual, representation and ideas that the human race uses to make sense of our existence. In this case, culture would be the things we produce that animals do not. And culture is the outcome of collective thought. Lots of people would argue with this, incidentally. Whole books are devoted to just trying to answer the question – what is culture? (see Jenks 2005) – so we should be given the benefit of the doubt here for trying to come up with a working definition. Jenks describes four definitions of culture:

- As a state of mind (an aspiration – the 'cultured' person)
- As a collective pursuit of civilisation (as part of progress)
- As artistic and intellectual activity (this is perhaps the most common use of the term)
- As a social category – the things that people do, our ways of life (which is more like where we started – how we are not mere animals).

The important thing for media students to remember is that in this subject we are mostly interested in 'popular culture', and we do not distinguish between what is and what is not 'cultural'. For us, everything we might study in the media and produce for the media is culture.

Social groups

Wherever it is possible to give people a label based on collective characteristics or traits, as opposed to their individual or biological make-up, we can say they are part of a social group. Examples range from very broad groups of people, such as gay men or Asian women, to more specific groups, such as teenage players of *World of Warcraft*.

Social values and cultural languages

What might these new social values and cultural languages look like? Here is an example. Depending on the theme you study (though they are all related to each other), you might consider the impact of broadband internet on how people use media. For example, do people 'watch television' in the traditional sense anymore? Are there any distinct 'media institutions' in the era of convergence? If you can share music on a social network with your 'friends', and they can purchase it (or take it for nothing) online and access the video within a few clicks on YouTube, what does this do to the music industry as we know it? And most importantly, is there such a thing as 'audience' in this postmodern 'we media' age?

Another version of this theme comes from Dan Gillmor's book *We, The Media* (2004), and one of the OCR themes relates directly to this idea. Looking specifically at 'citizen journalism' in the form of blogs, Gillmor argues that web 2.0 enables ordinary people to participate in politics and news by producing their own accounts of real events and commenting immediately (and loudly) on 'official' journalism. Another media academic, John Hartley (2007), describes the shift from a demand-led market of creative industries to a social network market. Hartley describes these changes in the context of the shift to long-tail economics. This idea came from Chris Anderson, editor of *Wired* magazine, who suggested that businesses are increasingly realising that the best way to make money is to sell less of more, to create more niche markets, increasingly to diversify. This goes together with what is known as the 'long tail' of media production – the proliferation of small chunks of media content at the opposite end of the body to the head, where the big corporations make hugely popular media products like *Prince Caspian*.

Describing the implications of this long tail of media distribution, Hartley suggests that the liberating potential of web 2.0 might be equal not only to the emergence of 'mass literacy', but beyond that, to the introduction of mass public schooling. So this part of media studies is about exploring universal digital literacy and the we media phenomenon – 'one minute you're a fan, the next you're signing autographs'.

Taking these ideas together, we end up thinking of the media more as a range of networks via which the public can decide to participate to whatever degree in creative, communicative, collaborative and democratic activities, and less as a group of

In this example, online media takes centre stage. Beginning with a consideration of how the BBC has acted as a pioneer in the digital age, a case study on the iPlayer as an online development will very soon extend to a consideration of whether or not this is a good use of the licence fee – a cornerstone of public service broadcasting in a **democracy**. Also, whether or not the public have more access to the BBC and what this means set against more explicit examples of '**we media**'. Next, we will think about the **global** reach of the BBC's services, made possible by broadband internet, and what difference increasingly global dissemination of ideas makes to culture and **identity**. This takes us to a consideration of whether our identities are increasingly shaped by media in the online age and whether this takes up to a '**postmodern**' state of mind. And if this is a dangerous thing, then what kinds of regulation are adequate in this web 2.0 world, and what impact might these new modes of regulation have on the BBC, compared to more orthodox forms of **regulation** such as charter renewal and the role of OFCOM?

You could put any theme in the centre . . .

Figure 3.2.1 A mind map of how all the Critical Perspectives themes connect

powerful organisations influencing us. Actually, we are probably halfway between these two states – or at least the developed world is (don't forget that less than 20 per cent of the world has a broadband connection – a somewhat sobering riposte to the 'global village' discourse). The most popular web 2.0 sites are owned by huge companies, so every moment of democratic *we media* social networking makes money for the big corporations – the same ones that were making billions from web 1.0, in fact. Hitwise (2007) reports that 0.16 per cent of YouTube visitors upload video, 0.2 per cent of Flickr visitors upload photos, and Wikipedia is edited or expanded by 4.59 per cent of users. So most of us are using the web 2.0 sites to read, watch, play and listen (not to create and upload), which is how we were using 'old media', whatever using the media might mean. For these reasons, might we be more sensible to think of where we are now as web 1.5?

But this is just an example of a cultural studies approach. Not all the themes demand a direct study of these web 2.0 themes. Media and Collective Identity and Contemporary Media Regulation might involve consideration of how identities are disseminated online, and how the internet provides an enormous challenge for regulators; but equally it might lead you to look at British cinema and TV representations, or film censorship and press regulation. What these themes all have in common, however, is the emphasis on the active audience, on how people 'give meaning' to cultural products, otherwise known as media texts.

All the themes that you can choose from for Critical Perspectives are connected, as the mind map in Figure 3.2.1 shows you.

So you, or your teacher, might choose to focus on one theme in depth, and then branch off to explore related areas, as in the diagram. Doing things this way might lead you from Media and Collective Identity to research into how Global Media pose a threat to local and national identities, for example. Or you might start with Contemporary Media Regulation and end up in an exploration of how Media in the Online Age provide new regulatory challenges compared to, say, **terrestrial** television. Another approach is to look at two or three related themes – for example, We Media and Democracy coupled with Media in the Online Age, Global Media, or both. Whichever route you take to the final exam outcome, you are strongly advised to read *all* the content in the next section, as it is almost impossible to neatly separate the material along theme lines. In other words, whichever theme you are studying, most of the following section will be useful.

4.1

Media and Collective Identity

For this theme you need to learn about the following, in relation to at least two areas of the media:

- How media that are in public circulation now represent groups of people in different ways
- How these representations can be seen as different to historical representations of the same groups
- The **effects** in society of particular kinds of media representation of collective identities
- Ways in which people might use the media actively to form a collective identity
- Debates around the idea that our identities are increasingly constructed by, or through, or in response to the media (and arguments against this notion).

Identity is complicated. Everyone thinks they've got one.

(Gauntlett 2007a: 1)

Identity

Two names that crop up a lot in this book are David Buckingham and David Gauntlett. The reason we keep returning to their ideas is twofold. First, they are two of the most influential writers in media education, so A-level media teachers and students will be wise to make use of their theoretical contributions, whether you agree with them or not. Second, they are both concerned with the relationship between media and cultural identity, and the OCR specification places a clear emphasis on this, as we have discussed. So let's begin our analysis of identity for this theme with a statement from each of them.

> A focus on identity requires us to pay close attention to the diverse ways in which media and technologies are used in everyday life, and their consequences both for individuals and for social groups.

(Buckingham 2008: 19)

It is, of course, the second of Buckingham's 'angles' that we will be paying close attention to in this theme – the consequences of media use for social groups. Here we return to the quote from Gauntlett that started this chapter to have a look in more detail at his elaboration on the complexity of any discussion of identity.

> Identity is complicated. Everyone thinks they've got one. Magazines and talk show hosts urge us to explore our 'identity'. Religious and national identities are at the heart of major international conflicts. Artists play with the idea of 'identity' in modern society. Blockbuster movie superheroes have emotional conflicts about their 'true' identity. And the average teenager can create three online 'identities' before breakfast... Thinking about self-identity and individuality can cause some anxiety – at least in cultures where individuals are encouraged to value their personal uniqueness. Each of us would like to think – to some extent – that we have special, personal qualities, which make us distinctive and valuable to the other people in our lives (or potential future friends). But does this mean anything? Is individuality just an illusion? Maybe we are all incredibly similar, but are programmed to value minuscule bits of differentiation.

(Gauntlett 2007a: 1, 14)

Identity is one of those words that we all take for granted. We talk about our identity in a number of different ways in everyday life – think about the debate over whether innocent people should have any reason to worry about carrying an identity card; think about the information that Facebook encourages you to reveal about yourself, and the 'digital footprint' this leaves for advertisers to make use of. There is a humorous cartoon in circulation with the caption, 'On the internet nobody knows you're a dog', which relates to how we can construct an alternative identity for ourselves online if we want to. These are specific examples about how information about us is shared publicly. But there are more abstract ways of thinking about identity that we also employ every day – the clothes we wear, the media we consume, the people we

Production Tip

To succeed at A2, you must make explicit theoretical links between your research in critical perspectives and your creative practice. Whichever set brief you are responding to for your Advanced Portfolio, you will need to consider – in the research and planning, the evaluation and in your critically reflective writing about your creative work – how your media products relate to ideas about collective identity. For example, advertising works on the assumption that there are clearly identifiable markets that are different to one another, and your advertising package will be constructed with a target consumer group in mind. Soap operas are always concerned with representing recognisable, 'real' communities in fiction. And a local TV news programme has to be all about a sense of local identity and how this will shape the particular news values of the programme – a community 'ethos' entirely based on the notion of a collective identity.

like. The combination of these practices amounts to an idea we have of how others see us, described by Goffman (1990) as 'the presentation of self'. If you see one of your teachers socialising, it can seem strange because you are used to seeing her demonstrating a 'professional identity' – a way of 'being' that is different to her social identity. The stakes get higher for identity when people feel marginalised, victimised or in any way prejudiced against because of their identity. Minority ethnic groups, gay people, disabled people, the elderly, the police, people from Birmingham, teenagers (and countless others – this is just a selection) may all, at times, have cause for complaint about how others make assumptions about them because of their identity. For Muslims in the UK, this might be a visible issue – people make assumptions because of appearance. For gay men, there is the

Synoptic Link

TV drama

For your AS studies you will have analysed representation in TV or radio drama, and the exam will have asked you to consider how the micro elements of a short extract of one drama programme added up to a macro representation of a group of people. This was good preparation for this theme, and one option you have here is to extend this work to consider how television drama represents particular groups of people. Within this scope, you might research and analyse the contemporary representation of a particular profession in UK television drama. This is particularly important because such broadcasting is always the subject of close scrutiny on the assumption that the viewing public must be given an accurate representation of how that profession operates, despite the fact that TV dramatists are usually given far more 'poetic licence'. In other words, the audience's ability to view the programme as fiction is seemingly reduced in this case, and there can be great anxiety from the profession in question that it may be misrepresented. For example, the comedy drama *Teachers* was discussed at length in terms of the morality and lack of professional enthusiasm displayed by the characters (the series was far more about sex and relationships than it was about schools, and the writers defended this by saying that the school was merely a location for a drama about young adults), as was *No Angels*, which used a similar template to offer a post-feminist comedy drama about female nurses and their sex lives. Police drama has always been the subject of close attention, and arguably researchers in this area have to work more rigorously with the profession to ensure that the balance of drama and authenticity is acceptable to the police community. Most recently, the BBC drama *Criminal Justice* represented the legal profession as manipulative, dishonest and opportunistic, leading to a debate on GMTV featuring high-ranking solicitors debating whether events depicted on screen 'could really happen' and what impact the drama could have on public trust in the legal process.

Figure 4.1.1 *Criminal Justice*: accused of eroding public trust in lawyers

issue of whether 'straight-acting' is a safer 'way of being', particularly in the workplace, as being gay is not an immediately visible trait (though there are more complex semiotic choices to be made about clothes, icons and accessories that may be visual). Children with Birmingham accents might be instantly dismissed in comparison to their peers from Kent, and assumptions made about intelligence. These examples take us into the realm of **collective identity**.

Magazines and gender

Carrying on with the mind-mapping idea set out in Chapter 3.2, here is one that Nina Moore prepared earlier (see Figure 4.1.2).

The primary commercial function of magazines is to sell us to advertisers. Although print magazines are threatened by the internet, at the moment they survive, and as students of the media, we must recognise that their income is largely achieved through advertising space, and this works so well because magazines produce a readership that is consistently 'targetable' as a collective group. If the readership of a magazine were too diverse, this would not be so easy to do. So before we embark on an analysis of the relationship between magazine content and collective identities, we must take this as a starting point – magazines sell their readers to advertisers.

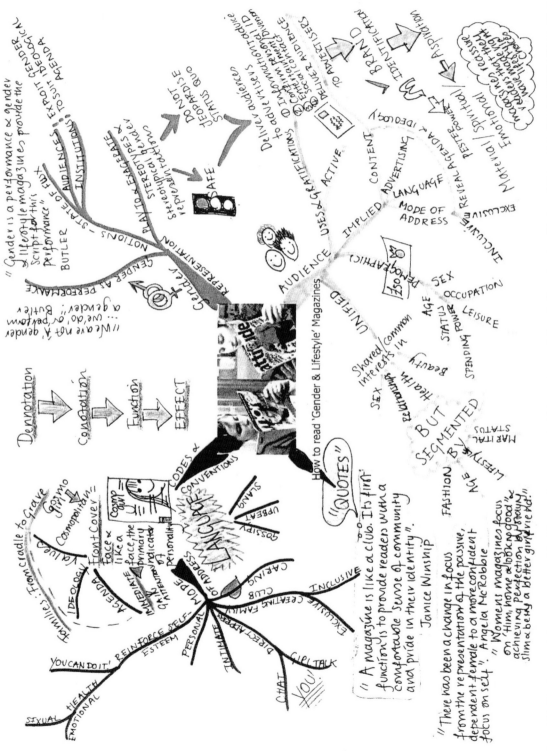

Figure 4.1.2 Nina Moore's mind map on gender and lifestyle magazines – you may find this visual representation of a theme area a useful approach to use across the whole of Critical Perspectives

The questions we need to ask about magazines that target a gender group relate to how editors, writers, photographers and publishers combine to create a sense of belonging based on gender codes and what social effects these might have. We need to assess the notion that there is a set of learned values and behaviours that is reinforced for the reader against the idea that the postmodern reader plays with gender identity and, as such, is able to pick and mix the meanings of the gender representations. (This is dealt with in more detail in the section on Postmodern Media.)

Although the vast majority of magazines can be studied in relation to collective identity, the most striking examples are those that are aimed at a gender group – men or women of a certain age bracket in a certain social stratification. So we can set the long-running woman's magazine, in all of its contemporary forms, against the newer market of lads' mags, and consider both a nature/nurture, positive/negative **binary**-structured approach, alongside a more postmodern conception of audience behaviour.

Activity

A sustained analysis of *Men's Health* may lead to the conclusion that the following four ideas are repeated in every issue, in which case we can say that these are the dominant discourses operating in the magazine:

- Quick-fix problem solving
- Male narcissism (and anxiety)
- New male sensitivity
- Male superiority/manipulation.

In a group of three, collect three editions (hard copy or online) of the magazine and map out articles and features in relation to these discourses.
   Try to separate them into the following categories:

- Those that fit obviously and neatly into one (e.g. a feature on steps to take to avoid prostate cancer or advice for various aspects of male grooming)
- Elements which appear to take a range of positions, meaning that they could fit into more than one discourse (e.g. a feature on sex in which advice for 'driving her wild' is combined with the sense of a 'trade-off' – if you do these things, in return she will…)
- Those which appear to defy these categorisations.

So you will end up with three sets of 'mapped' material.
   Once you have mapped the content to the dominant discourses, you can discuss the outcomes in your group and ask some critical questions about the positive and negative social implications of these discourses.
   Is this magazine 'setting a balance'? In other words, women have been subjected to anxiety about body image for decades, so is it about time men experienced the same thing? Or is it part of the same problem? If every cover features a man with a six-pack and every issue offers advice on transforming the male reader into the same, why would the reader need more than one edition?
   What do the readers really get out of the magazine, do you think?

All magazines strive, through hard work and strategic research by publishers and editorial teams, to create a sense of belonging on the part of their readers. But in order to avoid reducing the readership to a passive mass, we need to remember that readers do not necessarily really believe in this community. Some semiotic work can help to draw this out, looking at cover design in particular to address the simple question of how the reader is drawn in through the language of signs and symbols.

Let us consider two very different theoretical perspectives to apply to our semiotic findings. Winship (1987: 11) offers a feminist application of male gaze theory to women's magazine covers, arguing that 'the gaze between cover model and women readers marks the complicity between women seeing themselves in the image which the masculine culture has defined'.

This resonates with a much older theoretical concept: the **Marxist** idea developed in Althusser's (1971) notion of 'interpellation' – the social/ideological practice of misrecognising yourself. If we put these two together, a feminist-Marxist reading of magazine covers is straightforward – Winship's notion of complicity is about us being prepared, for the reward of gratification, to recognise the ideal version of ourselves, despite the anxiety this will cause (when we compare our real appearance to the ideal). For feminists, the male culture reinforces its power by defining women in this way and encouraging this anxiety. The alternative is to challenge it, but we all know from our cultural experience how difficult this is. The Marxist term for this is 'false consciousness'. Through a range of cultural reinforcements, of which magazines are just one, we are distracted from the inequality in our society. Instead of asking for equal pay and more positive representation in the media, women are reading *Hello* and commenting on the waistlines of celebrities.

To get further into this debate and to include an institutional angle, we require proof of how the constructed audience is 'made'. The easiest way to obtain this is by contacting publishers for advertising packs, which are easily available as downloads in PDF formats for most magazines, through their websites. These define the reader for potential advertisers – where she shops, what she likes, how she understands herself.

A comparison of *Nuts* with *Men's Health* helps us to review two very different examples within the broader category of male magazines. Whereas *Nuts* is explicit in its sexism and reduction of the male gender to its **stereotype** (whether knowing and playful or not), *Men's Health* lays claim to a more sensitive, aspiring version of the gender. However, we might argue that most of its quick-fix approaches to everything – from 'impressing the boss' to 'getting a six-pack' and 'making her beg for more' – are based on a traditional hunter-gatherer discourse about male behaviour. There is little complexity or subtlety in its pages, so whereas the mode of address is very different to *Nuts*, perhaps the discourse, or **ideology**, in both magazines is closer than it appears at first glance.

As stated at the outset, we are going to need a triangular approach to consider the representation of, and perhaps thus the construction of, collective identity in gender magazines. Three questions should be asked of each magazine you study.

- How does it represent its 'own' gender to the reader?
- How does it represent its 'own' gender to the 'other' gender?
- How does it represent the 'other' gender to its readers?

This will pay explicit attention to female readings of *Nuts* and male readings of *Sugar*, as this duality of representation serves to reinforce ideas of the other. Bring in discussions of sexuality and the 'secondary reader' (e.g. the gay male reader of *Elle*, or the

Activity

To see how readers are constructed by magazines, collect a range of popular titles aimed at one gender in each case, and after spending some time reading them, work in a group to answer the following questions about the reader in each magazine, just off the top of your head. What consumption choice would the reader make in each case?

- What breakfast cereal?
- What car/mode of transport?
- What accommodation?
- What drink?
- What TV shows?
- What music?
- What vegetable?
- What sport to watch and what sport to play?
- Ideal partner?
- What holiday?
- Who to vote for?
- What bar/pub?

Next, join with a larger group and take it in turns to adopt the role of the reader of the magazine being discussed and take the 'hot seat'. The rest of the group will fire questions at the person in the hot seat (these must not be questions already asked above). Through this approach, you are raising important theoretical ideas about readership, audience complicity and stereotyping, and deliberately making assumptions about the readership of magazines as fixed, stable types of people whom we can second-guess in these ways.

After this activity, you can match the outcomes to the information produced for advertisers for the magazine, to see the 'fit'. But crucially, as we are engaged here in a theoretical study of culture rather than just the kind of institutional knowledge acquisition we are concerned with at AS level, this way of thinking about magazine readers will need to be set against a more complex postmodern approach.

female reader of *GQ*), and things get more interesting, reminding us again of the *complexity* of representation. An interesting fact to be aware of is this – cover models on *Men's Health* are always in black and white, because the editors assume that the heterosexual readership will feel more secure with this as the black and white male torso is viewed as less sexual and more mechanical. Alongside this fact – which comes from the editorial team and is thus beyond mere academic speculation – is a question: why is it that, with a few exceptions, both women's and men's magazines feature female cover models?

Media and Collective Identity is a theme within Critical Perspectives, so we come to the point where you need to form an intellectually secure point of view on a debate with no 'right answers'. Consider these two opposing perspectives.

Synoptic Link

OCR Media Studies for AS featured a case study on *Monkey* magazine, a men's magazine that exists only online. From the AS angle, the focus was on the institutional context, but here we are concerned with magazines as potential agents in constructing social identity. *Monkey* is relevant for this also, so here is the case study reproduced and slightly adapted, but you will need to read it from a different perspective now, and place *Monkey* alongside *Nuts* and *Men's Health* as examples of men's magazines that may or may not influence the male reader to (mis)recognise their gender traits.

Monkey is an online-only magazine which offers a similar diet of material to *Nuts*, but with the added bonus of moving-image clips and sound. Given that the lads' mags format has a pornographic element, it is easy to see how this might appeal. The way it works is described on the website (www.monkeymag.co.uk/registration – accessed August 2008), which is the magazine, of course.

The world's first weekly digital men's magazine has arrived and it's 100% FREE forever! Yes! Give us your email address and every Wednesday you'll get a link to the latest issue of *Monkey*. It's honestly the best way to break the back of your week! *Monkey* is the first men's magazine in the world to bring you full, living, breathing, singing, dancing, stripping, and exploding video. You can watch videos and movie trailers, listen to the latest in music and share incredible stuff with your friends. To get your *Monkey* every week you need to sign up. Signing up is easy and free, we just need your name and email address (plus postcode if you live in the UK) and that's it. Join the *Monkey* party today!

But *Monkey* is not the product of an alternative, independent web distributor. Instead, it is produced by Dennis, one of the big companies, and a publisher already highly prolific in the lads' mags sector, with such titles as *Maxim* and *Stuff*. This is an example of a big media corporation realising that the best way to compete against a perceived threat is to harness its potential for yourself, in the same way that Rupert Murdoch recently acquired MySpace, and the music industry started offering legal downloads.

These days, the insinuation that all gents are satisfied by 29 cans of Stella and a slightly stained copy of *Razzle* is as quaintly outmoded as the suggestion that the lady loves Milk Tray. Nevertheless, *Zoo* and its brethren seem to act like some elaborate cultural muck-spreader, coating everything in an impermeable layer of tits and ass and porn and fighting. And the intimation is that any bird who can't handle that can feck off and take her scented candles with her.

(Barton 2004: 16)

Barton, Althusser and Winship (see above) offer variations on the theme that gender magazines do some damage, and that there is a correlation between the representation of gender in their pages, the readers' acceptance of them and problems in society.

A different view comes from David Gauntlett, who articulates the idea that we pick and mix our media and select in more or less regular ways how we form our identities in relation to them. This theoretical intervention, it is important to add, is the outcome of sustained audience research.

I have argued against the view that men's lifestyle magazines represent a reassertion of old-fashioned masculine values, or a 'back-lash' against feminism. Whilst certain pieces in the magazines might support such an argument, this is not their primary purpose or selling point. Instead, their existence and popularity shows men rather insecurely trying to find their place in the modern world, seeking help regarding how to behave in their relationships and advice on how to earn the attention, love and respect of women and the friendship of other men. In post-traditional cultures, where identities are not 'given' but need to be constructed and negotiated, and where an individual has to establish their personal ethics and mode of living, the magazines offer some reassurance to men who are wondering 'Is this right?' and 'Am I doing this OK?', enabling a more confident management of the narrative of the self.

(Gauntlett 2002: 180)

Kendall (2008: in press) researched young people's reading habits and, predictably, magazines featured heavily. She was concerned with students' ideas of themselves as particular kinds of readers. Kendall found that male readers adopted a less critical stance than their female counterparts.

The magazines functioned, as for female readers, to offer prompts and possibilities for representing self through negotiation of symbolic codes. However, the male readers were characteristically less critical and more acquiescent to the identities inscribed through the modalities of their 'hobby' magazines.

Why this would be so is open to debate. Perhaps males take a less negotiated position in response to these texts, or perhaps the longer history of the woman's magazine is a factor. Either way, both Gauntlett and Kendall remind us that, ultimately, the only viable approach to these debates is audience research. So it is very important that you follow up this introduction to the debate by conducting your own audience research with magazine readers, so you can illustrate your understanding of the theoretical perspectives you have read about here with your own 'empirical' evidence from 'real live magazine readers'.

Celebrity and collective identity

There are a range of theoretical perspectives on the cult of celebrity, and there are certainly many fascinating questions to ask: why can media producers make so much money out of telling us what celebrities are eating? Why do we care? What is missing in our lives? And, as we will explore in the We Media and Democracy section, as we are given more and more opportunities to become celebrities ourselves, through reality TV and TV talent contests of various kinds, something interesting happens. Rather than seeing this as 'devaluing' celebrity and thus losing interest, members of the public become even more obsessed with celebrities, even those (or particularly those) 'celebrities' who a few weeks before were stacking shelves in supermarkets, and who may well be going back to that in the same amount of time.

Case study

Heat magazine

Heat's circulation is around 500,000. Owned by Bauer Consumer Media, the main competition for the magazine comes from *Grazia* and *OK!* In relation to the discussion above, the fact that the market can bear three titles which we might place in the 'celebrity magazine' genre demonstrates the level of public interest in famous people. The editor of *Heat*, Julian Linley (interview in Brook 2008: 5), describes the magazine's mode of address as follows.

> I approach every single picture and every single story with the same attitude – what does this mean to the reader and her life? And I don't see my reader in a trashy way at all.

This defiant statement is clearly at odds with the perception of *Heat* as a key agent in the 'dumbing down' of media to the point where people who are only famous for being famous, or wanting to be, see *Heat* as a platform for their exposure. Linley's view of his audience relates well to Gauntlett's idea of the pick-and-mix reader, and Kendall's research findings where female readers of magazines were seen to have developed a metadiscourse in relation to their reading. In this postmodern sense, the readers of *Heat* are able to enjoy the trivial **pleasure** afforded by the magazine at the same time as being aware of the problematic nature of celebrity culture. Ruddock (2007) writes about the hard work of meaningless consumption, and this is a good example – the readers of *Heat* invest effort in defining the material as 'trivial' and as such they are far from passive in their reading of the text. On the other hand, in the interview referenced above, Linley talks about the commodification of celebrities by explaining that *OK!* has more money to offer famous people, but *Heat* has a more developed relationship with many of them, and this 'logistical' aspect of how this media product comes to exist can hardly be seen as progressive or empowering for anyone. So there is a debate to be had here about the social implications of the shared interest in celebrity culture as a collective identity, and what this might mean for ordinary people and how they make sense of their lives.

Sexuality and the politics of absence

While it is both educational and ethically important to analyse the ways in which mainstream media represent gay men and women, it is possibly even more enlightening (and sobering) to consider the absence of 'neutral' representations of people from minority sexuality groups. What this means is simple. While there may be increasing numbers of media images of gay people – from the success of Graham Norton to the postmodern 'playful' humour of Catherine Tate's Derek ('how very dare you'), alongside more serious films and TV such as *Brokeback Mountain* and *Sugar Rush*, it is a matter of concern in gay communities that gay characters tend to appear *as* gay – that is, their sexuality is the subject of the drama they find themselves in; or in non-fiction, they play up to camp stereotypes, however satirical or laden with pastiche. Consider how far we are from equality in the media by asking yourself this question: what would be the reaction if an action film hero like Bruce Willis in *Die Hard* had a male partner in danger rather than a female wife? Would the film work? Would it be successful? Would it seem strange? If you think it would, this is because sexuality is not neutral. When gay people are represented in media, it is too often as the objects of heterosexual curiosity, which reinforces marginalisation, and, at the more serious end of the debate, oppression and prejudice.

Case study

The Heinz Deli Mayo ad

In June 2008, Heinz withdrew an advertisement after feedback from both gay and heterosexual consumers indicated that the advert had failed in its attempt to be humorous and had offended people on all sides. The advert was for mayonnaise, and the premise of the narrative was that if you buy this product, you will have a New York Deli chef in your kitchen making the sandwiches, instead of a housewife. So when the husband leaves for work, he is kissed by the male chef instead of a female spouse. Whether this is progressive in relation to the politics of absence (see above) is something you can debate. As the idea of the male kiss is for comedy, possibly not. And after all, we are not supposed to believe that the chef is really the 'mother figure' in the house – it is a metaphor, a symbol for the 'authenticity' of the product. The more interesting area

for your attention here is the reaction of the audience and the decision by Heinz to respond. The decision to pull the advert was taken before it was reported that the ASA had received around 200 complaints. Further analysis shows that the majority of complaints came from religious groups, and that one common concern was that children would be given a 'dangerous' message (that homosexuality is normal). This is ironic given that the Ofcom regulations stipulate that the ad was not shown during peak-time children's viewing hours due to the sugar content of the product. So why this reaction? What does it tell us about the times we live in? How does this work in the context of our study of media and collective identity – how is 'normal' being defined and reinforced, and what implications might this have for our social lives?

British cinema

To explore the ways in which British films might serve to construct, reinforce or challenge notions of British identity, we need to approach this theme from three angles. In *OCR Media Studies for AS*, we dealt in detail with the British film industry and how contemporary production, distribution and exchange of film in the UK are shaped by new patterns of convergence and technology. We will not repeat all that here, since we are now working in an A2 context, but some of that material will be relevant, since the ways in which Britain is represented on screen are hugely influenced by economic and political contexts, such as funding, the relationship of British film to the USA and the rest of Europe, dilemmas for producers, audience shifts, government agendas and the relationship of culture to commerce. Second, we need to consider British films as cultural products and look at a range of commercially successful and critically acclaimed films on release, with regard to directors, styles and audience responses. And then we need to come to some conclusions about how films represent the changing nature of Britain and its people – in particular, how different films do this in different ways, how this has changed as the notion of being British has changed, and the question of whether British cinema has always suffered, and still does, from a 'burden of representation'. We must avoid simplistic binary oppositions here between 'cultural' UK films and 'commercial' Hollywood, as this is problematic for all sorts of reasons. There are commercially 'huge' UK films that offer little 'serious' cultural reflection, and there are Hollywood films which offer provocative and challenging 'artistic' representations. With a film like *This Is England*, which managed to achieve both, the debate is over critical acclaim in relation to commercial imperatives, and the importance of cultural reflection alongside the feel-good depictions we might associate more with costume drama and literary adaptation, or Hugh Grant and Julia Roberts falling in love in a Notting Hill which bears little resemblance to the 'real' location (although reading the section in this book on Postmodern Media might make you question this distinction).

The British film industry

If you studied the British film industry at AS, this will be a recap. The British Film Institute defines British films under four categories, in which Category A is an entirely British film, funded by UK finance, and staffed by a majority of British personnel; Category B is majority UK funded; C is the more common co-funding scenario; and D describes US films with some creative input from the UK.

In relation to the USA, sharing a language with Hollywood has been simultaneously a benefit and a stumbling block for UK cinema, and people's opinions on this vary, depending on whether we view films as cultural documents, artistic texts, commercial products or all three. Roddick argues strongly that 'Every memorable achievement to come out of UK cinema since the war has come out of someone's desire to say something, not to sell it' (Roddick 1999: 3). His point is that our media and government define success on the Hollywood model – 'bums on seats' and sales of DVDs and related merchandise. Because of this, films get money from the Film Council and the National Lottery, but are usually expected either to compete with blockbusters or to settle for low budgets and inadequate marketing. Thus, some argue that the bottleneck in the system is preventing more 'serious' films that represent Britain in more challenging ways from getting larger audiences.

So anyone making a film has a dilemma. The USA shares our language, and we are a tiny collective of people by comparison. So the impulse to aim for the international market will always be there. Alongside this, it is probably fair to assume that your film culture (alongside TV, games and, to a lesser extent, music) is increasingly American. Under New Labour, the Film Council, administrating lottery spend on films, has created some more visible resources for UK production, but the dilemmas faced by the likes of Shane Meadows, Ken Loach, Michael Winterbottom and Mike Leigh are summed up clearly here by Stafford (2002: 6).

> The choices for British producers are: make low-budget British films targeted at mainstream British audiences, hoping that the 'peculiarly British' subject matter will attract overseas audiences who will see the films as 'unusual'. A low-budget film could cover costs by careful sale of rights in the UK and Europe. Anything earned in the US is then a bonus. Or make low-budget films for a 'niche' arthouse audience in the UK and abroad. Or look for partners in Europe and/or America and aim more clearly for an 'international audience'.

The burden of representation

The 'burden of representation' is a phrase that cannot be ignored if you are studying British film in relation to collective identity. It describes the way that the history of social realist British film can weigh on the shoulders of new film-makers and producers. Looking at a range of films which aim to represent how Britain is changing as a result of immigration, we can assess how cinema has tried to do this in more or less commercially 'translatable' ways.

Bend it Like Beckham

Analysing *Bend it Like Beckham*, the interesting questions are around the blend of **realism**/authenticity and stereotyping. Some Muslim critics of British films such as *East Is East* have been concerned about the representation of 'traditional' Muslim values through the depiction of inflexible patriarchs. *Beckham*, equally, represents Punjabi identity through the well-worn depiction of a wedding, and Jess is marked out as 'other' to this culture through her desire to play football (the most western of activities, and traditionally male) on this day. The feel-good narrative alongside the intertextual timing of the release (the 2002 World Cup and Beckham's celebrity) resulted in this film grossing ten times its production costs. The critical question for you is this: to what extent does the film balance its stereotyping of Punjabi life with a more complex discourse about gender and identity? Could it be argued that the film avoids some of the more important issues about racism in the UK? Perhaps the most interesting angle to explore is the way in which this film bridges the 'culture or commerce' dilemma – it achieved both – and to ask how it managed this. On the one hand, the film is absolutely a reflection of contemporary British culture, and is happy to carry the burden of representation. But on the other, it was produced with the USA in mind, in the knowledge that soccer in the USA is a game played mostly by females – the obvious audience for the product.

Activity

Here is a framework for research on contemporary British film and collective identity.

- Undertake some local audience research and some industry fact-finding. In your area, who goes where to see what? Who owns the cinemas? Who distributes the films watched? What alternatives are there which people do not make use of, and why not? Focus on the reasons people give for their choices rather than your own assumptions. The study resources section at the end of the book will provide some useful starting points for the industry aspects.
- What are the most successful British films of the past year, in both commercial and cultural terms? How is this distinction made and what conclusions can you draw about the way that Britain is represented in film?
- A case study on the representation of multicultural Britain and the experiences of immigrants and their children, asylum seekers and economic migrants (see the activity on this later in this section). Follow up the work in the activity with some institutional research to find out how each film was funded and distributed. Use the Internet Movie Database to do this (www.imdb.com – accessed August 2008).

British social realism

As the 'burden of representation' phrase suggests, the UK has a strong legacy of fiction – spanning theatre, literature, TV and film – that attempts to portray issues facing ordinary people in their social situations. This tradition has remained, despite problems with funding and the lure of the US market, as we have discussed.

Here we will consider some recent British films which we can analyse as texts that provoke a response in relation to collective identity – competing ideas about 'Britishness'.

Social realist film should not be thought of as a genre or a type of film, but more of an approach. Like most labels used in the media, film directors are often resistant to it. Ken Loach, the English film director most commonly associated with this style, prefers to talk about his films more in terms of storytelling, suggesting that he merely tells stories which he hopes will 'resonate' with the public. Mike Leigh, another director often tagged in this way, tends to avoid any suggestion that his unusual style of working (no scripts, total improvisation, not telling the actors what will happen until it does – which he shares with Loach) can be pinned down to a form of 'realism'. So we have to tread carefully. But what we can do is distinguish between films that lead to serious debate about the 'real world' and real current social issues that affect people at the margins of society, and films that do not make this attempt. Social realism, then, will be best understood as an approach to film which seeks to make explicit connections to matters of public debate – the economic system, social relations, relationships between ethnic groups, various forms of exploitation. For example, Ken Loach's recent film *It's a Free World* tells the story of a single mother who sees an opportunity to give her son a better future by setting up a recruitment firm supplying cheap immigrant labour in London. The development of the story comes when she realises that there is more money to be made in illegal supply, and the film then explores the various levels of exploitation and human rights abuse that follow. But the 'social realist' approach means that we have to confront the complexity of the situation. Angie, the female protagonist, is not a faceless, 'evil' human trafficker, whom we can simply despise in a straightforward good/bad binary. Instead, she is a mother with limited opportunities for aspiration, and she sees her business empire as no different to any other self-employed entrepreneur. So the real enemy is the capitalist system which leads to such exploitation. In terms of collective identity, then, the film represents economic migrants as victims, but like other Ken Loach films, the focus is on the way in which the poor or dispossessed exploit one another. Other recurring themes in his films are loan sharks, drug dealers and corrupt employers, but these are rarely middle-class or executive characters – his interest is in how the system forces those at the bottom of the pile to turn on one another.

Murray (2008) identifies a range of very different kinds of films as examples of a 'new social realism' – *This Is England* and *London to Brighton*, both of which featured as case studies in the OCR AS textbook, alongside *Red Road, Ratcatcher* and *Kidulthood*. You are encouraged to view all these films in order to understand her argument more fully, but we will outline some key points here.

Synoptic Link

This Is England and *London to Brighton*

In **OCR Media Studies for AS**, both these films were explored as institutional case studies. Here we will take a more theoretical position, exploring their status as texts which represent the nature of British social life, but a recap on each film as a commercial and cultural product will be useful.

This Is England is directed by the Midlands director Shane Meadows. The plot could not be more indigenous, but this is not the England of *The Queen*, *Notting Hill* or *Pride and Prejudice*. Instead, the 1970s skinhead movement, its uneasy relationship with West Indian culture (from respect for which it grew) and its distortion by the racist National Front form the backdrop for a story about the adolescent life of a bereaved boy.

Previously, Meadows had varied box office and critical success with a range of other films, all based on domestic life and relationships in the Midlands – *Twenty Four Seven*, *A Room for Romeo Brass*, *Once Upon a Time in the Midlands* and *Dead Man's Shoes* – in which the presence or absence of fathers and older male authority figures, and the effects of such on young working-class men, are depicted with a mixture of comedy and sometimes disturbing drama. Another major difference between Meadows' output and the more commercially 'instant' British films from Working Title and similar companies, is the importance of cultural reference points – clothes, music, dialect – that only a viewer with a cultural familiarity with provincial urban life in the times depicted would recognise.

This Is England was produced as a result of collaboration between no fewer than seven companies – Big Arty Productions, EM Media, FilmFour, Optimum Releasing, Screen Yorkshire, the UK Film Council and Warp Films – and distributed by six organisations – IFC Films, Netflix, Red Envelope Entertainment and IFC First Take in the US, Madman Entertainment in Australia and Optimum Releasing in the UK.

The critical response to *This Is England* has largely been to celebrate a perceived 'return' to a kind of cultural reflective film-making that was threatened by extinction in the context of Hollywood's dominance, and the government's preference for funding films with an eye on the US market.

London to Brighton, released at the end of 2006, follows a long tradition of 'social realist' British films that, like the films of Gary Oldman, Shane Meadows and more established directors such as Ken Loach and Mike Leigh, reflect on the less palatable, but arguably more important aspects of contemporary, divided and uneasy British social life.

Clearly, the film has British cultural content, depicting two females attempting to escape to the coast after involvement with a gangster and a pimp, and fearing revenge. The locations are those often described as the 'underbelly' of London. The producers raised the initial budget through a group of private investors, and eventually it cost £80,000 to shoot and edit the film. Several scenes were then shown to the UK Film Council, who subsequently provided £185,000 to complete post-production and create all the materials needed by a production company. The cast was made up (by necessity) of unknown actors, and the style of filming was determined not only by the aesthetic desire to be 'gritty', but also by resources.

Final production credits are shared by Steel Mill Pictures and Wellington Films, and *London to Brighton* was distributed by Vertigo Films in the UK, MK2 Diffusion in France, Paradiso in Belgium and Noble Entertainment in Scandinavia, to name but a few territories. The film won several awards at film festivals, and was critically well received. The outcome is an interesting example of what is sometimes called 'guerrilla' film distribution, and time will tell whether Williams' strategy will act as a blueprint for other aspiring directors on a shoestring budget.

Murray (2008: 35) offers this working definition of new social realism.

The work of film-makers today who may be creative, but are always grounded in the actuality of the events within their social contexts – wanting to examine the social realities that these fictional stories and people grow out of. Our experience as audiences is a constant frisson of recognition – of places, of people we have varying degrees of contact with.

This idea of 'frisson' is very helpful, as it leads us to the idea that social realism is often uncomfortable to watch, especially when set against 'escapist' cinema, and this is probably a reason for its relative failure at the box office. As Murray goes on to illustrate, *This Is England* explores social breakdown, isolation and fear; *Red Road* deals with the victims of 'Big Brother Britain' – our contemporary surveillance culture and state of anxiety and suspicion (the Big Brother idea is from Orwell's novel *1984*, which the reality TV show takes its name from). *London to Brighton* is a very painful viewing experience, as we see a 'chase' unfold, where a drug dealer and pimp pursues a 12-year-old unwilling prostitute to the coast. Like many social realist films, the complexity of exploitation is the theme again here – the pimp is a 'low-level' player, caught in the middle – he has to pursue the girl to save himself, as a much more serious criminal above him is seeking revenge for events beyond his control. In reference to collective identity, on the one hand, the films represent different issues so cannot be lumped together as being universally typical of how the UK is viewed on screen in 2008. But the themes they explore are common, as Murray (2008: 50–1) demonstrates in relation to locations and environments used.

> These places represent an everywhere of Britain, where relationships have broken down and where people have become isolated and disconnected. *This Is England* celebrates community; *Red Road* gives us the faint possibility of its return through individual acts of connection… *London to Brighton*'s social message is bleaker, since it sees escape as the only option. Their Britishness is in their culturally specific address to audiences at home.

Films that make such culturally specific domestic addresses, then, will offer a version of 'collective identity' that is very different to the kinds of British films that are explicitly seeking an American box office return. But that is not to say that these more commercially minded products are any less significant for the kinds of collective identity they represent. Indeed, if so many more people see *Notting Hill*, *Atonement* or *Pride and Prejudice* than the social realist films we have discussed here, or the critically acclaimed material from Ken Loach and Mike Leigh, which is more successful in the rest of Europe than in these directors' home country, then who is to say which version of our collective identity is the more powerful or has the most impact?

Activity

View all the following films:

- *Ae Fond Kiss*
- *Bend it Like Beckham*
- *Dirty Pretty Things*
- *In this World*
- *Last Resort*

These films all deal with people with **hybrid** identities, or who are trying to survive in the UK as 'outsiders'. As such, they represent Britain itself and the idea of British identity, as well as the identity of these 'visitors'. For each film, these are the questions to explore.

- Who is being represented?
- Who is representing them?
- How are they represented?
- What seem to be the intentions of the representations?
- What range of readings are there?

Next, watch *Saturday Night and Sunday Morning*, a film from the 'kitchen sink' drama period. Again, ask the same questions: who is being represented, by whom, for what purpose and with what range of responses? Albert Finney's portrayal of Arthur Seaton in *Saturday Night and Sunday Morning* had an impact at the time of its release because it was seen to put new people on the screen, within a wider discourse about working-class male ideology. Crucially, the character of Arthur understands his alienation, there is no 'false consciousness' here, and the audience is placed within his mind as we hear his thoughts – there is a clear 'preferred reading' or dominant discourse which he carries through the film. Combining comedy to depict the existence of 'kinds of people' previously absent from the screen is something also evident in *Bend it Like Beckham*. *In This World* stands alone in this activity, since Michael Winterbottom (discussed at length in the Postmodern Media section) offers a partly documentary approach (he went to a refugee camp in Afghanistan and asked two of the residents to be filmed making the journey to London), to set up a more complex and troubling version of this 'representation of the new'. This is outlined by Stafford (2003b: 16).

> We see the characters 'as is' – they are 'ordinary' and 'extraordinary' and we are forced to wonder what we would do in their situation. The drama comes from the situation and the way the characters struggle to respond to it. This is the classic neorealist approach – the opposite of a story 'imposed' on the real world.

Your job here is to develop an understanding of how each of the five films compares to *Saturday Night and Sunday Morning*, in relation to cultural identity and nationhood, developing an analysis of each film as a site of conflict between different discourses or world views. To do this, simply ask yourself (or discuss with your fellow students) which characters carry which discourses – ideas of how the world works and what matters, what is positive and what is negative, and which discourse seems to be the one that is supposed to be dominant. Most importantly, look for moments where discourses are in conflict and it is possible to respond in a number of different ways. And most important of all, consider how possible it would be for someone to start watching the film with very fixed views on immigration, British identity and culture, and to have these ideas challenged during the viewing experience.

Exam-Style Question

Looking at two media, describe the ways in which a particular group of people are collectively represented or provided for, using specific examples to support your response.

Examiner's Tip

This is relevant for any theme in Critical Perspectives. When writing about two media, it is not necessary to devote exactly half of the time to each one. One may be more significant than the other. For example, for Media and Collective Identity, you might spend most of your time writing about British film, and a shorter chunk of your essay might be devoted to the changing representation of Britain on the small screen. However, whichever way you choose to construct your answer, you *will* gain extra marks for comparing, linking and contrasting the two media, rather than writing about them separately.

4.2
Global Media

For this theme you need to learn about the following, in relation to at least two areas of the media:

- A variety of media which we can consider global in terms of how they are distributed and shared
- The historical development of media **globalisation**
- The impact of global media on audience behaviour
- Debates about the pros and cons of global media.

Before we consider the media as global, we need to understand what is meant by globalisation in more general terms.

What has happened? What is happening?

In 1960, Marshall McLuhan wrote *Explorations in Communication*, and in this text he introduced the idea of the 'global village'. McLuhan was writing before cable TV, digital media, the internet, mobile phones, MP3 and pretty much everything we now call 'the media'. But McLuhan was a 'prophet' in that he predicted the process of globalisation as the product of society being increasingly 'mediated'. Globalisation could not work without people being more aware of global culture, and this happens through the media. Robertson (1994: 8) describes globalisation as 'both the **compression** of the world and the intensification of consciousness of the world as a whole'. This separates the two mutually dependent aspects of McLuhan's idea of the global village like this: it is only possible for us to watch films and listen to music and buy things that are not produced locally or nationally if we know they are there for us to watch, listen to and buy.

What difference does it make?

In a globalised world there will be a single society and culture occupying the planet ... it will be a society without borders and spatial boundaries. We can define globalisation as a social process in which the constraints of geography on social and cultural arrangements recede and in which people become increasingly aware that they are receding.

Waters (1995: 3) describes globalisation here in geographical terms. Put simply, as we become more 'globalised', we care less about local or national culture, and identify more with attractive, persuasive ideas and ways of living, regardless of where they come from. But not everybody agrees with this. Moores (2005: 66) argues that our idea of the specific place, the local, is not 'marginalised' (made less important) by globalisation, but is instead made 'instantaneously pluralized' – in other words, we just visit (virtually) a lot more local spaces rather than one big virtual global space. Another example Moores uses is the person walking down the high street talking on a mobile phone to somebody in another country, which we might think of as being in two places at once. So we end up living in lots of spaces – local and global, at the same time.

Globalisation divides as much as it unites; it divides as it unites – the causes of division being identical with those which promote the uniformity of the globe. What appears as globalisation for some means localisation for others; signalling a new freedom to some, upon many others it descends as an uninvited and cruel fate.

Here, Bauman (1998: 2) is reflecting on the 'winners and losers', stressing that not everybody is included in the global village, in which – in reality – the rich and powerful share ideas, exchange trade, buy and sell, and dominate markets of various kinds. For those 'left behind', local culture becomes impoverished and desperate. We must always remember, for example, that less than 20 per cent of the human race has broadband internet access. In a place like the Gambia, culture is very local, and very poor.

How can we study it?

Although the new electronic networks have partially replaced the relatively stable and enduring traditional communities with which we are accustomed, they also facilitate countless highly specialised social and cultural connections that otherwise would not take place. Millions of people all over the world are taking advantage. As technological and cultural landscapes evolve, the sense of belonging and community does not disappear; it changes shape.

Lull (2006: 56) here gives us the focus we need for Critical Perspectives. There are three areas for our research:

- How are specific areas of the media changing to become more 'globalised' in terms of how media are produced, distributed and exchanged?
- Who are the 'winners and losers' in this change, with Bauman's concerns in mind?
- How, as an outcome of these changes to how media 'happens', do ideas about culture, community and society change in the ways that Lull describes?

Activity

For one week, keep a media journal. This needs to cover media consumption of all kinds and any media production or distribution you are engaged in. While media consumption generally includes a whole range of experiences, ranging from planned and deliberate (e.g. going to the cinema to see a specific film) to indirect and accidental (e.g. an advert seen on a train or on the side of a bus), in this case you should focus only on the direct, deliberate side of things.

At the end of the week, identify the country of origin of each media product you consumed – this may take some time and require some internet research. When you have this information, consider the following questions:

- How much of the media you use is made in the UK?
- How much comes from overseas?
- How much is difficult to locate (e.g. made in the UK but distributed by a foreign organisation)?
- Express the amount of UK media you used as a percentage of your total media consumption for the week.
- Finally, consider how typical the week was – for example, if you watched a whole 'British cinema' season on a digital channel, this will have skewed your findings.

For this theme, you need to do two things. First, you have to show that you understand how the media has become more global in terms of how it is distributed, and you must have examples from two forms of media to back this up. Second, you must engage with the debates that arise from this increasing media globalisation – what difference does it make to people if their media is no longer controlled and organised locally or nationally?

Media studies has always been concerned with the difference made to culture and identity by the worldwide success of

Hollywood, the spread of international music, TV and news networks, and the importance of 'dispersed' media consumption like **Bollywood** cinemas in Birmingham. But there is no doubt that global media has become much more of an issue for debate since the internet arrived, or more specifically since broadband became accessible to the public. The reasons for this are obvious. The broadband internet is – with a few exceptions, like China's restricted version of Google – a global network for the distribution, consumption, critique and remixing of media products. At one end of the continuum, major corporations like Disney and the BBC use the internet to reach wider audiences than was previously possible. At the other end, school students share videos on YouTube and achieve playback from viewers all over the planet. The first example is organised, commercial, corporate and strategic. The second is an example of *we media* – organic, random, creative and much harder to analyse. Irvine (2006: 5) offers this explanation of how global digital media transform the social world.

At the extreme, modern media simply dissolve time, distance, place and local culture that once divided the globe. Perhaps the best examples are computer games and pop videos. Routinely their content blurs boundaries of history and geography in a mix that denies the specificities of actual locations and particular chronological periods. In effect, we are putting all our cultural eggs in one basket.

While Irvine seems to take a negative view of global media here – there being an inference in this statement that perhaps geographical and cultural boundaries are important and their erosion is damaging – others celebrate the 'shrinking world', especially on economic grounds. It is so much easier now to disseminate cultural products across the world, to physically travel on cheap flights and to use technology to communicate with people from all nations and walks of life. So this is a debate – the world is now said to be a 'global village' and the media are playing a huge part in this trend. But there are positive and negative outcomes. And we must remember that not everyone is invited to this global gathering – it is worth stating here again that less than 20 per cent of the world, at the time of writing (2008), has broadband access, so if we are saying that high-speed and quality downloading is what makes global media possible, then we must bear witness to this considerable 'digital divide'.

As the internet is itself a fact of convergence, finding two media to compare for this theme should be easy. Indeed, some commentators say that the internet transforms media distribution so much that the boundaries around separate media forms blur beyond recognition. Nevertheless, this section will take three examples, each from a different media, in order to find answers to these questions from the OCR A2 specification.

Case study

Federico

Read this blog posting from Federico Leopone, an Italian student in Birmingham for three months. Here he describes how he uses web 2.0 to communicate with friends in Italy, and how his media consumption is divided between Italian and American media.

I think the TV I see is about 40% made in Italy. The other 60% is produced by foreign companies (most of them are American). Almost every TV series I can see on Italian TV is made in USA.

The music I listen to on the radio is mostly foreign (70% foreign music; 30% Italian music). I think the English and US music industries have a lot of success in Italy because they have a lot of money for advertising! And honestly I really can not understand how people can love songs of which they do not know the meaning!

I really love Italian movies but usually when I go to the cinema with friends, we prefer (or they prefer and I follow them!) to see American productions dubbed into Italian. I usually see Italian films on DVD at home.

The internet I use is 50% based on foreign websites (YouTube, Facebook, MySpace) and 50% based on Italian websites. I use Italian websites to search for information or university news. On the other hand I use foreign websites to have some fun.

Finally I can say my Italian media consumption is dominated by foreign media, mainly coming from USA.

Production Tip

Whichever brief you choose for your Advanced Portfolio, you will develop an idea, based on research, of the 'reach' of the products you are distributing. You need to consider the place of your media products in the global media world, which can mean one of two things. Either you will be designing your products as global commodities, to be disseminated beyond the UK, or you will see your creative work as domestic in outlook and therefore you will consider risks and threats from globally dispersed competition. Either way, you should link the outcomes to the debates about local, national and global media in this section – how are your media products to relate to lived experiences of people in this increasingly fragmented **mediasphere**?

- What kinds of media are increasingly global in terms of **production** and **distribution**?
- How have global media developed in **historical** terms, and how **inclusive** is this trend in reality?
- What kinds of **audience** behaviour and consumption are increasingly global?
- What are the arguments for and against global media, in relation to **content**, **access**, **representation** and **identity**?

The three examples we will explore in relation to these questions and debates are television, news and cinema. As your own approach must span more than one media area – this is a requirement of the Critical Perspectives exam – you might choose to combine two of these, in which case you need to make some comparisons between them. Or you can take one of the areas and conduct a second, less developed case study to bring in along the way. Either way, you will probably find that the converging nature of the contemporary media does some of the work for you. For instance, the global distribution of video games will relate to the practices of the international film industry. And global online news impacts on television and print news.

There are some broader theoretical considerations which come from cultural studies which we need to keep in mind when analysing this material. Crucially, it is important always to have specific examples at our disposal, and not to overgeneralise about 'global culture'. What we are dealing with here is essentially the interplay in people's lives (including your own) *between* the local and the global. It is far too simplistic to assume that global media are dominant and that we get all our cultural reference points from those powerful corporations which have managed to distribute their media products worldwide. There is always resistance to this trend. And we need always to remember that our own cultural perspective is not universal – there are many countries where global access is limited, either for political, economic or cultural reasons. In these societies, the nation state, controlled by government, will be far more central to **media access** than is the case in the UK. And there are societies in which religious faith competes with the 'lure' of western media. So we are engaged in investigating what McMillin (2007: 180) describes as 'the cultural and social implications of global market strategies', and 'examining globalization processes from the ground, from the level of lived experiences'.

Global television and hybrid programming

It is important to resist the idea that media used to be national and now it is global, as though this were a neat, **linear**, historical development. In fact, as Hartley (2007: 63) reminds us, 'globalisation is as old as the media themselves', and what has really happened is that we have begun to realise how cross-cultural media have always been, and we have given a name to this – globalisation. Clearly, whether or not it is a new thing, we can see that there are advantages and disadvantages to the global distribution of television, represented here as a basic list.

Pros	Cons
Cheaper hardware (televisions)	Erosion of national culture
Ability to consume TV from elsewhere	Cultural dominance of the USA
Ability to compare own nation's television with other TV	Market forces funding
More choice?	Less choice?

We will look at each of these in more detail. The pros probably need less explanation, and they are partly economic and partly cultural. The economic benefits are obvious – companies like Sony compete in the global marketplace and the price of technology reduces far more than it would if we had nationalised industries which could fix a price. And in cultural terms, global media might look more attractive if you live in a nation where the government controls the flow of information. When Free Tibet protestors disrupted the procession of the Olympic torch in London in 2008 (the year of the Beijing Games), access to images of the events was denied to the Chinese public. But the cons of global television are serious concerns – it is argued that US culture had become the norm across the world and that as a result, specific cultural ways of life are threatened. This makes it easier for the West, and particularly the USA, to justify forceful imposition of economic and political structures on other nations. So we have to see television as something more significant than just entertainment, as it may be an agent in more far-reaching operations. The issue of choice is interesting – in quantitative terms, access via broadband to a host of global TV channels clearly increases your options. But the question is whether we end up with a diet of much more of the same, whether we are overfed what we seem to like in terms of formatting, rather than having our tastes broadened – this development is known as 'narrowcasting'.

To return to the theme of how the local and the global work together in the case of television, we must consider some examples of hybrid programming.

A hybrid programme is one which is sold across cultural and national boundaries, with changes made to the original format to accommodate local cultural differences, either to avoid offence or to attract more viewers. One very well-known example is *Who Wants To Be a Millionaire?*, which has been broadcast in Korea as *I Love Quiz Show*, in China as *The Dictionary of Happiness* and in India as *Kaun Banega Crorepathi*. These examples, which are assessed in more detail by McMillin (2007), are easy to export and import as they require very little adaptation – or can be described as 'culturally transparent'. An example of a format that needed more local adaptation is *Survivor*. When imported to Hong Kong, the programme moved away from a focus on hard competition between the contestants and instead foregrounded collaboration and good relations between the protagonists. This reflects the difference in cultural and moral ideology which survives the globalising trend.

Perhaps the most striking example of a hybrid programme offering a fusion of the global and the local, or of 'instantly plural localities', is the Beijing domestic drama *Joy Luck Street*, based on Granada TV's *Coronation Street*, but with a great deal of cultural adaptation.

Life on Mars might appear at first to be a programme that would resist hybrid export even more than 'Corrie'. After all, once you have replaced Northern England with Beijing, the soap opera template can translate to any context; the format is concerned with 'everyday life', and it does not really matter who is involved or where it takes place, as long as the audience is comfortable with the **verisimilitude** – the believable sense of reality and authenticity constructed by the text. But *Life on Mars* is different, because the juxtaposition of police life (in its broader social context) from the twenty-first century and that of the 1970s is particular to England in the drama. But this did not prove to be much of an obstacle for distributors in the global media sphere, who were able to export the original version to Canada, France, Germany, the Netherlands, New Zealand, Australia and Finland, and adapted versions for the USA (set in LA) and Spain (where the context will be post-Franco society in 1978).

Examples of TV shows that the UK imports include *Takeshi's Castle*, which is imported as filmed but altered for the UK audience. In Japan, where the show is filmed, the game is interspersed with comedy sketches and Japanese commentators. In the UK, the show is reduced to half an hour, with the sketches cut out so the focus in entirely on the games, with commentary by Craig Charles. In the USA, the show is called *Most Extreme Elimination Challenge*, with dubbing and commentary in English that effectively spoofs the original show. A more mainstream show is *Dragon's Den*, which originated in Japan as *Money no Tora* (Money Tiger). The UK, Australia, New Zealand, Canada and the Netherlands all use the same title, *Dragon's Den*, but in Israel people watch *Hakrishim* (Hebrew for The Sharks), and in the USA it is called *The Shark Tank*. It seems that many of the programmes that are the most culturally transparent are those with a global capitalist emphasis (i.e. making money is good and business is extremely competitive and ruthless). It is no surprise, then, that *The Apprentice* is another highly formatted global export. The franchise originated in the USA in 2004, hosted by business tycoon Donald Trump, and the UK version, hosted by Sir Alan Sugar, has needed very little local translation. Similarly, the show has seamlessly reached mass audiences in Germany as *The Big Boss*, and in South Africa, India and Arabic nations, with similar titles and famous tycoons firing contestants in each case.

Activity

Use the internet to find three examples of hybrid TV programmes not used in this book. Your three examples must be different to each other in the following ways:

- One must be culturally transparent.
- One must be an imported format with some minor cultural changes.
- One must be an imported format with more significant cultural changes that reflect ideological differences between the nation where the product was first shown and the new host nation.

Share your examples with three other students, so that you each have four of each.

Next, in your group of four, carry out the following two creative tasks.

- Plan the export of a popular TV show for a very different cultural context. What would be easy to keep in place and what would you need to change for the new audience?
- Create a pitch for a completely global, culturally transparent TV show that could, subject to language, be distributed to any nation on earth with the format entirely in place. Can such a show be designed?

We must be careful, then, to distinguish between hybrid programmes where specific cultural adaptation is required (such as *Joy Luck Street*) and those transparent exports where the format stays in place, but names and presenters change. The former are programmes which seem to prove and disprove globalisation theory at the same time, while the latter set of examples can easily be used to defend the global village idea.

Hybrid programming is fascinating for the student of media and culture because it shows us how global and local cultural influences on people can 'intermingle'. This connects to several of the other Critical Perspectives themes, but especially Postmodern Media, because this mixing of cultural reference points for people is one of the defining features of postmodern culture. For example, the music channel MTV is 'remixed' for a great many different countries, a technique described by Brown (1997) as 'glocalised' programming. Again, here we must return to the important fact, as established at the start of this section, that globalisation only works if the audience recognises the difference between the local and the global, or at least recognises the possibilities of a culture beyond the country they live in. This playful mixing of culture, described on page 76 by McMillin (2007: 112), is key to understanding the postmodern condition.

Hybrid programming becomes a key strategy in the latter domain, to meet the rising demand for programs that contain elements of the global, yet are charged with local relevance in terms of language, themes, actors and contexts. Hybrid programming allows lighthearted combinations of global and local programming elements. The average consumer is able to appreciate the humour in the caricature of both global and local and recognise his or her membership in a media world that transcends national borders.

Global news and journalism

In 2008, the five leading players in the global news arena were **Al Jazeera English**, which was reaching 100 million viewers globally (outside the USA); **France 24**, available in French or Arabic; **CNN**, with double the audience share of Al Jazeera, with a clearly US news agenda; **Russia Today**, generally considered to be frequently state-biased; and our own **BBC World**, which enjoys the status – legitimate or not – of being the most objective. Each of these broadcasters has a global objective and news agenda, but a culturally specific starting point, and our interest here is in the impact of that tension for the news we are provided with.

As with so much of the content of Critical Perspectives, there is a huge overlap here with We Media and Democracy, since we are considering not only whether our news is increasingly international in nature, but also the emergence of 'citizen journalism', whereby ordinary people produce news via the internet, which is of course a global network. News is interesting as a case study for global media because we tend to be more sensitive about where our news comes from than we are about what we perceive to be entertainment. Here is an example: if most of the films we watch come from the USA, then some of us will worry about cultural representation, but it will not be treated as a really big issue for our democracy; but if our news comes from the USA, that would be a different matter for most people. Alongside this, the rise of user-generated video on YouTube is considered by most of us to be an interesting new form of media that sits quite happily alongside commercial film and television. But citizen journalism – ordinary people producing news via blogs and eyewitness video – provokes debates about truth and the law. According to John Hartley (2008: 53), we cannot think of the internet revolution in news journalism purely in terms of space (news that is distributed beyond national boundaries); we also have to consider how the internet revolutionises 'news time'.

Traditional journalism and broadcasting have pitched their tent, as it were, in the temporal rhythm of the day and the week. But this is the frequency that seems the most under attrition in the present developments. There may be a challenge to traditional daily/weekly journalism and broadcasting in this scenario. People are responding to different speeds of public communication, but this doesn't necessarily mean the end of democracy. It's not dumbing down but speeding up.

But what about news and space, which is more our focus here? The distribution of news has in this decade been increasingly global in some aspects, due to the emergence and success of a small number of global news services, a trend that has been labelled 'CNN-isation'. The American news network, along with Sky, Fox and the BBC, produces and circulates news via digital technologies and, crucially, satellite, to geographically diverse and in some cases remote parts of the Earth. If we view news as a locally or nationally produced service, which we have tended to, then we will be used to the news being selected and constructed in relation to a particular narrative (running order of stories) and

Synoptic Link

News Corporation

At AS, you may have studied News Corporation in the context of institutions and audiences. Here, we might usefully return to some amended **data** from the AS book on News Corporation as a case study for our assessment of global media.

The Australian 'tycoon' Rupert Murdoch started owning media institutions in the early 1950s and since then he has come to acquire for his News Corporation a vast array of newspapers, TV channels, radio stations, film companies and websites. In the UK he owns BSkyB, 18 per cent of ITV (and he is after Channel 5), *The Sun*, *News of the World* and *The Times*, and globally he dominates the press, owns the Fox Broadcasting Company and Twentieth Century Fox, and most recently he purchased MySpace. News Corporation has a gross annual income of approximately $20 billion and employs around 40,000 people worldwide. The music industry is the only sector of the mass media that Murdoch's company does not have a major stake in, although the acquisition of MySpace may be a move towards this. Murdoch's huge 'media empire' is the subject of much concern, with people thinking that the deregulation of media ownership in the UK, started by Margaret Thatcher when she was Prime Minister and continued by Tony Blair and Gordon Brown under New Labour, has allowed him to become so powerful that he now has influence over the way political events in particular are reported. For three different accounts of

Murdoch's power, see the film *Outfoxed*, the extracts of Alastair Campbell's recent diary *The Blair Years* which chronicles Murdoch's relationship with the Prime Minister, and Anthony Sampson's *Who Owns this Place*, a book about power in contemporary Britain, who has it and how it is exercised.

The documentary film *Outfoxed*, directed by Robert Greenwald, is highly recommended for this theme. You should view the whole film, but one particular sequence stands out as a challenge to the idea of news/current affairs broadcasting as a neutral 'window on the world'. It features the appearance on the Fox network's *Bill O'Reilly Show* of the son of a New York Port Authority worker killed on 9/11 who refused to sanction the 'war on terror'. The guest is told to 'shut up' by O'Reilly and is escorted from the studio; he later becomes the victim of a sustained campaign to discredit his views about the Bush administration's response to the attacks on 9/11. The key issue is about audience and distribution. If we agree (as the makers of *Outfoxed* certainly want us to) that Fox News is anything but impartial, then the fact that Fox is a global network – thanks to satellite and digital access – has international implications. The concern is that the American perspective on news events comes to determine what is seen as newsworthy, what gets reported, how it gets reported and how the aftermath of news events is discussed. Crucially, the American treatment of events and the American ideology come to be seen as the norm across the globe.

specific news values that correspond to editors' ideas about what a specific audience, in a specific time and place, is interested in. But if the news is produced elsewhere, then all of that is up for grabs, and there are some democratic issues raised about who determines which events are newsworthy, who edits the news, who the news

Figure 4.2.1 *Outfoxed* points the finger at the Fox global news service

Case study

BBC Online

Despite being a **public service** broadcaster, which is often wrongly associated with traditional, non-commercial operations, the BBC is the most successful internet news provider. BBC News tops the average monthly UK audience chart for news articles, entertainment and sport (Gibson 2008: 260). Whereas *The Sun* dominates the circulation figures for hard-copy newspaper readership, the BBC attracts 7.2 million visitors per month online, compared to 1.9 million users of the online version of *The Sun*. The BBC has an increasingly global reach for its news output, as the online press statements from the Corporation reproduced here demonstrate, with the important statistics in bold type for your consideration (BBC Press Office, press release, 21 May 2007, at www.bbc.co.uk/pressoffice/pressreleases/stories/2007/05_may/21/global.shtml – accessed August 2008).

> The BBC's combined international news services attracted a record global weekly audience of more than **233 million** during 2006/7, according to independent surveys. The global audience figure for the combined services of BBC World Service radio, BBC World television and the BBC's international online news service bbcnews.com is up 23 million from 210 million last year.

BBC World – the commercially funded international English language news and information television channel – now has estimated record audiences of **76 million viewers** a week, up from 65 million in 2005/6.

The BBC's international-facing online news sites attracted a record 763 million page impressions in March 2007, up from 546 million in March 2006. There were a record **38.5 million unique online users** across the globe during March 2007, up from 32.8 million a year ago.

BBC Global News Director Richard Sambrook said: 'This is a strong and welcome indication that the BBC's news services are strengthening their impact with audiences around the globe in the highly competitive multimedia age. People around the world are increasingly turning to the BBC when they need quality news and information that is independent and trusted.'

The questions that arise here for our analysis of global media are to do with origin and circulation. We must include the BBC alongside Sky, Fox and CNN in our list of big global players in the digital news arena, and ask the same questions of the BBC's service that we ask of these commercial rivals which do not work in the same public-funding context. Who decides on what the news is and what the audience is entitled to in a global context? What are global news values?

represents and who it excludes, and, ultimately, who the 'we' is that the news is speaking to – there are links here with another theme, Media and Collective Identity.

If news is considered a global commodity, this means that it does not just happen, but it is produced, purchased and sold on like any other commodity. To understand how this works, we need to know about news agencies. These are organisations such as the Associated Press, Reuters or World Television News. These bodies supply international news supposedly from the point of view of 'pure information' (if such a thing is possible); then, when the news is purchased by the big news providers we have heard of, the news agenda is 'applied' to the information. To go back to the Tesco analogy, this is like a supermarket buying meat from a farmer and then packaging it with their own brand identity.

Case study

Al Jazeera English (AJE)

Al Jazeera cannot be ignored in any study of global news. For background on the context for this case study, go to http://english.aljazeera.net (accessed August 2008) or go to YouTube and search for Al Jazeera.

The news agenda of the network is clear – to use the same global strategies employed by western corporations to challenge the perspectives they offer. In other words, Al Jazeera's relatively new English language network (AJE) seeks to offer a balance to the 'global news supremacy' so far enjoyed by Fox, CNN and the BBC. This statement from Dave Marash (in Goldkorn 2006: 1), the Washington news anchor for Al Jazeera, is interesting, as Marash is situated at the centre of the strategy – working from the heart of the USA for a news service based in Qatar.

'All of our competitors, CNN International, BBC World and the American networks, concentrate about 80 percent of their news gathering resources in Western Europe and North America,' he said, sitting in his small office at the network's Washington hub. 'Al Jazeera English is going to concentrate about 80 percent of our news gathering outside of North America and Western Europe.'

It must be stated clearly here that Al Jazeera is as critical in its reporting of Arab governments and military action as it is of American interventions. The station is not a mere propaganda outlet for Arabic states. Indeed, the popularity of the service arises from its offering of an alternative to both western and official Arabic news offerings. However, if the globalisation of news is the inevitable outcome of capitalism – just as the Tesco

chain became dominant in the food retail market in the UK by controlling a market and swallowing up competitors, so the global news networks reduce their opposition by the same logic – then the Al Jazeera response is to use the same tactics from a different starting point. The result is that the idea of news as objective and neutral is dispensed with for broadcasting, just as it has been for newspapers. Consumers can choose which news agenda to consume. However, critics would argue that news hegemony operates so powerfully that only the most media-literate citizen is actually able to make such an informed choice. The majority of people consume a news service which they assume to be reliable, honest and transparent. Consider this comment from Badreya Al-Jenaibi (2007: 2).

The thoughtful audience member would hopefully watch Al Jazeera and other broadcasts like CNN and BBC. The way to counteract bias from one program is to not rely on just one source of news. In the past, the Arab and non-Arab audience had little choice, however, but to listen to either Western-dominated news with its particular bias, or to receive news of the Arab world from Arab regimes. Al Jazeera has offered a revolutionary alternative that has helped to create a new Arab discourse and alter the Arab media experience. It is obviously biased, but it does present an Arab perspective in a world where Arab voices were not particularly distinct. Al Jazeera changed that, and for that reason, it is a worthy source of news and opinion, even though the news and opinions are often quite biased.

But news analysts and academics argue that although the news agencies do not explicitly share the news agendas of the western networks, because they know that Fox, CNN, Sky and the BBC are their main 'customers', they will seek news which they perceive to be 'client-friendly'. In this way, news production becomes circular, and the concern is that non-western events are marginalised even at the first stage in the cycle. News is business.

Boyd-Barrett and Rantenen (1999) suggest that a series of events have shaped the development of global news, and as there is not sufficient space here to cover these in factual detail, you are strongly advised to research each one yourself. These are, in chronological order, the protests in Tiananmen Square, Beijing in 1989; the collapse of the Berlin Wall in the same year; the Gulf War in 1991; and 9/11. Each of these instantly became a 'global news event' because of the way the images were circulated. According to Boyd-Barrett and Rantenen, the global news coverage of each can be seen very easily as American rather than neutral – the first two events were celebrated, as a rival political/economic system to US capitalism was challenged in each case, and the latter two were

Synoptic Link

Local newspapers

This amended set of institutional data from **OCR Media Studies for AS** about the ownership of local papers will also be useful for this discussion about the survival of local print media in the age of global online news.

Ten regional publishing institutions control 90 per cent of the total market for the local press. This is a clear example of 'concentrated ownership' which has in recent years come to define the 'behind the scenes' institutional structure of the mass media, often without much public awareness. Ask yourself these questions – do you read a (paid-for) local paper? If so, who owns it? You might not think it matters, but it may well have implications for the extent to which the publication reflects the community to whom it is sold. Trinity Mirror have roughly 20 per cent of the market, owning 234 titles. Newsquest Media Group weigh in with 219 (15 per cent share). Johnston Press have 282 and 14 per cent share, Northcliffe Newspapers are close behind with 111 (12 per cent) and Associated Newspapers have 10 per cent of the market with just 11 papers (clearly these are bigger selling titles in bigger regions). So close to 70 percent of the regional newspaper audience is catered for by five companies. The source for these figures is the Newspaper Society (July 2006). While the 'freesheet' threat is not a new one for local papers, the way in which *Metro* is circulated is proving to have an impact: an average of 10,000 sales of paid-for papers are reportedly lost to free papers in the major cities. Unlike national newspapers, some of which are maintaining sales as a result of a host of strategies and innovations, the average net circulation of every paid-for regional paper is in decline. However the regional press is still a very lucrative media sector, just slightly less so than in the linear news era.

portrayed via a simple binary opposition of good/evil, hero/villain. So if we combine this range of contingencies, we can arrive at a history of global news, arising from developments in technology affording global news first and 24/7 news second; the emergence of global news networks such as CNN as a response; and a series of news events that were 'Americanised' in their media circulation.

But now we need to return to the question: is our news increasingly global, as opposed to local or national? To do this, we have to turn our attention to the most old-fashioned of media products – the local paper.

In 2008, almost every local newspaper in the UK reported declining sales, and this is generally perceived by industry commentators to be a linear trend – the local paper looks doomed in the face of global, online, 24-hour news media. However, there are many examples of local newspapers turning the threat of the

Activity

Your local rag

Rather than provide a case study on a local newspaper to consider in contrast to the global media examples above, it is far more effective for you to carry out your own case study using this template. Work in a group (or even the whole class) to collect this information and to evaluate the findings. If possible, invite (via your teacher) a journalist working on the paper into school/college to share her/his experiences of the 'community service' the paper provides.

For the journalist's visit, good preparation is essential. You will need to get their thoughts on the following areas:

- Who owns the paper
- How the paper seeks to reinforce or even create community values
- How it makes money
- What the relationship is between ownership and the editorial agenda (who selects the news and decides how it is presented?)
- What the paper considers the greatest threat to its existence.

Split into five groups and take one theme each. Each student within each group should produce five questions, and then each group chooses two questions from the 25 on the table. This is an important process, as it will create a clear agenda for the interview and the desired outcomes.

The next step is to agree on who will ask the questions, in what order and with what recording mechanism, and then to rehearse so as to avoid badly phrased questions or answers going unrecorded on the day.

Although this may seem to put pressure on you, we tend to find that many local journalists are happy to help, as you will be demonstrating an interest in the work they do, and you are, after all, part of their audience.

If it is not possible to arrange a local journalist visit, or to visit the paper yourselves, then you can get the 'cold information' from the internet or by contacting the paper, and you may be able to ask the questions via email.

internet to their advantage, by enhancing their community focus with online elements, allowing readers to connect with one another as well as with the paper. In guerrilla warfare, the trick is to make your weakness your strength – small armies can hide. This is a very different example, but the idea of identifying a weakness and making it your niche is the same here – the internet can offer global reach or local activity. The strategy now is called ultralocal provision, where readers of the 'local rag' can follow the minute detail of very specific issues that affect them directly, and can use the online version of the paper to blog, respond, refresh and update this information, which would be of little interest to anyone more than five miles away. Wainwright (2008:1) explores this concept.

> Given the threat of the web and the growth of freesheets, people might well ask – why should anyone buy one of those local papers anyway? But look past the across-the-board sales declines and there are pockets of success, where the age-old values of a town or country source of information are alive and well. Moreover, they are harnessing the power of the web to succeed.

Global cinema

There are three strands to this theme within the broader study of Global Media. First, we must assess the idea that films are increasingly made for a global audience, and this will lead us, once again, to discuss cultural imperialism. Alongside this analysis, we need to pay attention to diaspora – a term which describes people dispersing across the world and, to some extent, taking their 'home culture' with them. This provides a challenge to the cultural imperialism 'version' of global media theory, so we will be into a debate at this point. And third, but perhaps most importantly, we need to be aware of the range of films made around the world that may or may not attract the attention of audiences in other countries. This approach is sometimes described as the study of 'world cinema', but the problem with this, as Stafford (2007) points out, is that we can end up creating a simplistic binary opposition between Hollywood films and everything else, so 'world cinema' is only understood in terms of its perceived difference to the Hollywood films that dominate the box office in most countries. Instead, we should see 'global cinema' simply as a very varied collection of film industries, so we will look at a range of examples here in their own right.

To address the idea of the global audience, let us consider some statistics provided by Stafford (2007: 20) that may or may not surprise you. The Indian cinema audience is the largest in the world, more than twice the size of the US audience (source:

European Audiovisual Observatory, 2004). But Hollywood is hugely successful at reaching audiences outside the USA, generating revenue for the major studios of $15 billion annually. The exceptions to the 'Hollywood hegemony' are China, Japan, South Korea and India, where in each case under half of all box office returns are currently for US films. Britain, as you will know, has, for a variety of reasons (which are explored in detail in the section on British cinema in relation to Media and Collective Identity), allowed Hollywood to become hugely dominant at the box office, but it is important to recognise that this is not universal, as Stafford (2007: 20) points out.

> When we think of the typical cinema audience, we usually think now of a multiplex showing a Hollywood film and that does indeed happen around the world. But we should perhaps also consider the millions watching films in a variety of Indian languages (not just Hindi) in many different types of cinema auditoria. Hollywood has the richest film industry because it has the most affluent 'domestic' audiences. However in the last ten years it has become apparent that the market outside North America is much bigger and potentially more lucrative.

So our first way of thinking about global film looks like this. Hollywood films are, compared to other film industries, more successful at reaching international audiences. Whether this is just inevitable capitalist economics at work (the USA is a rich nation and lots of people worldwide speak English, so it is not rocket science that we prefer to watch expensively made, lavishly promoted films in English, because we can), or whether there is a more sinister outcome (cultural homogenisation leading to a US ideology dominating world culture and 'othering' huge groups of the population into the bargain), is a matter for debate. Let us consider an example in order to unpack some of this.

Our second approach concerns diaspora. Later in this section, we will consider research by Durham (2004), which produced interesting findings about how people connect the global to the local in relation to their own highly specific life contexts. Diaspora is described by Ruddock (2007: 72).

> Diasporic audience research emerges from the fact that the media's role in cultural mediation is influenced by the movement of people as well as goods. The vast audience for Indian and Chinese media, in its various dialects, exists on an international as well as national level.

This poses a challenge to the 'cultural imperialism' idea, as the logic of that theory would suggest that this would not happen – that the lure of American media would reduce any desire to cling to any notion of cultural heritage through media consumption.

Pirates of the Caribbean: At World's End

Here are the box office statistics for the third film in the *Pirates* franchise. The total US box office gross figure comes to $309,404,152, with international box office returns of $643,000,000, so in this significant case, the international revenue doubles that acquired from the domestic market. In the 2007 box office chart, *Pirates* was top in a top 50 list where the first 45 films were American, so this gives us some perspective on the global reach of Hollywood. (Source: www.the-numbers.com/movies – accessed August 2008, and Pulver in Gibson 2008: 216)

What are the implications of *At World's End* being seen in cinemas alone (so disregarding DVD viewings) by enough people to generate almost $100 million from just this one film?

Purely on the level of distribution, it means that in all the countries in the world where the film was shown on a large number of screens at the same time, domestic films were in competition with *Pirates*. In other words, people were not watching films that might relate more to their own cultural experiences. On the other hand, as this film is a fantasy with global themes, that argument might be limited – after all, you do not have to be American to be interested in pirate myths.

But if we look at the film as a representing text, there is an argument that the film does portray some key themes in very pro-western ways. The film was made in St Vincent, by agreement with the government of Dominica, but the representation of Caribs caused offence in Trinidad and other Caribbean communities, due to the reinforcement of a long-standing binary opposition created in western fiction between civilisation and savagery. This is more serious than it might appear at first from our UK vantage point, as there is a highly specific, local battle in the Caribbean over the need to educate children about their ancestry in order to challenge these stereotypes. So for the Carib communities, the global media reach of Disney offers a direct threat to the struggle to revise offensive and disempowering versions of their history.

So we can see in this example how what seems like a piece of 'mere entertainment' can be viewed as an example of both capitalist domination (the domestic exclusion of domestic cinema, seen here as no different to Tesco putting the local grocer out of business in the name of 'business development' and 'consumer choice') and also cultural imperialism (the imposition of biased and oppressive representations of people as 'truth'). How seriously we take these claims is a matter for debate, of course. They are presented here as a challenge to the notion that *At World's End* is 'only a film'.

Bollywood in the UK

The best example of diaspora in the UK context is Bollywood, which we looked at in some detail in **OCR Media Studies for AS**, within the study of audience. Here we return to that detail, as it connects well with our focus here on diaspora in relation to global media.

Consider this description of current access to Bollywood films and music in Birmingham, from Somak Raychoudry (from an email exchange, 31 August 2007).

There are lots of channels you can access now. Many of them are free. On Sky I get Zee and B4U music, which are essentially film music channels, and several regular channels that do Indian TV programmes – soaps etc. And if I were to pay I could get B4U, Zee and Sony's three premium movie channels. Then there are channels for other languages – not strictly Bollywood – Punjabi, Gujarati and Bengali.

The scale is amazing. I watch them often. Sometimes the premium channels are free on weekends. The advertising on these channels is phenomenal, which shows the extent of the audience. Like Sunrise FM radio, for instance. I haven't seen Chak de India yet but it's on at Star City I hear and is highly recommended. In Birmingham it seems every major cinema has a Bollywood movie showing.

The Edukators

The Edukators is a German film in which a group of politically motivated young people, who are angered by the capitalist system which keeps the poor in poverty to feed the rich, develop a form of protest whereby they break into the homes of rich people. But rather than steal their goods, which would do little to threaten the system, they rearrange the furniture and leave a message – 'Your days of plenty are numbered' – seeking to disturb and frighten those who live in affluence. When one such break-in goes wrong, the group is forced to kidnap a victim and a thriller plot develops with some twists, not only in terms of plot, but also in terms of how we feel about the characters.

This is an interesting film in the context of our study of Global Media because it is much more than just an alternative to Hollywood. In fact, there is no point trying to understand it within a general understanding of 'independent' or 'world' cinema. While it may be the case that there is a more developed youth politics in Germany than in the UK at present, the film's themes are more global than culturally specific, given that capitalism is defined by its global force. When watching the film, consider the oppositions it sets up between rich and poor, empowered and disempowered, radical and 'distracted'. As a media student, you should be especially interested, fairly early on in the film, in the Marxist discussion of television – seen as a brainwashing facility for the people in power, leaving the dispossessed with no time for revolutionary thoughts. Consider how the oppositions become less clear as the film progresses, and discuss the variety of possible responses you might have to this film, and how this might depend on your age and your sociocultural situation. Assess the degree to which you think these themes are global, and whether you agree with this comment from one film critic (Dudek 2005: 1).

The characters and their ideas are considered dangerous by the state, but their symbolic actions are a threat to no one but themselves. Although The Edukators is a German-language film, it is set in a global village where all politics are local.

Finally, our third method for considering global cinema is more to do with awareness – becoming familiar with films that are made in different countries, not just as 'different to Hollywood', but as interesting media products on their own terms. To do this, we turn our attention to the German film The Edukators (directed by Hans Weingartner, 2005) – see the case study above.

Local, national, global

How can we pull together these case studies and perspectives to make an informed judgement on the idea that the media are becoming increasingly global? It is surely a question of balance, and also a question of vantage point. In other words, how you see the globalisation debate will depend on where you are and what you prioritise.

Academics developing research in the area of media globalisation are usually in agreement on the importance of ethnographic research methods. These methods involve spending time in the social context of the audience group you are researching in order to 'go native' and get to grips with the specific local context as far as possible. There is no way that you have time for this on your A2 course, but it is nevertheless very important that you understand the interplay between the local and the global, rather than assuming that everyone is experiencing the media in the same way in some idealised global village, as this is simply not the case. One illuminating example is Durham's (2004) research into teenage girls of Hindu cultural heritage living in Florida, who were using the media partly to construct a hybrid identity. Durham discovered, through the ethnographic endeavour (spending time, observing from the location) that the girls were using *Friends* alongside Hindi film songs to switch and combine the two poles of their identities, as paraphrased here by Ruddock (2007: 71).

> Both of these experiences were meaningless on an explicitly textual level; *Friends* was just 'stupid', where Hindu musicals probably mean something, but the girls did not know what. But on a cultural level, both resources helped the girls mediate the different worlds they inhabited; *Friends* accessed a high school (language) where musicals contained a sense of Indianness shared with parents. The girls found themselves being Indian in Florida due to forces beyond their control. They had to figure out what this means, partly by using media products made by multinational systems of production and delivery. But it was up to them to make these power dynamics real by embodying them in specific ways.

This specific embodying of cultural meaning is crucial. We cannot understand globalisation merely by imagining that everyone

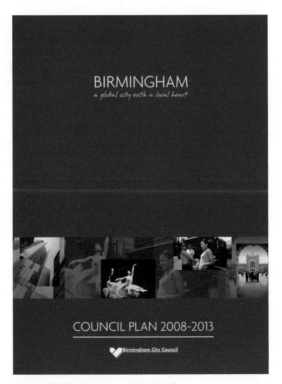

Figure 4.2.2 Birmingham – a 'glocal' city?

ends up attaching the same kinds of meanings to the same cultural products. Global media is always-already used by people in highly specific local contexts, and we are better served by understanding it as an infinite number of 'small stories' rather than a simple 'grand narrative' of cultural imperialism. Consider Birmingham City Council's new slogan for the city – 'global city, local heart'.

On the other hand, we cannot deny the development of global media and the potentially serious implications of an increasingly US media agenda being 'naturalised' and made to seem neutral. This is power at its most dangerous – when it looks like truth. Al Jazeera's attempts to redress this balance might look like an important political intervention, but equally we might worry that 'two wrongs don't make a right', if it is true that its news agenda lays no more serious claim to objectivity than that of Fox and CNN. On the other hand, why does the local paper survive? The longevity of this old-fashioned media format might seem like proof positive that there will always be a need for media that support a community, where the editorial agenda resonates with the values of the location. In each case, the more important questions are about access and ownership. Even local papers are usually owned by bigger companies which do not operate in the locality – so the concentration of ownership that pervades global media is mirrored at the level of the local rag also. You will need to come to your own informed, academic position on this, as once again there is no right answer. What we must remember is that there are two versions of media globalisation. One is hard to contest – the fact that there is more and more availability of media, which is distributed across national and cultural boundaries, following the logic of capitalism and arising from concentrated ownership. In this context, it is fair to say that it is harder to cling to local cultural identities – which is not to say that people do not do so. The second version extends this assessment to conclude that this increase in global media leads inevitably to a 'cultural homogeneity' (McMillin 2007), whereby people in an ever increasing number of countries consume the same cultural material, which tends to be produced by major power-holding corporations within a western capitalist ideological framework. The 'third way', which we have explored with regard to global cinema, diaspora and hybridity, bears witness to the complex ways in which people 'mix and match' the local, national and global. These different versions of the globalisation theory are described here by McMillin (2007: 11).

In the political economy view, 'global' is often considered synonymous for a 'site of cultural erosion and destruction' and the 'local' as a site of pristine cultural 'authenticity' (Ang 1996: 153). The second view, held by cultural theorists, is a little more nuanced, and regards globalisation as including processes of cultural appropriation where people take what is relevant to their own contexts and orient or adapt it to their local needs.

Your task, having used the material and case studies here as a starting point, is to assess the value of each of these approaches. Is globalisation really happening and having a real impact on your life, through the media? And if it is, then what difference, if any, is this making to your identity and the way you see yourself as belonging to a community? And are you able to pick and mix appropriate global media to adapt them to your own local situation?

Examiner's Tip

There is one very easy thing that A level media studies students rarely do in exams, but compared to other skills, it is quite straightforward. It will certainly impress the examiner. In higher education, this is expected, so as well as getting you more marks in Critical Perspectives, it will be useful preparation for the next part of your educational career. It is called referencing. All you have to do is remember the year of publication of each book, article or online publication that you want to quote or paraphrase. Then, when you write about someone's idea, you put the year in brackets – for example, McDougall (2009), if it were this book. The idea is that the reader of your contribution can use your essay as a starting point for more research, so they are easily able to locate the source you are referring to by looking up the various publications of the writer by year.

4.3
Media in the Online Age

For this theme you need to learn about the following, in relation to at least two areas of the media:

- The historical development of online media
- Examples of how media production has been transformed by the internet and broadband access (and examples of media that have remained untouched by these developments)
- The impact of broadband internet access on audience behaviour
- The importance of media convergence and the role of the internet in accelerating this
- Debates around the future of the media in the web 3.0 era.

The new generation of UK media power players are ditching the traditional gatekeepers and going straight to their audience via the web.

(Plunkett 2008: 2)

Broadband internet distribution has changed, if not everything, then at least a tremendous amount of how media products are shared with audiences. If you have grown up in a broadband world, then this will be a 'history lesson'. The over-30s are starting to realise how little choice they had compared with today's audiences. Rather than nostalgically bemoaning the absence of 'collective viewing', they are waking up to the fact that they would probably not have organised their lives around weekly broadcasts of 'classic' TV programmes in the 1970s if they had been able to stream an entire series of a more interesting show with BitTorrent!

The long tail

Whichever two media forms you choose to research for this theme, Chris Anderson's (2006) theory of 'the long tail' will be useful. Indeed, it would be conspicuous by its absence in your work if you were to ignore it. But equally there is no compulsion for you to agree with it, so your task here – as for all the theories and ideas you encounter during your work for Critical Perspectives – is to understand Anderson's contribution, apply it to some of your own examples of how media is produced, distributed and exchanged, and then decide on its merits and/or limitations. This is deeper learning, as it obliges you to form an informed position on a range of issues, and it is this that makes this part of the OCR Media Studies course the 'stretch and challenge' element.

So what is 'the long tail'? In 2006, Chris Anderson, editor of *Wired* magazine, published his theory – a description of the way that the internet has transformed economics, commerce and consumption. Anderson was not setting out to write a book for media academics and students, but because his most significant examples included iTunes®, YouTube and social networking sites, interest in the book spread quickly, via word of mouth in academic circles, which Anderson calls 'viral marketing', and references to the long tail have been a feature of much writing about the changing nature of the media since – including what you are reading now.

Anderson's idea summed up in very convincing terms what had been happening for a few years, since broadband was rolled out to consumers. Whereas in the pre-broadband era, companies and distributors were interested in blockbuster hits and best-selling products, now there is a realisation that adding up all the niche consumption might amount to as much revenue as the units sold of the peak material. In other words, if you think about it in spatial terms, on a graph, there is a longer, flatter, low end of the market – this is the 'long tail'.

Anderson's idea was revolutionary because up to his intervention, economics had usually been ignoring the end of the tail, concentrating mostly on 'above-the-line sales'. His simple point is this: as broadband internet allows more and more people to look for and share or buy a wider variety of material and products, what happens is that people buy less of more. So instead of ignoring all the small sales of obscure products in favour

of concentrating on huge mass sales (more of less), businesses ought to consider both routes and give equal weighting to both ends of the tail. Here is an explanation of the idea in Anderson's own words (2006: 52).

> The theory of the Long Tail can be boiled down to this: Our culture and economy are increasingly shifting away from a focus on a relatively small number of hits (mainstream products and markets) at the head of the demand curve, and moving toward a huge number of niches in the tail. In an era without the constraints of physical shelf space and other bottlenecks of distribution, narrowly targeted goods and services can be as economically attractive as mainstream fare.

The point about shelf space is key. In the 'old days', shops would not consider it worthwhile to stock one copy of loads of CDs, DVDs or books. They would prefer to stockpile better-selling titles, and you might be able to order other products from a warehouse. As the internet is really a virtual warehouse, there are fewer overheads associated with niche distribution, and therefore 'infinite choice' becomes an essential commodity. Think about it from your own experience – would you not expect to be able to buy pretty much any media product online within a few clicks? Whether you can afford the purchase or not is another matter, but essentially we expect 100 per cent availability these days.

Anderson went on to describe the detail of what the long tail is doing to our culture and to our economics.

Figure 4.3.1(a) The fact that a picture of Camper Van Beethoven appears in a media studies textbook in 2009 is evidence of the long tail and the rise of niche culture

He suggested that this dominance of 'niche' materials will continue because it is now very cheap to distribute niche products to the people who want them – this is directly the opposite of how things were before broadband, when niche was considered an expensive luxury. Next, people develop a range of filtering services to help consumers find niches – recommendations, lists, customer reviews, blogs. On the one hand, this is a democratic development – we get to have a say and share our ideas – but clearly it serves a commercial function for media distributors as well. Whereas in the past a shop assistant might have recommended some music to a customer, or you might have chatted about a new band with friends in the pub, and in both cases you might have followed up this word of mouth and made another purchase, in the online age it simply happens more quickly and more often. Consider the 'ilike' application used by Facebook users, and this example from my own experience. The illustration that follows is a slide I used at a conference for media teachers at which I was discussing the media studies 2.0 debate – to what extent has the broadband, web 2.0 internet transformed the media so much that we need a new way of studying it? The point I was making then, and will do again here, is that I am, compared to most media students, old (or at least middle-aged). So if I can do this without thinking about it, then surely this will soon be – if it is not so already – ordinary, instinctive behaviour for young people (the key market for media)? The long tail in action, surely?

Anderson goes on to argue that the effect of this filtering is that the 'demand curve' flattens. There are still huge hits and these still get most of our attention, but in economic terms they are only equally significant to the 'flattened' tail of niche sales – again, more of less (Anderson 2006: 53).

All those niches add up. Although none sell in huge numbers, there are so many niche products that collectively they can comprise a market rivalling the hits. Once all of this is in place, the natural shape of demand is revealed, undistorted by distribution bottlenecks, scarcity of information, and limited choice of shelf-space. What's more, that shape is far less hit-driven than we have been led to believe. Instead, it is as diverse as the population itself.

The point in the quote above is the most striking in terms of culture. Anderson is arguing here that broadband has allowed us to behave in ways that fit better with our instincts. Before web 2.0, we did not have sufficient access to things, so our tastes and interests were 'channelled' for commercial ends by elite producers who wanted us to consume more of less. Now we are able to choose from 'infinite variety', so while there is certainly a capitalist thrust to all of this – there are still profit margins, shareholders and hugely rich people exploiting the 'value chain' – there is also a democratising effect: in the brave new world of the long tail, the niche consumer is queen and she has a potentially limitless choice of places to buy from.

In 1985 I bought this record. Now it reminds me of being a sixth form student. Long time ago. For Xmas 22 years later I got a USB turntable. This week I converted this song to mp3 and then put it on my ipod. Then I went on facebook and told everyone I was listening to it. If my 'friends' are remotely interested they can download it from facebook through another application. Then I found the video on youtube which took about 10 seconds, so I decided to play it here. Is this 'we media' or 'me media'? I don't know. But it's me giving meaning to media. The text, or texts, in question are clearly less important than the dissemination – the chain. But is this kind of stuff, which is going on in many parts of the world, every minute, relevant to Media Studies? And what kinds of theoretical concepts could work to analyse this? A big chunk of Media Studies is an extension of English and that's OK if you are looking at something like TV drama because you can use genre, narrative, representation etc and really it's a bit like a book, only a moving image version. But lots of people, not just young ones, don't actually watch television in the traditional sense these days. So maybe my indulgent playing around with Camper Van Beethoven is actually a more typical bit of 'media consumption' than watching Corrie? So is it OK to marginalise this kind of stuff under 'new media' and leave the 'Englishey' bits alone? And can we keep calling it 'new media' when the people we are teaching were born into it? What do you think?

Figure 4.3.1(b)

One of the Examiner's tips in this book encourages you to make full use of the *Media Guardian* in your research for A2. For this theme, which is all about the rapid pace of change, it is particularly vital to stay up to date week by week. On 7 July 2008, the three main features in the supplement all related precisely to the impact of the internet on the media.

- The front page reported a huge loss in advertising revenues for three large newspaper companies (including national and regional owners), as companies migrate to online advertising.
- The editorial assessed the idea that the BBC is becoming more commercial by the day and that the licence fee is threatened more than ever, with the corporation's pioneering role in web distribution of TV a major factor in this.
- An interview with Robert Greenwald, director of *Outfoxed* (a film we deal with in several sections of this book), explored his decision to switch from feature films to **online video** as his medium of preference.

In all three cases, the immediate impact of online distribution compared to other ways of reaching an audience is shared as the major catalyst of change. This was one edition of *Media Guardian* on one day, but it really focuses our minds for this theme.

Activity

Apply the theory of the long tail to one of the following:

- Films
- Magazines
- Music
- Newspapers
- Radio
- Television
- Video games.

Rather than relying on published data for sales figures, you need to work in a group on a small-scale research project for this task.

Target a research group of 50 people between you. This can either be a broad, representative cross section of people in your local area (a range of gender, age, social status, ethnic origin and occupation) or a very specific group of similar people, but it *must* be one of these and not something in between.

Through whichever research methods you wish to use, find out the proportion of media consumption by this group of 50 people in your chosen area that you would describe as 'hits' (big, well-known media products), compared to the proportion that you would describe as 'niche'.

When you have the results, your group can collate the data and apply Anderson's theory. If you find that the niche consumption is equal or just less than equal (i.e. 40 per cent or over) to the consumption of hits, then his ideas will seem about right. If not, then you need to consider whether your research group is untypical of the whole population or whether Anderson's ideas are overstated.

Either way, you will have a very interesting and useful piece of applied audience research to include in your Critical Perspectives exam answer.

Figure 4.3.2 Wikinomics – another idea about online media that you need to be familiar with

Wikinomics

Don Tapscott and Anthony Williams published *Wikinomics* in 2006. Along with Chris Anderson's *The Long Tail* (discussed above), this is the other 'big idea' about business and commerce in the online age. The chapter headings are similar to Anderson's: 'Peer pioneers', 'The wiki workplace', 'Collaborative minds' and 'Enterprise 2.0' are added to 'Viral marketing' and 'Endless niche'. You might take a cynical view of all this discourse and assess it as nothing more than a bandwagon, or you might take this more seriously as a summary of the changes. But either way, these two 'big ideas' are useful for us because they take us beyond the media text or the study of media products into the realm of economics. The subtitle of Tapscott and Williams' intervention is *How Mass Collaboration Changes Everything*, so we could just as easily use this material for the We Media and Democracy theme. These arguments are about the media (distribution in particular), but also about consumption and exchange (buying and selling – the meat and drink of capitalist economics, as *The Apprentice* demonstrates every year), and about human behaviour. So perhaps for the first time, web 2.0 has brought cultural studies and economics together, and that is important for media studies, as explored by Tapscott and Williams (2006: 46).

> As people individually and collectively program the Web, they're increasingly in command. They not only have an abundance of choices, they can increasingly rely on themselves. This is the new consumer power. It's not just the ability to swap suppliers at the click of a mouse, or the prerogative to customise their purchased goods (that was last century). It's the power to become their own supplier – in effect to become an economy unto themselves.

Activity

On page 94 are listed five 'big ideas' from **Wikinomics**. Your job is to apply each one to a different example of online media, so you end up with five examples spanning five media areas (although given that you are studying the converged mediasphere, these are likely to overlap).

If you wish to work in a group of five and research one example each, that will save you some time. The easier it is to apply each idea and find an example, the stronger the wikinomics theory. Conversely, the harder you have to work to relate the ideas to examples, the weaker the argument. The most important element of this activity, then, is the discussion about the outcomes. When you get to the exam, you will not simply be listing your examples. Additionally, you will be able to offer your own researched critique of wikinomics in the online media world, and this will impress the examiners.

Here are the five ideas.

continued

- **Peering** – the free sharing of material on the internet – is good news for businesses when it cuts distribution costs to almost zero, but bad news for people who want to protect their creative materials and ideas as intellectual property (IP). So the 'roar of collaborative culture' will change economics beyond recognition, and corporations are forced to respond or perish.
- **Free creativity** is a natural and positive outcome of the free market, so attempting to regulate and control online 'remix' creativity is like trying to hold back the tide. The happy medium is achieved by a service such as Creative Commons, which provides licences which protect IP while at the same time allowing others to remix your material within limits.
- The media is **democratised** by peering, free creativity and the *we media* journalism produced by ordinary people. (See the chapter on We Media and Democracy for a substantial extension of this idea.)
- Web 2.0 makes **thinking globally** inevitable. The internet is the 'world's biggest coffeehouse', a virtual space in which a new blog is created every second. In this instantly global communication sphere, national and cultural boundaries are inevitably reduced.
- The combination of three things – technology (web 2.0), demographics (young people are described as 'digital natives' – they have grown up in a collaborative virtual world which to them is natural and instinctive) and economics (the development of a global economy where business can, and must, think of its market as international, given that traditional, national production structures have declined as we have entered the knowledge economy) – results in a **perfect storm**, which creates such a force that resistance is impossible, so any media company trying to operate without web 2.0 will be like a small fishing boat on the sea during this freak meteorological occurrence.

But this is the really important bit: lots of people disagree with all this. It is a debate on which you need a critical perspective. For every 'wikonomist' there will be a sceptic. The sceptics believe that things are not changing as quickly and profoundly as Tapscott and Williams would have us believe. They think the idea of digital natives assumes too much, and that in fact many young people feel left behind and alienated by web 2.0 – they might just feel too embarrassed to tell anyone. The sceptics think that the wikinomics argument ignores inequality and the fact that the vast majority of the world's population does not even have access to broadband, so thinking globally is a luxury of the rich nations, not a worldwide ecological reality.

Collect your examples, assess the merits of the wikinomics ideas in relation to the media and then debate the pros and cons of the broader argument – the author's bold claim that mass collaboration 'changes everything'. This quote from the book (Tapscott and Williams 2006: 315) should get you started – see if you can apply it to media companies and the ways they operate and succeed.

> Winning companies today have open and porous boundaries and compete by reaching outside their walls to harness external knowledge, resources and capabilities. They're like a hub for innovation and a magnet for uniquely qualified minds. They focus their internal staff on value integration and orchestration, and treat the world as their research and development department. All of this adds up to a new kind of collaborative enterprise – an Enterprise 2.0 that is constantly shaping and reshaping clusters of knowledge and capability to compete on a global basis. Is your mind wired for wikinomics?

Production Tip

It would be almost impossible to avoid relating this theme to your production work. Whichever brief you are responding to, you will have to pay attention to the way that your media products either rely on the internet for dissemination, make partial use of the online mediasphere or are competing against it in more of a media 1.0 context. For example, if you are producing a website, what is the relationship between the site and the world of social networking, peer sharing and user reviews? At the other end of the scale, if you are producing a radio play, what elements of the play will the website feature, and are you planning to release the play online, or set up a forum for listeners? For a short film, how will you distribute the product online? In addition, your research, planning and evaluation will themselves be constructed and shared online in many cases, so you can share your work in progress via the internet, and invite responses and suggestions. And when you write about your production work in the exam, you will be well set to explain how your media products as micro examples relate to the broader macro ideas discussed here – wikinomics, the long tail and viral marketing, for instance.

Charles Leadbetter and We-Think

If you thought we were done with the 'big ideas' after the long tail and wikinomics, think again. Charles Leadbetter's intervention – We-Think – takes a similar view on the revolutionary nature of the internet, but develops this further – beyond business and consumption – to argue that the way we think and make sense of 'knowledge' is fundamentally shifting in the online age.

For Leadbetter, open-access knowledge-building communities on the web allow ideas to be shared and tested much more quickly and effectively. Ultimately, this leads to us becoming more creative and innovative, as we are liberated from the usual institutional constraints on how things are invented and changed by scientists and academics. Leadbetter (2006: 26) uses *World of Warcraft* to make his point and extend it to challenge the world of education, which might be of particular interest to us.

> In such games it's the players who create the content. A computer game with a million players only needs 1 per cent of them to create content for other players to use and the game has an unpaid development team of 10.000. If we could persuade 1 per cent of Britain's pupils to be player-developers for education, that would be 70,000 new sources of learning. But that would require us to see learning as something more like a computer game, something that is done **peer to peer**, without a traditional teacher.

You might be thinking – what does this have to do with media? It is significant in the sense that video games, so often seen as a media form partly responsible for reducing young people's capacity for learning, are in this view (and Leadbetter is by no means alone in this position) perceived as a template for learning. So the boundaries between media and the rest of social life are blurred and contested.

Synoptic Link

Online newspapers

This A2 theme asks you to go much further than the AS analysis of institutions and audiences, so will be assessing the difference made by the internet in more theoretical and **sociological** ways. But that does not mean that the knowledge base you acquired at AS on the factual stuff – the changes to industry practice – will not be relevant. So here is an amended recap from *OCR Media Studies for AS* on the challenges faced by newspapers in the online age.

> The local press relies on its established reputation for representing a local community to resist the threats of the more globally focused internet. In addition, national news is often 'cherry-picked' from local stories, with broadcast news following newspapers, so local news maintains a

continued

protected status to some extent. However, the internet hosts an array of free listings and public selling sites (Gumtree and eBay being the most notable) which do pose a challenge to the role of the local rag in providing classified ads, entertainment listings, property details and job vacancies. The response to this has been widespread development, by regional papers, of small, local sites offering free listings alongside their existing paid-for classified ads.

National papers do not enjoy such a protected status among the general public, having no equivalent sense of community to cling to. The development of new media versions of their new provision has, then, been far more rapid and substantial. A key shift in 2006 was the decision by *The Times* to release news on the internet first, whereas previously there had been an agreement among newspapers to publish in printed form first. Since then, online news, blogs and **podcasts** have become the norm.

Here are some recent statistics and talking points to extend our understanding of how online newspapers are taking off (taken from *Media Guardian*, 25 February 2008).

- *The Mail*, *The Guardian*, *The Times*, *The Sun* and *The Telegraph* have all enjoyed incremental growth in web audiences year on year since launching their online versions.
- Almost three-quarters of unique visitors to Mail Online are from outside the UK, and the figure is over half for all the papers listed above.
- The newspapers, given this new information, are now considering how they can combine their UK news agendas with 'glocalised' agendas and advertising, for obvious reasons.
- A further strategic aspiration is for these newspapers to compete with international rivals, so we may see a time when people in London will read *The New York Times* online and vice versa. Clearly this is relevant for our analysis of Global Media also.

Online TV

When the BBC launched iPlayer, many media commentators heralded this as the beginning of the internet TV era for real. Whereas there had been divided opinion about whether TV through the internet would catch on, the incredible success of online video and the newer development of **internet protocol television** are combining to make online TV an inevitability. It is worth pausing here for a moment to ask yourself how long you think YouTube has been around for. Look up the answer on the internet and you may be surprised. Then consider its degree of success in that space of time, and, however young you are, you might get a sense of why the older generation see the internet as so revolutionary – it is a simple equation of the amount and the impact of change in relation to time. Compare this development with, say, the development of the motor engine.

iPlayer

The BBC's iPlayer service was launched in 2008, and each month downloads have increased by a fifth. Within weeks, Virgin Media had included the service in its digital TV package, so immediately the on-screen context was transformed. Virgin customers simply press the red button and go straight to iPlayer, so the web context becomes 'invisible'. This is already pretty revolutionary – the archetypal public service broadcaster contributing so explicitly and enthusiastically to the 'death of the schedule'. But the next step is even more radical, as the Corporation makes available software that allows iPlayer to be viewed on portable devices such as the iPod or PSP. This technological urgency for the BBC can be viewed in many ways, but ultimately it is a public service response to a commercial threat, the BBC placing itself at the heart of online video in order to survive in the wake of its commercial competitors – by being free, wide-ranging and having a very high picture and content quality by comparison. Not only does iPlayer increase audience share for the BBC – in 2008 the statistics showed that the *EastEnders* audience grew by 2.5 per cent overall with the addition of downloads – but it also acts as a market surveillance tool, as the Corporation can monitor downloads and thus gauge viewer preference more 'smartly' than before – after all, downloading a programme is a more active choice than simply having the TV on.

Virgin Media's statistics for March 2008 provide us with an interesting insight into viewers' use of online TV in the relatively early days, with 35 per cent of content viewing represented by people catching up with programmes broadcast over the previous week. The same amount of viewings were of music video, and another 20 per cent accounted for viewings of episodes of older TV series on demand. Only 3 per cent of viewing was paid-for film, which seems to indicate that that market is threatened, in particular, by the archive TV series offer. In a feature in *The Guardian*, the CEO of Virgin Media Content, Malcolm Wall, described the Virgin offer as 'TV for the iPod generation' (Sweeney 2008: 6), and the amount of music video viewings would appear to support that.

This question is designed to test your media literacy, not in terms of theory or textual analysis, but in terms of how well you understand the power dynamics and commercial practices of the contemporary media. Have a go, and if you are at a loss, ask your teacher, or turn to the definition of internet protocol television Glossary for the answer. Think as cynically as you can.

As internet protocol television (IPTV) is developed alongside online video, and TV viewers increasingly personalise their TV viewing so they can watch what they want, when and where they want, who stands to benefit the most?

Synoptic Link

Web radio

In the section on Institutions and Audiences in the AS textbook, we considered the development of radio 3.0, which is of great relevance for this theme as well. Radio 3.0 is (yet another) buzz-term that describes the next generation of radio, with radio 2.0 describing the advent of digital radio (**DAB**). The following commentary, from James Cridland on the 2007 radio 3.0 conference, is from BBC Radio's Pods and Blogs website (www.bbc.co.uk/blogs/podsandblogs/radio – accessed August 2008).

> The Radio 3.0 event in London aimed to look at where radio goes next in an increasingly competitive marketplace. Jenny Abramsky, BBC Director of Radio, opened the event revealing the launch before the end of the year of DAB plugins for MP3 players, a way to keep the next generation in tune with the wireless. There was a lot of talk during the day about the ongoing growth of digital radio, although Phil Riley of Chrysalis Radio was keen to point out the commercial sector is paying for digital development out of their own profits. He also likened multiplatform to high stakes gambling, having to decide whether to back Sky, Freeview, mobile or online with development money. He went on to pretty much dismiss online listening, pointing out the BBC's 15 million online listening hours per month is a tiny fraction of the 1 billion listening hours per week across the whole sector. Last FM and Pandora were dismissed as 'inconsequential', along with any other online radio station. Commercial radio is alive and well according to Riley, with Galaxy in the Midlands reaching 54% of the teenage population. Didn't look so healthy though an hour later, when the man in the expensive suit from Ofcom revealed that commercial radio revenues are down 4.5% year on year and 40% are actually losing money. He also predicted many small stations may not survive. Digital listening is now at 14%, but predicted to rise to 90% in the next ten years. Although I did begin to think he was making stuff up to see if we were paying attention.

James Cridland is Head of Future Media & Technology, Audio & Music Interactive at the BBC. Elsewhere on his blog, which can be accessed through the Pods and Blogs site, he suggests that radio is actually the most successful medium there is in terms of evolving to survive under the threat of digital and online media forms. The examples he cites are podcasts – with the BBC in particular making a selection of its programmes available for downloading and transferring to an MP3 player for several years already. Radio streaming is a more established trend, with listeners using their PC or laptop to access radio at work or on holiday, for example. The one aspect of the digital revolution that has not, to date, had an impact on radio is the subscription/pay-per-view environment, as there are no predictions yet in relation to 'pay-per-listen' radio or even subscription to radio channels. And a more low-tech but equally radical development has been the ease of downloading and saving audio files in comparison to taping radio, which was always much clumsier than recording from the television.

Here we turn our focus to web music radio. Music radio online now includes radio stations, podcasts and web feeds, and what they all offer is a new listening experience, ranging from traditional station broadcasts linked to podcasts and web streaming, to music blogs where listeners post MP3 tracks to share and comment on them. Here are two examples from either end of the spectrum. At one end, AOL radio (www.music.aol.com/radioguide/bb – accessed August 2008) offers a huge range of free streamed music, with no DJs. At the other is Resonance FM (www.resonancefm.com – accessed August 2008), using live streaming and podcasts via iTunes, with an agenda to broadcast music that would normally be hard to find. As with all the online media examples we are discussing, as well as the case studies you will find in the Global Media section, the big change with web radio is simply the lack of local or national boundaries, making it possible to listen to music from anywhere in the world directly, without the corporate radio station and record label 'middle men' **gatekeeping** distribution across national boundaries.

GTA IV online

If you have looked at more than one theme area here, you have probably noticed that they overlap, which is an outcome of the converged mediasphere we are studying. So no apologies for yet another mention of *Grand Theft Auto IV*, which also appears in Contemporary Media Regulation and Postmodern Media.

For a much more detailed analysis of *Grand Theft Auto IV* as a media product and immersive experience for game players, see the Postmodern Media section of this book and the Institutions and Audiences case study on Rockstar Games in the AS book. For a history of the *GTA* franchise and more detailed debate about 'effects' of the game series, see *Studying Videogames* (McDougall and O'Brien 2008). What we need to know right now is this: the biggest difference between *GTA III* and *GTA IV* is the internet. Players have the opportunity to access the internet within the game in order to access 'hyper-textual' information or to buy *GTA*-related items (ringtones, for example). And they can play in multiplayer mode, taking part in a range of missions with friends. One outcome – perhaps unexpected – is that players have the chance to just hang out in the gameworld with their friends, as well as taking part in more strategic missions with an endgame in mind. Here is *PSW* magazine's take on the online *GTA* (Keating 2008: 91).

> It's not even like Rockstar had to try too hard; putting you in its city playground with a bunch of mates was always going to be amazing (as is proven in the simple Free Mode set up, which lets you and 15 others roam the city unchained), and now they've finally got the technology to pull it off. A motorbike race through the airport is another grin-inducing spectacle, as 16 of us speed underneath moving 737s with guns-blazing and tyres burning. Absolutely awesome.

Case study

Audiobooks

It is useful here, in order to remind ourselves of the broad impact of the internet on cultural production and consumption, to look at a media form seemingly far removed from the various immersive pleasures available in *Grand Theft Auto*'s Liberty City – the novel. By the time you read this, if industry 'futuregazers' are correct, it will be possible for the average mobile phone to download a four-hour audiobook in four minutes. Audio, distributed via the internet instead of on cassette or CD, looks set to dominate the publishing industry. The distributor Audible, owned by Amazon, supplies iTunes and makes available over 20,000 audiobooks using digital rights management. Audible and other companies are striving to develop converged audiobooks, so that a user can switch between reading an e-book on screen and listening to it being read without losing their place. It is possible that the novel might enjoy a perhaps unlikely renaissance in the online age, despite initial fears that the internet would kill reading as a pastime.

As has been stated many times, we cannot separate this theme from the others, so if you are studying Media in the Online Age, you really need to read all the Critical Perspectives sections in this book. This is why this section is much shorter than the other themes – to avoid duplication. The full range of themes will give you more coverage of the impact of the internet on media distribution, participation, access and representation, to accompany the coverage of 'new media economics' (the long tail and wikinomics) above. But for the rest of this section, we will focus on the impact of the internet on media content specifically. And there are two key ways in which this has changed since broadband was rolled out. First, media producers can now distribute existing content much more quickly and on a wider scale than before – so old media can be shared in new ways. Second, new kinds of content can now be produced and shared much more cheaply than before. It is the second category we are more interested in here, but we are going to consider new media content in relation to the legal minefield that is **copyright** law.

Case study

Copyright law in the online age

Kung, Picard and Towse (2008: 120) map out the problem.

> There seems to be no simple solution to the problem of how to encourage creativity when one click can send an author or performer's work all over the globe in a split second. Copyright is, after all, a system for getting users to finance creativity. For some, rewards can be appropriated indirectly: free distribution of your music can act as advertising for your concerts at which you can exclude anyone who does not want to pay for entrance, but that does not apply to other artists; writers, for example, do not have such means available. However, strong enforcement may invade privacy and alienate and criminalise ordinary people, most problematically children. This could have a greater social cost than is gained by the copyright incentive and protection of authors. These are the difficult social choices that digitalisation and the Internet in combination with copyright law present to national governments everywhere.

Exam-Style Question

What difference has web 2.0 made to the two media areas you have studied? And are the bold claims that 'everything has changed' accurate in both cases?

Figure 4.3.3 The *Media Guardian* website – an essential study resource

Examiner's Tip

As for all the examiner tips, you can apply this to any of the Critical Perspectives theme areas, but perhaps it is particularly important for this one. And it is very simple. Add the *Media Guardian* website (www.guardian.co.uk/media – accessed August 2008) to your favourites, subscribe to the Media briefing and any RSS feeds and podcasts that are available, and read every word every week. Use what you find out about online developments in your chosen media areas as your micro examples to relate to your macro themes. Unlike other subjects, where you are told not to revise any later than a week before the exam – 'if you don't know it now, you never will' – media studies is different. There might be a brilliant case study emerging the night before. So as long as you have your template prepared, it can do no harm to try to be as contemporary as possible with the facts you have at your disposal.

4.4

'We Media' and Democracy

For this theme you need to learn about the following, in relation to at least two areas of the media:

- The *we media* theory and associated claims that the media is becoming more democratic
- Examples of where you think *we media* is developing, and examples of where you think it is not
- Debates around the impact on our culture and daily lives of *we media*, in terms of power, access, truth and freedom.

The US is spending hundreds of billion dollars on a war to bring democracy to Iraq. Yet only 4 per cent of people in the Arab world have broadband access. The most potent way to promote democracy in the Middle East would be to get that figure above 50 per cent.

(Leadbetter 2008: 26)

At the risk of repeating the same point beyond reason, these themes converge. Just as we cannot think of media industries or media hardware as being separate from one another anymore, nor can we think of Media in the Online Age, Global Media and We Media and Democracy as being distinct areas of knowledge or analysis. So you have to read every section. Think of this book as being like an iPhone in that respect – don't only use the phone bit and ignore the MP3. Leadbetter makes the point above that access is the key issue in assessing the potential of media to make the world a better, fairer place. Access to broadband internet, then, becomes a matter of social justice. This theme asks you to consider the social world in terms of fairness and equality. What is the role of the media in promoting democracy, and when is the media a barrier to democracy?

Dan Gillmor and citizen journalists

The name of this theme comes from a book published in 2004 by Dan Gillmor, founder of the Centre for Citizen Media. This institutional affiliation is important because it is a profoundly democratic social intervention. You will have studied citizenship in school, so you will know that the government sees 'being a citizen' as something which has to be learned or developed – it does not just happen. Gillmor's view is clear: what he calls 'Big Media' (the huge corporations we have studied at AS and elsewhere at A2 – News Corporation, CNN, the BBC, Emap and now Google, to name but a few) have for years enjoyed control over who gets to produce and share media, and the effect of this on democracy is that we get a concentrated choice of media, leading to profits for an oligopoly (small cluster) of companies. And if you look at who owns and controls those companies, then you can see that this is unrepresentative of the cross section of people who make up our society. Large groups of people only ever get represented by other groups, to put it simply. This mirrors the political arena, where the same thing takes place. Even though we live in a democracy and we are able to vote for the people who will make big decisions – from the amount of tax we pay to whether we invade Iraq – and anyone can stand for election, the choice the system throws up tends to be between a group of very similar people – largely white males with a private school education. The big media corporations are owned by a similarly narrow group. But Gillmor sees the internet as a catalyst for a challenge to this establishment hegemony, as ordinary citizens use blogs and other online communication tools to share their own news, which he calls 'citizen journalism'.

Gillmor calls bloggers 'the former audience', and writes about news blogs as a new form of people's journalism. His book, which you should read for this theme, details blogs from Iraq which offered an alternative to the western media's accounts – a range of collaborative wikispaces, children's news blogs and Persian networkers using the internet for a collective voice in a country where free speech is curtailed, at least from Gillmor's western perspective. Here he summarises starkly how this sea change will

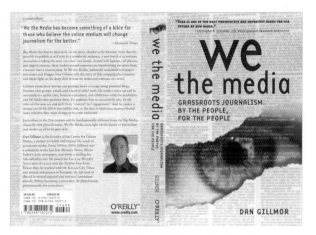

Figure 4.4.1 Gillmor's *We, The Media*, which lends this theme its name

develop in the near future (Gillmor 2004: 42–3). Time will tell if he is right.

> The spreading of an item of news, or of something much larger, will occur – much more so than today – without any help from mass media as we know it. The people who'll understand this best are probably just being born. In the meantime, even the beginnings of this 'shift' are forcing all of us to adjust our assumptions and behaviour.

Taking *we media* together with wikinomics and the long tail (the latter two are both explored at length in the section on Media in the Online Age), we get a rounded celebration of the power of contemporary online discourse to challenge the corporate stronghold, and your job will be to assess the validity of these claims in relation to your two chosen media.

Reality TV

At first, this might seem like a riposte to Gillmor. On the one hand, if he is right, we are increasingly empowering ourselves by creating our own citizen news agendas, free from the corporate news hegemony of the pre-online age. But at the same time, we cannot deny that reality TV, seemingly the most trivial of media formats, is more popular than ever. If *we media* is really happening, why do we not turn off our televisions and do something more interesting, like write a blog? Why do we tune in, collectively, to *Britain's Got Talent* in such huge numbers? And reality TV challenges another claim made by advocates of the web 2.0 'cultural shift'. We are told that people increasingly use television as 'pull media' and watch it on demand, when they want to, where they want to, even through the web in many cases. But the viewing figures for *Big Brother, I'm A Celebrity … Get Me Out of Here!* and *The X Factor* still prove that a huge number of people sit down together at the same time to watch these shows in a very media 1.0 way.

We could just as easily locate this focus on reality TV in any of the other themes: these shows are increasingly global (with local variations); they certainly take us into debates about postmodernism as they test our sense of reality to breaking point; their use of online elements is important; they are at the heart of debates about deregulation, choice and quality; and perhaps most clearly, they offer us an interesting representation of ordinary people – ourselves, as a collective group. In this sense, we are portrayed in the media as 'wannabees' – the myth that is perpetuated is that fame is the ultimate aspiration for all of us, more so even than money in our capitalist system.

Our interest in reality TV in relation to democracy is all about the issue of access. Clearly, more ordinary people are on TV than ever before, and this trend looks set to continue. So we are moving away from the idea that 'being on telly' is for an elite group of talented individuals, and moving towards the idea that the television is an arena for 'the masses', and that fame is obtainable with or without a clear reason for being famous. Whether this is a good or a bad thing depends on your view of what television is for, what the implications of our celebrity culture might be for social life, and what is meant by talent. Let us consider the history of this incredibly popular media form.

In 1965, the BBC broadcast *Man Alive*, a documentary about working-class people and how they live, which at the time seemed groundbreaking but is now derided – especially by Peter Bazalgette, credited with creating the *Big Brother* franchise for Endemol – as patronising in the way it featured middle-class reporters 'investigating' how people live in working-class communities. A decade of similar documentaries about 'ordinary people' followed, but things got more interesting in relation to our times when the subjects of *The Family*, broadcast in 1975, became celebrities at the same time as the programme was still being filmed, which was unheard of at the time. So a family wedding happening in the 'real world', but being filmed for the documentary, which was by now a huge success, became a media event, and the Wilkins family became a 'normal family' and an Osborne-esque TV family simultaneously.

The late 1970s and 1980s saw the further development of the integration of the public into television, with a series of candid camera shows and game shows making temporary stars out of contestants and unsuspecting participants alike. Camcorders created the opportunity for video diaries to dominate screens in the early 1990s, and in 1997 a cluster of 'docusoaps' merged the soap opera, documentary and video diary genres to great effect, most famously with *Airport*. For the first time, members of the public who featured in such shows realised that they could, like Jeremy Space, develop a character for themselves which would appeal more generally and lead to contracts for other TV/radio shows and magazine features – something the contestants of *Big Brother* are increasingly in tune to with every series. As the narrator of the BBC series, *How TV Changed Britain*, put it, television was by now 'making ordinary people famous by casting them in their own lives'. The next step was to develop the 'social experiment' model, which we are now so familiar with. This started with *Castaway* in 2000, which, unlike *Big Brother*, allowed contestants to be aware of the public reaction to them while still competing. But this BBC pioneer of the reality TV format was of course eclipsed by *Big Brother* in July 2000, just a few months later. The influence of webcams on the internet distinguished *Big Brother*, which dispensed with a film crew in favour of the 360-degree camera set-up.

While the success of *Big Brother* might have been predicted, what was less expected was the convergence of reality TV with the music and performance industries that followed. After the success of the Spice Girls, a 'manufactured' pop group, *Popstars* was the first programme to make this construction of a band the subject of a television series, with Hearsay emerging as the successful 'product'. Rather than deride this blatant exposure of how music is marketed and created to order, the viewing public demonstrated such an appetite for more that *Popstars*, which next created Girls Aloud, was followed by *Pop Idol*, *The X Factor* and *Britain's Got Talent*, thus creating a lottery culture in which the American dream idea of a level playing field, whereby anyone's dream can come true, is the subject of more and more entertainment, especially on Saturday evenings. The postmodern angle on this becomes more significant when we consider the way that celebrities themselves have 'joined the party'. The contestants on *I'm A Celebrity ...* clearly have the intent of resurrecting their profiles by winning the show, and we can read this almost as a revenge on celebrity culture. As they eat bugs and expose their flesh for our entertainment, we get to decide whose career is salvaged by this circus act. Ricky Gervais's treatment of this issue in a Boxing Day special edition of *Extras* is discussed in this context in the section on Postmodern Media.

And so to where we are now, and the current debate. Those who wish to uphold the idea of television as enrichment – to educate, inform and entertain in equal measure, as Lord Reith of the BBC declared almost a hundred years ago as a template for public service broadcasting's obligations – see reality TV as a 'dumbed-down' year zero for our culture, distracting us from more serious matters and using the public as a freak show. So these shows are criticised as dehumanising and immoral, as well as

Figure 4.4.2 *Britain's Got Talent* – democracy in action or cultural year zero?

being of low quality – whatever that might mean. Therefore they are counter-democratic in so much as they serve to disempower citizens from the political arena. Instead of challenging the political status quo, we are voting for Signature to win *Britain's Got Talent* (they didn't). The riposte to this comes most robustly from Peter Bazalgette, who accuses the critics of class snobbery – they do not like to see ordinary people getting so much attention on television because they preferred it when the working class were only on our screens as the curious subjects of such patronising series as *Man Alive*. He gives the striking example of a miner being asked what he ate at dinner parties, and compares this to the fact that in recent editions of *Big Brother* the public have voted to victory people of various ethnic origins, sexual preferences and disabilities, unlike the formal political process, as we discussed earlier. Your job, then, is to weigh up this debate: are reality shows just TV, democracy in action or agents in cultural decline? I cannot resist using this catchphrase – *you decide*.

Fan media

Fan media is covered in the Postmodern Media section in some detail – the boundaries between these themes really are fluid when we get to the detail, as you will have gathered by now. So you are advised to use that part of the book as well. In this section, we will consider the development of anime music video. More generally, fan culture has a long history but has increased greatly in the broadband age. Anime music video is one media form within the much broader category of fan media, which describes any 'remixed' piece of media content, where a fan of a commercial media product has put her or his own spin on the material and shared it on the internet. Fan video is a huge area and within this, anime is itself a subgenre of the unofficial music video (UMV). According to Milstein (2008), UMVs are produced with a range of motivations, including the subversion of copyright law, countercultural politics, or broader notions of paying tribute or just being creative – just producing, because you can. The reason why we can include this media activity within a study of we media is very nicely spelled out by Milstein (in Sexton 2008: 33).

> What do UMV-ers want that they cannot have? Certainly, they no longer want their MTV! Rather, they crave the time, talent and freedom to re-envision music and video – to play, blur genres, contradict 'pop' meanings, and revitalise what has become a slowly dying, ever greedy, talent-lacking industry. Thus, the internet has become home to many types of UMV-ers. Some use spliced clips to enhance music with poignant imagery (and vice versa). Others jumble or mock traditional associations in ways that result in funny, political or nonsensical videos. Still others focus exclusively on showcasing their technical prowess. Regardless of motivation or ability, the underlying intent is to form a community in which everyone and anyone can participate and contribute.

If you are looking for a definition of democracy, then 'a community in which everyone and anyone can participate and contribute' comes pretty close.

Anime music video (AMV) is a more specific form of UMV, as it is defined by being animated. Arguably a more technical, skilled enterprise, AMV-ers use a range of effects to either further develop the perceived meanings of a music video, or to subvert or challenge them. When shared on the internet, playback and reviews are more commonly achieved by the AMVs that are perceived to be more original, more radical, less imitative. One critically acclaimed AMV is *Jihaku*, by Yann J., which won the 2005 award for AMV Video of the Year, and reworked a Foo Fighters song ('Best of you') by incorporating over a hundred amime elements. A textbook cannot reproduce the complexity of this media text, so the activity that follows is essential.

Activity

View the *Jihaku* AMV at www.youtube.com/watch?v=KuPruxFfugE (accessed August 2008).

View the Foo Fighters' traditional music video (TMV) at http://ie.youtube.com/watch?v=ynn9iqFVSJE (accessed August 2008).

Discuss with fellow students how the AMV departs from the TMV, but also how it pays tribute to the TMV and adheres to the themes of the song and its visual representation in the TMV. Assess the relative percentage weightings you would give to 'fan tribute' and 'we media remix' for this text.

'Hyperpublic' youth identity

Is social networking, facilitated by sites like Bebo, MySpace and Facebook, a democratic development? Or does the corporate ownership of these sites and the way that personal information is shared with advertisers compromise this spirit? The certainty is that social networking is incredibly popular, particularly with teenagers. Boyd (2008) researched teenage use of MySpace in relation to how users engage in forms of peer-to-peer sociality, and the implications of this for youth identity. Most interestingly, Boyd explored the various different kinds of public and private space that can be understood as operating in and around MySpace. For example, the research found that the pressure to fit in with peer preferences in a public arena was intimidating, and that the conflict between peer interaction and parental surveillance added extra pressure. An obligation to participate in a public culture and an erosion of privacy emerged as key findings, as Boyd sets out here (in Buckingham 2008: 137–8).

> Teens today face a public life with the possibility of unimaginably wide publicity. The fundamental properties of networked publics – persistence, searchability, replicability and invisible audiences – are unfamiliar to the adults that are guiding them through social life. Few adults could imagine every conversation they have sitting in the park or drinking tea in a café being available for hyperpublic consumption, yet this is what technology enables.

The chances are that you are in the age group Boyd observes, and that you are very familiar with these features of modern life. You can, if you wish to, reach a global audience with a meme, but equally you can be the victim of more localised, unwanted online attention if caught unawares on a phone camera. Boyd is suggesting that you are unlikely to get much help from your parents or teachers if you get into trouble in this new world, and that can only be a serious problem in a democracy. On the other hand, Boyd is part of the 'adult culture' that has always defined youth on its own terms. Young people rarely recognise themselves in the ways they are described by adults, a phenomenon Barham (2004) calls 'the disconnect'. So perhaps this anxiety over the way you and your peers are left to your own devices to survive in social networks is not such a big deal as Boyd thinks. Herring (in Buckingham 2008: 80), in another piece of research looking at youth identity and digital technology, found that users of MySpace were able to articulate the duality of its positive and negative aspects, and were annoyed by the parent culture assuming the worst.

A male high school student recently blogged – 'STOP BLAMING EVERYTHING ON MYSPACE! America, give your children some credit. They're relatively intelligent, and they're pretty rebellious when they want to be. They will have their MySpace regardless of what you say, and by telling them they can't handle it, you're not helping the situation at all'.

Activity

Over to you. Assuming you are a MySpace user, get together, preferably on MySpace (it would make sense), and discuss Boyd and Herring's research. In your experience, do the positive opportunities enabled by MySpace outweigh the dangers and pressures? Do you feel more able to participate in a collective culture and have your voice heard – which would be a democratic outcome? Or do you feel that this participation is an obligation, a pressure and that there are risks involved? Or both?

Power, control, hegemony

Hegemony is quite an old-fashioned idea in these postmodern media times, but despite that, it is arguably as important as ever. Here is a definition to get us started (Watson and Hill 2003: 126).

A state of hegemony is achieved when a provisional alliance of certain social groups exerts a consensus that makes the power of the dominant group appear both natural and legitimate. Institutions such as the mass media, the family, the education system and religion, play a key role in the shaping of people's awareness and consciousness and thus can be agents through which hegemony is constructed, exercised and maintained.

There are three Marxist theorists we need to get to grips with briefly here. The first is Karl Marx himself, who famously declared that the people who rule in any society do so by controlling not only the means of production (the ways of making money – in his day this would be land and factories, but in our times we can think

Figure 4.4.3 Gramsci's classic theory of hegemony is perhaps more important than ever in the deregulated broadband era

about Rupert Murdoch, Richard Branson and Bill Gates, who own the means by which information is exchanged), but also the production of ideas. In other words, they keep the rest of us in our place by making sure that we share their ideas about 'the way things should be'. Our monarchy still proves this. If we wanted to, we could throw the Royal Family out of their homes and demand that we no longer fund their lives through our taxes, but we do not do this, because of a consensus shared by many that this elitist hierarchy is understood as 'heritage' and 'tradition'. And we do not do very much about the unfair nature of the capitalist system because we are convinced that everyone has the chance to become Alan Sugar (which is clearly not the case, as the system cannot allow everyone to succeed), and because we cannot think of a viable alternative.

Althusser was a Marxist who developed this idea by distinguishing between two forms of state control: repressive state apparatus (RSA) – these are physical, 'concrete' ways of controlling us, such as the law, the police and the army; and ideological state apparatus (ISA) – the media, the church and education. The point is simple: you do not need the RSA if the ISA works. People will not challenge the system if the ISA is working to make it seem natural and fair – so the ISA, including the media, works to create consensus.

Case study

Google China

The People's Republic of China, being a Communist country, offers an interesting contrast to our capitalist media set-up. The three main TV networks in China are government controlled, and the government also monitors various kinds of broadband internet activity. At the time of writing, just before the Beijing Olympics 2008, the attention of the world is on China, and on the issue of whether this global focus, combined with the availability of new media that are almost impossible to regulate – the mediasphere – will break down the state control of Chinese media once and for all.

The relationship between Google China and the rest of Google is interesting. At first, Google was blocked in China, but in return for accepting a limited version, Google was granted a licence for a Chinese-language version of the search engine. The limitations are in the form of government banning of certain subjects from the search listings. In the lead-up to the Olympics, Free Tibet protestors disrupted the progress of the Olympic flame around the globe, and in London the Chinese political context was visually represented by the farcical media images of a group of security officials fighting with protestors, while bemused British flame carriers did their best to run with the flame amid the madness. According

to the western media, the Chinese TV stations did not broadcast any of these images, so the Chinese public was unaware that the Olympics were proving so controversial internationally. But on a trip to China, an English academic colleague searched in Google (English language) for 'Olympic flame protests' and found news results amounting to 1,800,000,000.

The question, in any case, is whether Google's move into restricted Chinese webspace is a small step in the right (democratic) direction, or whether the principle of free speech is a sacred absolute that cannot be compromised. Bill Gates, perhaps the ultimate advocate of the free market, believes that the former is the case and that the internet is contributing to an incremental reduction in state censorship. On the other hand, China is still described by the pressure group Reporters Without Borders as 'the world champion of internet censorship', referring to the so-called 'Great Firewall of China' and the fact that two key words allegedly blocked are 'freedom' and 'democracy'. On the same trip mentioned above, our academic colleague also tried to access a YouTube clip relating to Tiananmen Square and was unsuccessful, but it could not be ascertained whether this was technical or content-specific.

Exam-Style Question

Is the media really getting more democratic?

Gramsci was the Marxist intellectual who developed the idea of hegemony, which we started with, to explain the importance of this constructed consensus. In a famous documentary about the media's role in all of this, Noam Chomsky described how consent is manufactured. You can study this at www.youtube.com/watch?v= O_uXGCZenwY (accessed August 2008). And a much more recent example of the manufacturing of consent is dealt with in the *Outfoxed* documentary, which is discussed elsewhere in this book.

This relates to our study of *we media* because we need to look for examples where we can say that people's access to the production of ideas is increasing, as is suggested by Dan Gillmor, Charles Leadbetter and, in more commercial times, Chris Anderson (all of whom are covered in this book, across various themes). But we need to balance this with examples where we might think the media are playing an active role in suppressing access.

Examiner's Tip

Writing about your own media culture is very useful if you do it well, and very dangerous if you do it badly. This theme really lends itself to some personal reflection, but the safe way to do it is to always make sure that you relate the relevantly anecdotal aspect of your answer to an idea written by someone else. So you might link Gillmor's ideas to your own use of blogs; or comment on your own voting habits in response to political elections and reality TV, but link this to Bazalgette's claims about the democratic nature of *Big Brother*; or you might include your own fan productions, but connect this to Millstein or the work of Matt Hills (2002). It is not mandatory to do this, but it helps to 'discipline' your writing, so that you cannot go off on a personal tangent, which may be interesting, but might risk losing you marks when the examiner has to weigh up the relevance of the material in relation to the specific question set.

4.5

Contemporary Media Regulation

For this theme you need to learn about the following, in relation to at least two areas of the media:

- How media regulation now is different to the past – the historical angle
- The different kinds of media regulation and how they all seek to 'protect' people in some way
- The efficiency and impact of various forms of media regulation – how well do they work, and what difference do they make to people's lives?
- Debates around the role of the regulator in a democracy – arguments for and against various forms of media regulation.

This theme takes you into the heart of public discourse and debate about the media. Whether a government should, or can, regulate the media, and if so, how, is one of the most important **political** questions we can raise about the media, and this kind of analysis really disarms the notion that media studies is a trivial subject that should not be taken seriously. Alongside these political issues, there are crucial **economic** decisions to be made. The media is big business, and if it is unregulated, companies and corporations can gain a great deal of power and influence through acquisition of media organisations. And there are, of course, the well-known **social** factors relating to the media and how we use it (or are used by it), so there are always heated discussions in the public forum about the need for the powers-that-be to regulate the content of media and,

All the set briefs for the Advanced Portfolio ask you to produce media materials which take you into questions of regulation and the law. For example, a news programme will have to be produced with journalistic codes of practice in mind; a new video game will need a **classification**, and this will impact on the marketing strategy; and a children's drama will have to be very carefully constructed, to avoid – or invite – controversy, but with an eye on Ofcom. Whichever brief you respond to, you should include a section on regulation on your website, blog or other electronic format, to keep a record of the decisions you are making in relation to the critical question of how your products will be shaped by your understanding of the regulatory and legal frameworks for the area you are working in.

more importantly perhaps, people's access to it, especially children, who are more vulnerable to media effects. This leads us to a general 'way-in' to this theme. We can say that, one way or another, any case study on contemporary media regulation will be contextualised by the debates around various kinds of 'media effects'.

Media effects

Some case studies are more directly concerned with effects – the classification and regulation of video games, television and film are notable examples that are all to do with the need for the authorities to 'protect' people from material which might cause social harm of one kind or another. This will be achieved either through classification – preventing people from accessing material that is deemed to be unsuitable for their age – or through censorship – removing material from public access altogether. These are very different approaches and it is extremely important that you do not confuse them or lump them together as one and the same. At the other end of the regulatory spectrum, we find forms of regulation that at first glance appear to be unrelated to this 'protective' obligation. For example, regulating the amount of shares businesses can acquire in media companies might seem to be the stuff of politics, economics and law. Likewise, creating new legislation to try to curb illegal downloading of music and film might seem to be a simple matter of 'policing'. But each of these examples connects to the notion of protection from effects in a different way. There is a concern that a business tycoon like Rupert Murdoch, if allowed free rein with the British media, will be in a strong position to influence our thinking in relation to key political issues that will then serve his business interests – so we are being protected from the effects of potentially biased news reporting. And the music industry will tell us that **piracy** threatens musicians who are just starting out more than the likes of Radiohead, as it will become less possible for people to make a living from their music if we carry on expecting to get it for nothing, so there is another 'effect' here that can be controlled or reduced through regulation. So while we are always thinking about effects in one way or another, it is useful to distinguish between three kinds of media regulation:

- Regulation of **media content**
- Regulation of **media access and distribution**
- Regulation of **media ownership and commercial practices**.

Media audience theories

According to Barker and Petley (1998: 2), there is an obsession with trying to prove that the media are responsible for a range of social problems, and the researchers who want to find this link carry on despite the lack of evidence to support the idea.

> Predictably, each new claim comes with an imprimatur of 'this time we've done it, this time we've finally proved it' – but never does an admission follow, when their claims fall apart (as they invariably do), that they were simply wrong in the first place. We have to uncover and hold up to bright daylight the unstated assumptions that come camouflaged within these claims. We have to show the ill effects of the campaigns run by the 'effects' campaigners – including their effects on those whom the campaigners frequently insult and denigrate as morally debased – the people who enjoy and enthusiastically participate in the movies, TV programmes, video games or whatever that the moralists are so certain are 'harmful'.

The effects approach is one of a variety of approaches that media researchers work in. One extreme variant of effects theory is the **hyperdermic syringe** model, which viewed audiences as passive recipients of 'injected' messages – this is largely rejected today. Another version of effects is **cultivation theory**, which tries to prove that we form views and opinions about people over time as a result of exposure to media, and thus people become stereotyped. Another familiar theme is **desensitisation** – the idea that the more violence we see, the less shocked we are by it in real life. And another that resonates with the public is **copycat theory**, claiming that individuals may act out what they see 'modelled' on the screen – this gets a lot of media attention and can often be a helpful theory for vote-hungry politicians. Famous examples are the Jamie Bulger case and the Columbine killings. More complex audience theories include the now slightly outdated, but still popular (among media teachers, so be careful!) **uses and gratifications** theory, which is more about what people do *with* the media to satisfy various individual and social needs that we have; **reception theory** (showing how we make different **polysemic** meanings from the same media); **ethnography** (looking at people's responses to media from their point of view in their reading contexts); and **postmodernism**, which looks at how the boundaries between reality and media have become blurred. To bring things right up to date, and maybe to stretch and challenge you even more, Gauntlett (2007b) now argues that web 2.0 media erodes the boundary between producer and audience, to the extent that it makes little sense to talk about media audiences in this way anymore. He calls this new approach **media studies 2.0**.

Regulating video games

The Byron Review (2008) found no direct evidence for the harmful effects of violent video games on children, yet the public discourse of concern arising from the release of *Grand Theft Auto IV* in April 2008 shows that broader society will continue to look for such a link. In *Studying Videogames* (McDougall and O'Brien 2008), *GTA* is used as a major case study within a much fuller discussion of the 'social effects' of video games, the nature of the psychological studies into 'effects' and other social factors relating to gaming – health concerns, the changing nature of literacy and the identity-play made possible by online gaming and multiplayer experiences such as *Second Life*.

Byron (2008: 149) came to the following conclusions:

- There is no evidence of 'desensitisation' as a result of playing video games.
- The specific sociocultural and psychological context of the individual game player is crucial.

The lack of firm evidence for negative long-term effects from video games on attitudes, beliefs and behaviours, means that we need to consider the question of harm and risk of harm within the broader biological, psychological and social context of the child or young person playing the game. This approach can help to highlight specific potential areas of risk for some vulnerable children and young people.

- The idea that video games are addictive for children is based on prejudice about the activity rather than any evidence.
- While the media, including games, may have some influence on negative behaviour displayed by children, they should not be singled out as a cause.

Byron's (2008: 158) study went on:

It is vitally important that the sole or primary cause of violence or other behaviours such as excessive use in children is not identified as the media or video games per se. Neither should the media be seen as playing no role. Many researchers are now arguing for a more comprehensive approach to these questions of social importance, which begin with an account of the problem or behaviour of interest (e.g. aggression) and carry out a comprehensive examination of all the factors that might impact on that, including the influence of the media.

Video game classification

In 2008 an action plan was produced as the outcome of the Byron Review, for the classification of video games. You will be able to review the progress being made towards some of the targets outlined in this action plan. As you can see via http://www.dcsf.gov.uk/byronreview/actionplan/index.shtml, changes to the system itself, and to the ways in which games are advertised to the 'illegal' age group, are recommended. So what is the current system like and why is it seen to be failing?

The British Board of Film Classification's (**BBFC**) guidelines to game developers will give you a sense of how complicated things are in comparison to films. You can access these guidelines at www.bbfc.co.uk/customer/cust_procDigi.php (accessed August 2008). Part of the reason for this is that games include **cut scenes** as well as gameplay, and part of it is due to the unique nature of each gaming experience. At another web page (www.parentsbbfc.co.uk— accessed August 2008), you can find very clear information for parents about the required age for playing a video game, including a search facility where you can enter any game and be given the classification and a clear indication of content. And the BBFC website also contains a student area for people like you, where you can gather research information about particular grading decisions undertaken by the BBFC. *Grand Theft Auto* is an '18' game, and the parental information is very clear about the violence, sexual content and moral issues that the player can expect to encounter. The ratings for games are no different to the ratings for films and DVDs, so if the system is working, identification should be required at the point of sale or rental, and parents should be on guard to prevent 'illegal' access. Of course, internet distribution raises an enormous challenge for the regulator, but notwithstanding it must be remembered at all times that children are not the intended audience for a game like *GTA IV*, so if we have a problem with children playing it and being affected, then systemic failure is to blame rather than the game designers. This argument is only so robust though, when we bring into the equation the allegation that the distributors of such games deliberately develop promotional materials to target an underage audience, which is why Byron's recommendations include a review of the regulation of game advertising, along the lines of the promotion of tobacco and alcohol.

Here are some examples of video game ratings, accompanied by the BBFC content description in each case.

- *The Sims 2 – Double Deluxe*: rated 12

The Sims 2 – Double Deluxe is a strategy game which enables the player to create a range of human characters and build up whole neighbourhoods for them to inhabit and enjoy. The game contains moderate sex references.

The *sex references* include the suggestion that couples are having sex under the covers at some points in the game. No detail is shown, but as the player constructs the situation themselves by putting the characters together, this would be inappropriate for young children.

No-one younger than 12 may rent or buy a '12' rated game. Responsibility for allowing under-12s to play lies with the accompanying or supervising adult.

- *Grand Theft Auto IV*: rated 18

  This fourth generation of the series has players taking on the role of Niko Bellic, an Eastern European who comes to the United States in search of the 'American Dream', only to find the reality of his new life far from what had been promised. It has been rated '18' for **strong violence, very strong language, very strong sex references** and **drugs use.**

  Violence is a central theme of the game, with the character able to engage on missions which invariably involve killing in return for money and other in-game rewards. The character can gain use of a variety of weapons including machine guns, Molotov cocktails, a serrated knife and a rocket propelled grenade launcher. Injuries and death are shown with blood, including blood projected onto nearby walls, windscreens and the camera lens. The character is able to attack and kill any other character in the game, including 'innocent' non-player characters, although this carries a strong risk of being pursued by the police providing a negative consequence for such action.

  The game includes several uses of **very strong language** (e.g. 'c**t', 'motherf**ker'), and frequent use of **strong language** (e.g. 'f**k.). The very strong language occurs within 'cut scenes' in which the story and character development take place, in spoof television episodes and during a stand up comedy routine.

  Sex references also occur during cut scenes, including **strong references to sexual behaviour.** During gameplay the character can pick up prostitutes and pay for three different levels of service. What follows is an undetailed portrayal of masturbation, fellatio and intercourse. The character can also visit lap dancing clubs and request a private dance. While the game contains sexualised dancing and the portrayal of sex, there is no sexualised nudity.

  Reference is made to **drugs** trafficking and several cut scenes portray cocaine snorting. There is also a satirical reference to the domestic production of a hard drug, but it does not contain the detail necessary to reproduce this in the real world.

  '18' means suitable for adults only. No-one younger than 18 may rent or buy an '18' rated video game.

- *Harry Potter and the Order of the Phoenix*: rated PG

  Harry Potter and the Order of the Phoenix is a children's adventure game, based on the popular book and film of the same name. The game contains **mild violence**. There are also some **scary scenes**.

  The **violence** in the game largely takes the form of magical duels with wands as weapons and spells and charms being cast – the setting is quite clearly fantasy and a very well known fantastical world. Much of the game contains little in the way of violence, but the later levels of the game involve the player fighting against fantastical villains. These encounters are sometimes intense but undetailed and the outcome is reassuring.

The game also contains some mild **scary moments**, such as the appearance of the main villain, Lord Voldemort, and some of his followers. Again, the familiar fantasy setting lessens the impact of these isolated scenes.

'PG' stands for Parental Guidance. A 'PG' game should not disturb a child aged around eight or older. However, parents are advised to consider whether the content may upset younger or more sensitive children.

Video games only require BBFC classification if their material leads them to lose exemption. This exemption was traditionally based on the idea that the graphics were not sophisticated enough for games to be as 'realistic' as films, whereas now films are increasingly trying to look like video games!

The exemption is lost, if, in the words of the regulator, games 'depict, to any significant extent, gross violence against humans or animals, human sexual activity, human urinary or excretory functions or genital organs, or techniques likely to be useful in the commission of offences' (www.parentsbbfc.co.uk/ faqs.asp#How%20does%20the%20BBFC%20classify%20films%20 and%20videos? – accessed August 2008).

Where games include non-interactive material, such as cut scenes and trailers, then exemption may also be removed. So really it is only games that contain no violence or sex that are exempt from the BBFC, and these are regulated by the PEGI system, which is a European rating system, the UK version of which is the Video Standards Council (VSC). If a game producer is not sure whether they will need BBFC classification, the VSC can advise them.

Why are these details important? Because you are studying contemporary media regulation, and this is one example of a regulatory system that many view as failing in its duty to protect. So to really understand the critical perspectives on this, you need to know *why* there is a need for protection, *how* the protection is currently organised, and *who* has a view about how well it is working.

Here is a view on the effects of video games, from Gentile et al. (2004: 1). Gentile is a very vocal US critic of games.

Looking across the dozens of studies that have now been conducted on violent video games, there appear to be five major effects. Playing violent games leads to increased physiological arousal, increased aggressive thoughts, increased aggressive feelings, increased aggressive behaviors, and decreased prosocial helping. These studies include experimental studies (where it can be shown that playing violent games actually causes increases in aggression), correlational studies (where long-term relations between game play and real-world aggression can be shown), and longitudinal studies (where changes in children's aggressive behaviors can be demonstrated). For example, in a study of over 400 3rd–5th graders, those students who played more violent video games early in the school year changed to become more physically aggressive later in the school year, even after statistically controlling for sex, race, total screen time, prior aggression, and other relevant variables. Apparently practice does make perfect.

So according to Gentile, there is a compelling range of scientific 'proof' that antisocial and dangerous behaviour increases as a result of playing a violent game. But how are these studies conducted, and under what conditions? While there is undoubtedly some tangible evidence of increased aggression, we need to consider whether aggressive thoughts are necessarily dangerous. A lot of this research describes what people say rather than what they really do. Freud's psychoanalytical theories tell us that people are divided between their desires in thought (what they would really like to do) and their sense of self (what they think others will accept them doing and still like them). But most of the psychological effects research might convincingly be accused of ignoring this, and assuming a direct link between desire and action. Another issue is that a lot of this research is conducted in a laboratory context, so we need to ask how aggression was tested, in what conditions and with what kind of sample? How close can this laboratory context be to real life? And what are the dynamics at work in the experiment – might research subjects act more aggressively if they think that is what the researchers are looking for?

Activity

Australia and New Zealand, unlike the UK, regulate television content through on-screen classification. This is a more explicit approach than the 9 p.m. watershed. Research by the Broadcasting Standards Authority in New Zealand found that 75 per cent of parents were aware of this system and half of those were very active in enforcing the system with their children.

- Write a press release sentence describing the above research statistic as a positive finding that proves that parents in New Zealand are doing a good job when it comes to regulating their children's access to TV. Then write a negative version of the same statistics. This will serve as a tangible reminder that audience research can be spun in two ways in almost every case.
- Research, via the internet, how the on-screen classification system works in Australia and New Zealand, and visit the Ofcom website to research the regulation of television content in the UK. What are the key differences and why do you think we do not have on-screen classification here?

Case Study

Grand Theft Auto IV

When video game classification is discussed, there are two common occurrences. First, people mention *Grand Theft Auto*, usually as an example of a 'corrupting' game. Second, they ignore the fact that *GTA* is classified as 18, so the discussion should not be about the content of the game, which is already rated as inappropriate for children, but about the efficiency of the classification system. A third issue is the tendency for people who have never played the game to condemn its moral bankruptcy, without an informed understanding of how subject matter, play and behaviour may or may not be connected in the gaming experience. Media critic Charlie Brooker (2008) explores some of these issues in a review of the game.

> The one thing everyone knows about *Grand Theft Auto* is that you can kill prostitutes in it. That's because it's a 'sandbox' game in which you can kill anyone you like. Or you can not kill them. Or you can simply drive around slowly, obeying the traffic lights. If you break the law and the in-game police spot you, they'll hunt you down and nab you. Murdering innocent people is neither a) encouraged, b) free of consequence, or c) any more realistic than a Tex Avery cartoon. Nonetheless, Keith Vaz MP is probably standing on his roof screaming for a ban right now, confidently telling the world's press that *Grand Theft Auto IV* is a dedicated, ultra-realistic prostitute-murdering simulator aimed exclusively at easily corruptible three-year-olds. He means well, possibly. But he's ignorant. The irony is that every time I read some dumb anti-gaming proclamation by Vaz and co, I get so angry I have to fire up *GTA IV* and shoot 29 pedestrians in the face just to vent the frustration they've caused. Thank God these games exist, or I would be taking it out on real people.

Brooker is ironically turning around the 'effects discourse' here, but he makes a very serious point. As he says, the player of *GTA IV* knows, as the uninformed critic may not, that the headline features of the game are a matter of choice, and that actually the character of Niko Bellic, who the player inhabits, has a complex and critical relationship with crime and violence, as described here by the 'serious writer' Peter Conrad (2008: 14).

> *GTA IV* is about the revved up tempo and suicidal trajectory of our mechanised lives. But it has a more reflective dimension: games like this dramatise the interplay of fate and chance, or destiny and contingency. Niko's cousin asks what he's doing in America. 'What's anyone doing?', he shrugs. 'I'm just trying to make the right decisions'. That's also the game-ster's occupation. Do I go left or right? Forwards or in-reverse? Do I return the call in which the slinky Michelle begs for another date? Such decisions are quickly, unthinkingly made, but their consequences unfurl peripherally in a nuclear chain reaction.

Conrad highlights the non-linear, chaos-theory experience of the game and of the player's 'ideological' state. Clearly, this is not a hyperdermic-syringe relationship between reality and morality and a twisted game which influences and corrupts by desensitising. The important angle is this: if *Grand Theft Auto* were a Hollywood action film about crime, vice and violence in a dystopian city based on New York, there would be little interest in the 'corrupting' nature of the product, as long as it were classified correctly. It is the status of *GTA IV* as a 'game' that means it is taken less seriously as a text by broader reviewers of popular culture – as Brooker says elsewhere in his review, those who make a living analysing video games tend to be treated as 'big kids' compared to, say, theatre critics – but more seriously as a product in society. Without any specific evidence, as the Byron Review shows, it is assumed that playing *GTA IV* – in other words, being the protagonist – is somehow automatically more 'dangerous' than merely watching an actor playing out the role. So on the one hand it is treated as just a game, but on the other as 'training' for real-life immorality. Can the discourse of concern have it both ways? *Discuss!*

Regulating 'new media'

As we shall see, the Byron Review (2008) cannot be ignored for this theme, given that this piece of research was government commissioned and thus carries considerable weight in the public domain. Part of Byron's review is a summary of effects research, which was conducted by David Buckingham of the Institute of Education. Along with Martin Barker and David Gauntlett, David Buckingham is a 'key player' in serious academic research into media audiences and how they make sense of media products.

To get a full and balanced sense of the effects debate, you need to read a range of policy statements alongside academic perspectives like this book and the writers in the activity above. The most recent example – the Byron Review – is covered in detail in this section, but you should also research information provided on the internet by Ofcom and the BBFC. You will soon discover that the regulators operate in the middle of a polarised debate, between those who blame the media for the apparent decline in moral standards and those who seek to uphold freedom of speech and of access. The following two quotes are both interesting when considered within these axes of regulation.

> It is very hard to maintain freedom of speech in a culture which has become terminally infantilised. We've allowed the censors to view us all as children, and we've handed over the reins of responsibility for our viewing habits because we are not willing to accept that responsibility for ourselves.
>
> (Kermode 2001)

> The Internet is a reflection of our society and that mirror is going to be reflecting what we see. If we do not like what we see in that mirror the problem is not to fix the mirror, we have to fix society.
>
> (Vint Cerf 2004)

Writing about violent films and the internet respectively, both writers assert that the responsibility for media audience behaviour would ideally rest with citizens, and thus our ability to make appropriate decisions about the media we use and share would override any need for censorship. These both resonate with current regulatory attitudes, but there is a feeling that we are not, as Kermode suggests and Vint Cerf appears to agree, as responsible as we should be.

But there is a broader context in which we need to understand the effects debate, which is the more general nature of 'concern' over popular culture, described here in the pre-internet age by sociologist Stuart Hall (1980: 228).

> There is a continuous and necessarily uneven and unequal struggle, by the dominant culture, constantly to disorganise and

Activity

Part of the Critical Perspectives unit is about knowing which academic theorists said what and when. Compared to most media studies work, this is a pretty old-fashioned skill, but you need to balance this with the more 'creative' activities you will be engaged in elsewhere on your course. In other words, you need to do well with both. This task is about referencing, and you need to use the quote, paraphrase, comment strategy in order to do this well. This means that when you write about something someone has written in a book, journal or website (formal, published material), you need to do three things.

- Paraphrase the writer – this is where you tell the reader what the writer's ideas were all about, but mostly in your own words. You have to remember to **reference** the writer, though, or you will be guilty of plagiarism. So you say something like, 'Buckingham (2008) is of the view that much of the effects research is the result of experiments carried out in artificial conditions'. Some of these words will be his – he will have used the phrase 'artificial conditions' somewhere – but the specific wording here, the exact combination of words in sentences, is yours. You have told the reader that you are writing about Buckingham, you have referenced the year of publication so the reader can access his work if s/he wants to, so you have done your job and you cannot be accused of copying.
- Quote the writer – this is where you take the exact words the writer produced and put them in quotation marks, followed by the year of publication and the page number, so the reader can go straight to the source if s/he wants to. If you do this without quotation marks and the author's name, you will be in trouble, so be careful!

- Comment on the writer's ideas – it is no good just paraphrasing and/or quoting, without showing the reader that you understand the writer's ideas and have a view on them.

Referencing is a skill that will impress the examiner and prepare you well for higher education, so it is worth spending some time preparing this. This activity will help you.

Go to www.theory.org.uk (accessed August 2008). This is David Gauntlett's very interesting and useful website on all things related to media theory, especially audiences and identity. Go to the 'Trading cards' section of the website and you will find a 'top trumps' style trading card for a number of key philosophers and social theorists.

To help you remember what a range of academics have to say about media effects, produce a trading card, using the format you will find on the website, for the following writers:

- David Buckingham
- David Gauntlett
- Sonia Livingstone
- Martin Barker
- Dafna Lemish.

If you use Google images, or a similar image bank on the internet, you will be able to see what these people look like, so you can produce a visual caricature (like the trading cards at www.theory.org.uk). The key thing here, though, with your Critical Perspectives exam in mind, is to construct the trading cards so you can remember for your exam key information, such as:

- Key idea
- Name and year of most important book or article
- Useful quote (with page number)
- Your comment on the key idea.

reorganise popular culture; to enclose and confine its definitions and forms within a more inclusive range of dominant forms. There are points of resistance; there are also moments of supersession. This is the dialectic of cultural struggle.

Hall reminds us that we must not isolate the notion of the state censoring media content from power struggles over the function and limits of popular culture. Actually, media studies itself is located within this contested area – is it a 'proper' subject?

Film censorship and classification

A range of historical examples of film censorship will illustrate Hall's point for us – such as *Crash* (not banned in novel form), *Clockwork Orange* (banned by its director), *Battleship Potemkin* (banned for some social groups, but not others) and *Straw Dogs* (where there is a view that the censor made the images more disturbing than before). To focus on the politics of censorious claims, films like *The Magdelene Sisters*, *Dogma* and *The Passion of the Christ* help us to analyse the ideological nature of debates over faith and the media, and then we can realise that all censorship is actually based on power claims, and there is no single text that is universally offensive. For example, as Kermode has argued recently, the BBFC (which, it should be noted, is funded by the film industry rather than the government) appears more heavy-handed when dealing with English-language films compared to subtitled arthouse movies with controversial content. The assumption about audience is obvious here – the censor assumes that the intelligent, middle-class audience for foreign cinema can 'cope' more easily with sensitive content than 'the masses' who watch the more accessible films. As always, the most productive, active strategy for your work in this area will be to carry out some small-scale audience research – not to try to 'prove' whether your friends and/or family are influenced negatively by film images, but to collect qualitative data through interviews and focus group discussions about films and censorship – so you can analyse the discourses articulated (the assumptions and ideas that people rely on when talking about this theme) and compare these to your own responses to 'shocking' films. Davey (2005: 30) offers a really interesting student view.

> Films are a form of expression, and many forms of expression are prompted by sorrow and loss which, in many cases, are prompted by violence. Therefore, without violence, a vast number of films would never have been made. If violence has played a part in the making of a film, then it's understandable that in the content of the film, violence may play a part. We cannot distinguish between violence and film, because that would mean distinguishing between violence and life.

It is also useful for you to reflect on the issues your teachers may have to wrestle with if they bring films into the classroom which society has expressed concerns about. With reference to the controversial film *Crash* – which was banned by some local councils but not others, due to different responses to Cronenberg's film adaptation of the Ballard novel (which, interestingly, nobody wanted to ban) – about people who are sexually aroused by the victims of car crashes, here are two teachers offering very different views about whether media students should study the film.

> A film, by an important director, of a book by a great novelist, which has generated much media heat (and of course, very little light) should be dealt with in the Media Studies classroom because if we're not doing it then sure as hell nobody else is.

(Lacey, quoted in Stafford 1997: 7)

> Inevitably, trying to understand what people 'do' with media products will involve discussing the issue of violence in moving image products. This does mean analysing the views of both those who maintain a direct 'cause and effect' relationship between 'violence' on screen and violence in society and those critics who reject such a crude model or way of describing the debate. There are enough examples from recent years to enable a thoughtful, intellectual debate. I just don't think a film about obtaining sado-masochistic sexual pleasure from car crashes is one of them. It is just too extreme for use with 16–18 year olds.

(Kemp, quoted in Stafford 1997: 7)

If even media teachers cannot agree on this, then one thing is certain: we cannot expect you to come to the Critical Perspectives exam with all the answers. Your job will be to intelligently weigh up the debate, with lots of examples, and then give us your informed, academic viewpoint.

Children and television

These are the key critical questions to address when researching ideas about children watching television – what they watch, how much they watch and what effects this might have.

- How are children defined and by whom?
- What research methods have been used to produce these findings?
- What model of audience behaviour is evident?

Primary research with parents and children is incredibly enlightening here, as long as you ask your teachers to support you with the ethical issues. Outcomes are only useful if you are aware that parents cannot be treated as objective subjects if they are asked questions about how much television their children watch, as this is an emotive area with an underlying subtext about parental neglect. In other words, people will not always be honest about how much TV they or their kids watch, because they will worry about the impressions this will give of their parenting, their lifestyle and their intelligence. Having said that, children are great subjects for open-ended discursive work, especially in response to images. You should be discouraged from trying to answer simple questions (e.g. are children influenced by TV advertising? the answer is probably yes), and encouraged to find out about the range of different responses out there. Some interesting examples of research questions might be:

- In what different ways is television considered to be educational? (Note: this question is *not* asking if television is educational or not.)
- How do children understand the function of advertising?
- How do children and parents discuss the suitability of television?
- What are children's responses to TV drama representations of family life?

By carrying out this kind of research, as long as you are *very* careful, you will be giving voice to children, which happens too rarely in media research, as Buckingham (2000: 206) suggests here.

We need to begin by exploring what children make of the films and television programmes that they themselves identify as upsetting or indeed as 'violent' – which, it should be emphasised, are not necessarily those that adults would identify for them. In a debate that is dominated by adults purporting to speak on children's behalf, children's voices have been almost entirely unheard.

Activity

With Buckingham's advice in mind, here is a framework for a research exercise on children and television.

Research methods: describe the purpose of research, the different kinds of media research in operation, the kind of research you are doing, your broader theme and your micro-theme within it. Justify your hypothesis in terms of what it will add to the broader field of research in this area. What are you doing that is new, or specific, or local?

Literature review: how have you 'mapped the field'? What literature did you identify as central and why? Summarise and synthesise from these sources, and identify one particularly useful source. Describe how your planning for the primary research relates to this secondary work.

Describe the **research methodology** for the primary work in detail, and any logistical and/or ethical issues you encountered.

Analyse the data you acquired, at a basic quantitative level and also in a more discursive, qualitative and interpretive dimension. What were your research questions, and what are the answers? What further research can other people now undertake from your contribution to the field? How does your set of findings relate to the literature you started with?

Ensure all your sources are referenced correctly, and that you guarantee anonymity where needed.

In 2008, Dr Tanya Byron produced a government-funded report on young people's use of the internet and digital media, with a series of recommendations for safeguarding these young and potentially vulnerable citizens from the perceived dangers of the information revolution. This review can be found and downloaded at www.dfes.gov.uk/byronreview (accessed August 2008).

Activity

View the cover of the Byron Review, accessed via the website mentioned above. The outcomes of the review were not sensationalist in relation to media effects. Indeed, balance was achieved in the findings and the conclusions were cautious and moderate, so we cannot accuse Byron of mobilising or accelerating a new or existing **moral panic**. But while the old adage that you should not judge a book by its cover remains, closer scrutiny of the cover of the report does anchor the outcomes in a particular way in the mind of the reader, who is unlikely to read the full text in most cases. Using your skills in semiotic analysis from AS level, deconstruct the cover of the review using the following framing questions:

- What are the **connotations** of the use of images produced by children?
- What public concerns are assumed by the images?
- What emotive impact might the mode of address have?
- What is the relationship between the outcomes and recommendations in the review itself and the cover images?
- What alternative images might have been used in order to link the outcomes and recommendations more closely to the front cover?
- Why do you think the cover was produced in this way?

Some of Dr Byron's key findings were these:

- Parents feel ill-equipped to protect their children in digital, online activities and spaces – she calls this a 'generational digital divide'.
- Classification systems for video games need to be improved and tightened up.
- Children need to be educated to become more media-literate, so they can make themselves safer (she uses learning to swim so you do not need a lifeguard as an analogy here).
- The only way to securely protect young people from material they should not be accessing is to link families, media industries and government together in a regulatory strategy.

Byron (2008: 206) expresses this as follows.

I believe that alongside new technology we need a new culture of responsibility, where all in society focus not on defending our entrenched positions, but on working together to help children keep themselves safe, to help parents to keep their children safe and to help each other support children and parents in this task.

This new culture of responsibility fits with the government of the time (Gordon Brown's New Labour Party). Their agenda is to gradually shift from regulation (controlling what people can do) to responsibility (expecting people to regulate what they do themselves).

Perhaps equally interesting for the media student – if not more interesting than the report itself – is the public response. Here are three examples.

From a journalist (Lilley 2008) – a positive response:

> This is not the stuff of tabloid pandering, nor is it the stuff of easy, spin-driven politics. The easy version of the review would have included a couple of headline-grabbing clampdowns, an overstatement of the risks and an understatement of the benefits of new technology, as well as a fair sprinkling of head in the sand. The actual recommendations are rooted in an unsensational, knowledgeable pragmatism that's just what the issues need.

From two bloggers (anonymous at http://blogs.guardian.co.uk/digitalcontent/2008/03/post.html – accessed August 2008) – one negative and one pessimistic about the outcomes:

> In her 5 Live interview this morning she was doing anything not to blame bad parenting for kids ending up with 18 certificate games, when it is clearly the dumbest of the dumb that buy their brats any game cos they are pestering for it and they want 10 minutes of silence.

> They want to enforce age ratings in stores, but by the time any legislation on it comes into effect many games will be distributed online from other territories, making the entire classification system useless. It talks about self-regulation of websites, but ignores the fact that most of them aren't UK companies and frankly just don't give a toss what our government thinks or does.

As Byron herself states at the start of her review, discussions about media regulation, control and danger are always emotive. In the three response examples above, we can find a range of ideas about people and the media, which we might call 'discourses'.

Lilley is positive about the report because it compares favourably with more sensationalist research and writing about the effects of the media. The pragmatic approach, according to Lilley, is usually lacking from reports, which overemphasise the threats posed by the media to children and to the broader social world. Why is there often such overstatement of risks? Perhaps because it is easier to blame the media, the internet and video games for things that go wrong in our society than it is to look for deeper-rooted social, cultural and psychological causes? If this is true, then the media is a scapegoat for more complex failures in individuals and society. An example of this would be the focus on

YouTube as a 'problem' in the wake of a campus shooting in America. When the public realised that the murderer had filmed himself before the events and posted this on YouTube, questions were immediately raised about the influence of the internet in such a terrible crime, and whether the killer would have done this had he not been able to reach an 'audience' through this unregulated online space.

The first contributor to the *Guardian* blog is clearly articulating ideas within a discourse of blame, which lies squarely with parents. So the video games themselves are not the problem, as they are regulated through a classification system. The problem is that modern parents are feckless and irresponsible, and thus cannot be trusted to observe the regulatory conditions and play their part in policing media consumption. So there is little chance of Byron's review making any tangible difference. This discourse is in opposition to the government's 'consumer responsibility through media literacy' discourse, which Byron's report echoes.

Activity

Read the Byron report, and produce a summary of its key findings and recommendations. Ideally, if you have the resources, produce this summary in a digital format – video or podcast, blog, website or wiki – and disseminate this to a carefully selected research group, which should include:

- Two children aged between 11 and 14
- Two parents
- One adult who is over 50
- Two of your fellow A level students
- One teacher.

Make sure you have permission to speak to the children and that their parents are present or have access to the discussions if they are online.

When they have had time to read the summary, either hold a research meeting or set up an online forum to get their views on Byron's recommendations – are they sensible? will they work? what alternatives might work better?

Next, apply basic discourse analysis to what the members of your research group say. How much of the discussion seems to connect to each of these discourses?

- **The discourse of 'effects'** (overstating the dangers, blaming the media for broader and more complex problems)
- **The discourse of blame** (of parents)
- **The discourse of blame** (of media companies)
- **The liberal discourse** (anti-censorship, trusting people)
- **The responsibilities discourse** (expect people to make sensible choices themselves about what they access).

You will find that many of the statements overlap and cover more than one discourse.

Finally, produce a visual representation of how the discussion maps onto these discourses.

The second blogger comes to the same conclusion, but lays the blame at the door of media distributors rather than consumers. So the suggestions are unlikely to work because, while the government and parents can be reasonably expected to work together, the media industries are demonised as irresponsible, cynical and unlikely to accept any responsibility.

Regulating power

How much media any individual or corporation should be allowed to own is a crucial question in a democracy. In recent years in the UK, this concern has arisen in relation to the BBC's relationship with government, and whether it has abused its privileges as a protected public service broadcaster, free from the pressures of commercial **market forces**. This arose when the Hutton Report concluded that the BBC was wrong to accuse the government of misleading the public over intelligence reports leading to the invasion of Iraq, in the aftermath of the suicide of Dr David Kelly, an intelligence official working for the government. Another very different example is the growth of News Corporation and whether Rupert Murdoch has been allowed, in the UK's newly deregulated media economy, to buy up too much of our press and broadcasting services. And this anxiety, in the UK context, has been further fuelled by the release of the documentary film, *Outfoxed*, directed by Robert Greenwald, which clearly accuses Murdoch of influencing the news agenda of this global service in order to support the Bush administration and suppress opposition to it, most notably in relation to the 'war on terror' (see the section on Global Media for more detail on *Outfoxed*, a film you are certainly recommended to see so you can form your own opinion on all this).

Regulating ideas

In the digital era, copyright and intellectual property have become much harder to own and control. As you may know from your own studies, the ease with which you can copy and paste digital material has revolutionised the construction of texts and made it much harder to keep tabs on who has actually originated what. Copyright is an entitlement, so as soon as you originate material you have the copyright and nobody is allowed to steal it, but proving you have it and that you were the originator is a different matter. The umbrella phrase **intellectual property** is often used to describe all the legal ownership of media material, but copyright, which relates to written words, is just one type. There are two other forms: patents, which are to do with new inventions; and trademarks, which relate to the branding of material. Music downloading is one area of study for which an awareness of intellectual property is essential, and while the legal ownership of ideas and creative output is not restricted to media regulation, it is certainly something you should research in relation to your chosen theme.

The law makes a distinction between counterfeiting – deliberate ignoring of trademarks (e.g. fake watches or football shirts) – and piracy – copying material onto a DVD to sell or downloading music illegally from the internet. According to the government, this is a more serious issue than we might think at first, as set out on the UK Intellectual Property Office website: www.ipo.gov.uk/crime-whatis.htmcy? (accessed August 2008).

Intellectual Property crime is a serious **economic** threat in the United Kingdom (UK), and is considered a serious threat to safety of consumers. No product is too cheap to copy, and no product immune. It is estimated that IP crime costs the UK economy around GBP £9 billion each year and it is growing considerably.

Regulating creativity

Case Study

Good Copy, Bad Copy

(Note: this case study is essential for Contemporary Media Regulation, but it is also very useful for Postmodern Media and Media in the Online Age.)
    Watch this Danish documentary film from 2007: www.youtube.com/watch?v=Osow49ROeAA (accessed August 2008). It will give you an excellent understanding of the issues arising from the changes to the way media is produced and distributed in the era of web 2.0. It covers the postmodern nature of new media material – where the original and the remix are blurred and people make new culture from 'recycling' what has already been produced. It covers the importance of the online context in changing what media is and how it is used. And it covers the legal and ethical debates arising from online media distribution.

    In the documentary, you will watch a section about a group of lawbreakers or countercultural activists – which they are is a matter for your own judgement – called Pirate Bay. Be warned – if you access their website and download material, it is not on the recommendation of the author of this book! But you are advised to visit this page of their website, where they have shared the legal threats made to them and their responses (http://thepiratebay.org/legal – accessed August 2008).

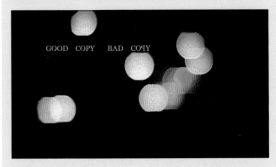

Figure 4.5.1 *Good Copy, Bad Copy* – this is essential viewing for this theme

Music downloads

The section on Media in the Online Age contains a more detailed set of case studies on this subtheme, so you are advised to read that material as well. The music industry has lobbied the government to develop new legislation to curb illegal downloading. In turn, the government, at the time of writing (2008), was threatening internet service providers (ISPs) with legislation as a sanction against the continuing avoidance by ISPs of any dialogue with the music and film industries, which had complained of a lack of cooperation. The government's strategy, seen by many industry commentators as unrealistic, involves a warning system whereby illegal downloaders are given notice that their activities are being monitored, and repeat offenders are then prosecuted. Previously, the French government introduced this system, with those found guilty having their internet access removed – but how workable this will be in practice over time is as yet unknown. The problem for the music and film industries, of course, is that ISPs are understandably reluctant to impose any limitations on their customers or to enter into any surveillance procedures, as they are not the victims of the illegal activity. The government's reason for trying to clamp down on this is economic. With the Blair and Brown governments both 'talking up' the creative industries as a key part of the UK economy, it is a major problem for the state if those industries report huge losses in revenue as a direct result of the practices of ISPs, which are, in many cases, operating globally. Like most of our debates in the online age, this is to do with where nation state ends and international communication and trade begin, and the fact is that any media regulation at the national level is increasingly hard to enforce.

Privacy laws and the press

The press (newspapers) in the UK regulates itself, and as a result, press regulation is considered 'light-touch' in comparison to other media regulation. If members of the public do wish to take action, feeling that regulations have been infringed, they can turn to the Press Complaints Commission (**PCC**), which is considered by some to be a weak body due to the fact that some newspapers perpetuate the practice of 'publish and be damned', in the comfort that they have far more money to use in a legal battle than individuals who may sue them. This way of working is described by critics as 'power without responsibility'. The PCC Code of Practice gives guidance rather than rules with regard to accuracy, right to reply, distinguishing between fact and comment, privacy, harassment, misrepresentation, chequebook journalism, intrusion (into grief or shock), the identification of the relatives or friends of convicted criminals, the protection of children, confidentiality and the definition of 'public interest', which is highly subjective. Investigative journalism into potential corruption by a government minister is clearly in the public interest, but the invasion of celebrity privacy might well not be. On the other hand, editors would argue that if we buy the papers then we demonstrate 'public interest' – end of story.

In 2007, the Press Complaints Commission responded to a record number of complaints. The reasons for this might be varied. Are newspapers breaking the Code of Practice more frequently or are people more aware of the PCC than before? In other words, are there more offences or just more complaints, or perhaps both? Or has the development of online news, as explored in other parts of this section, made a difference? Here is an explanation of the increase in activity from the Chairman of the PCC, Sir Christopher Meyer (from www.pcc.org.uk/news/index.html?article=NTExMA== – accessed August 2008).

Not only have we established ourselves as a fast and effective arbitrator of privacy disputes, discreetly settling over a hundred such complaints to the satisfaction of the complainant in 2007, but we also help prevent intrusions in dozens more cases with pre-publication advice and action to disperse media scrums. Additionally, we made almost 250 rulings on privacy under the Code of Practice to add to our case law. What is more, the flexible service offered by the PCC is clearly sought-after in resolving complaints about digital media. This is because, when information can go round the world in the blink of an eye, consumers are chiefly demanding quick solutions to their problems. The majority of complaints in 2007 – for the first time – concerned articles as they appeared online, not in the paper. I believe that 2007 has shown, more than ever before, the PCC to be worthy of the increasing confidence that is being placed in us, by the industry, by the political establishment and – most important – by the members of the public who use our wide-ranging services.

While not everyone agrees with this expression of efficiency and public confidence – as we shall see – in the last few years there have been some very high-profile examples of newspapers being punished for, or at least confessing to breaking the code. The recent set of apologies issued by national newspapers to Kate and Gerry McCann offers a highly relevant example for this area.

The tabloid representation of the McCann case was not mentioned directly in the PCC statement above, but it cannot be ignored. Of the record 4340 complaints to the PCC in 2007, 458 were about an article in the *Mirror* by Tony Parsons about the investigation into the disappearance of Madeleine McCann. But crucially, these complaints are not part of the large increase in prosecutions reported by the organisation, since in this case the article was found to be in compliance with the Code of Practice. An article deemed to be disrespectful to Katie Price's disabled child in *Heat* magazine prompted 143 complaints. In this example, the magazine published an apology.

It is very important that we spend some time reinforcing just how important this protection of the 'free press' is in a democracy. If we regulate the press more than we do at the moment, then we make it easier for people to use their power for unfair ends. The press are free so that they can monitor and report to the public on matters of national interest. In countries where the state owns the media, there is no expectation among the public that they will get anything other than a version of the truth circulated by those in power. But in Britain, wars were fought so that freedom and objectivity could be protected. This is not just a patriotic, sentimental discourse, but a reminder that a free press is a cornerstone of democracy, along with a free vote in a secret ballot and public information being available. Conflict of interest is avoided in a democracy, and there is no greater conflict of interest than powerful people owning media and avoiding regulation. Here are some statements to illustrate this (all from Brown 2008: 9).

> At their lowest, British papers can be brutally unfair, inexcusably intrusive and make terrible mistakes. At their best, they are incomparable. No form of regulation will make them perfect.
>
> (Les Hinton, former chair of the Press Complaints Commission)

> I believe self-regulation of the press is of fundamental importance in a democracy. We compiled 108 offending articles from four titles and demanded front page apologies and damages. If they had not been accepted, we would have issued libel writs.
>
> (Clarence Mitchell, the McCanns' spokesman)

> No commission funded by the newspapers upon which it adjudicates, and working to a code produced by the very editors liable to censure, can possibly inspire public confidence. Self-regulation is toothless and discredited statutory regulation a horrific thought. Reform is vital – involve more frontline journalists, not editors, give the regulator powers to hit companies in the pocket and make the system more accountable.
>
> (Jeremy Dear, National Union of Journalists)

> The Press Complaints Commission doesn't impose fines or indulge in histrionics, but it has steadied press standards of behaviour over almost two decades now. It's part of the landscape, increasingly referred and resorted to. And it works alongside the law, not in opposition to it.

(Peter Preston, former editor of *The Guardian*)

Activity

- Take the four statements above and identify which are in favour of keeping the current situation as it is (despite its flaws), which support a change to the regulatory situation and which seem to be on the fence.
- Then produce a more everyday-language version of each statement and conduct some micro-research with a cross section of people who read national newspapers regularly – at least ten people. Working in a group of five, this will add up to 50, a reasonable sample size.
- Ask each respondent to simply tick which of the statements (para-phrased by you) they most agree with. In your exam answer, you can now contextualise the statements from Hinton, Mitchell, Dear and Preston with some easy, straightforward, but nevertheless very relevant quantitative research data of your own.

Exam-Style Question

How effective is media regulation today at protecting the public in two media areas you have studied?

Examiner's Tip

It is very difficult to balance personal engagement – having an informed opinion on something as emotive as media regulation – with academic synthesis and critique. But this balance is fundamental to your success in the exam. You need to leave your own opinion until the later stages of the answer, and ensure that this opinion is clearly informed by the academic arguments you have encountered. And wherever you can, you need to make links and connections in your answer between the critics you have studied (whereas person A suggests that … person B argues against this by saying …). Then, when you get to the part of the answer where you weigh up the debate, you have already applied these perspectives to a range of micro examples and made comparisons. So your conclusions are clearly the outcome of study – not just the opinions you already had.

4.6
Postmodern Media

For this theme you need to learn about the following, in relation to at least two areas of the media:

- Definitions of postmodernism in relation to media products and media audiences, and which definition is the one you want to work with
- The difference between postmodern media and traditional media – what difference does postmodern culture make historically?
- Examples of media products which you think can be, or have been defined as postmodern, and the reasons for them being analysed in this way
- The impact of postmodern media on audiences and the ways in which we think about texts
- Debates around postmodernism and whether it is really a useful theory or not.

Although postmodernism seems at first like a very 'deep' philosophical idea, it is really a fairly simple theory. Media students are well trained in analysing the ways that media texts represent reality. So we usually think of the media as being 'in between' us and reality, hence the word 'media' and the idea of 'mediation'. Postmodernists claim that in a media-saturated world, where we are constantly immersed in media, 24/7 – on the move, at work, at home – the distinction between reality and the media representation of it becomes blurred or even entirely invisible to us. In other words, we no longer have any sense of the difference between real things and images of them, or real experiences and simulations of them. Media reality is the new reality. Some see this as a historical development: the modern period came before, during which artists experimented with the representation of reality, and the postmodern comes next, where this idea of representation gets 'remixed', played around with, through pastiche, **parody** and intertextual references – where the people that make texts deliberately expose their nature as constructed texts and make no attempt to pretend that they are 'realist'. Others say that postmodernism is just a new way of thinking about media, when really it has always been this way. One of these is Strinati (1995: 224).

> The mass media … were once thought of as holding up a mirror to, and thereby reflecting, a wider social reality. Now that reality is only definable in terms of the surface reflections of that mirror. It is no longer a question of distortion since the term implies that there is a reality, outside the surface simulations of the media, which can be distorted, and this is precisely what is at issue.

Here are some basic postmodern ideas to get us started.

- Postmodern media rejects the idea that any media product or text is of any greater value than another. All judgements of value are merely taste. Anything can be art, anything can deserve to reach an audience, and culture 'eats itself' as there is no longer anything new to produce or distribute.
- The distinction between media and reality has collapsed, and we now live in a 'reality' defined by images and representations – a state of simulacrum. Images refer to each other and represent each other as reality rather than some 'pure' reality that exists before the image represents it – this is the state of hyperreality.
- All ideas of 'the truth' are just competing claims – or discourses – and what we believe to be the truth at any point is merely the 'winning' discourse.

There are many media examples of texts or products which deliberately set out to explore and play with this state of hyperreality. These texts are said to be intertextual and self-referential – they break the rules of realism to explore the nature of their own status as constructed texts. In other words, they seek not to represent reality, but to represent media reality. Examples which we will look at are the televised images of the 9/11 attacks on the World Trade Center; *The Matrix* and *Blade Runner* as postmodern films; the music of DJ Shadow; an advert for Cadbury; the films of Michael Winterbottom, the Coen brothers and Wong Kar-wai; *Big Brother*; *The Mighty Boosh*; the television of Ricky Gervais; *The Wire* and *Echo Beach/Moving Wallpaper* as postmodern TV; postmodern magazine readers; *Grand Theft Auto IV* as a postmodern video game; and *Second Life* as the ultimate hyperreal media experience (so far).

So we are going to look at a wide range of media products which have been given the 'postmodern' label, but first we need to cover the basic philosophical ideas and get our heads round the two key thinkers in this challenging area, both of whom are French.

Jean-François Lyotard and Jean Baudrillard – both now deceased – offered different versions of either postmodernism or postmodernity. We are going to lump these two theories together for our approach, but just for the record, if you were studying philosophy you would need to have a more 'purist' comparative understanding of each one. What they share is a belief that the idea of truth needs to be 'deconstructed' so that we can challenge dominant ideas that people claim as truth, which Lyotard (1984) describes as 'grand narratives'. In the postmodern world, media texts make visible and challenge ideas of truth and reality, removing the illusion that stories, texts or images can ever accurately or neutrally reproduce reality or truth. So we get the idea that there are always competing versions of the truth and reality, and postmodern media products will engage with this idea. As Baudrillard (1988: 10) said:

> Truth is what we should rid ourselves of as fast as possible and pass it on to somebody else. As with illnesses, it's the only way to be cured of it. He who hangs on to truth has lost.

It is important to say here that many critics see Baudrillard's position as offensive. This is because they believe that it is a luxury of people who live in advanced, rich nations and democratic states to take this 'playful' stance on matters of truth, whereas people living in Iraq, Tibet or Zimbabwe cannot have such a frivolous disposition, given that crucial matters of truth, justice and human rights are contested on a daily basis. But Baudrillard is not attempting to deny this political reality; instead, he is establishing a philosophical position, and I would argue that oppressive regimes are the most expert in asserting a set of ideologies as 'truth'. The difference between postmodernism and a more 'emancipatory' theory such as Marxism, is that a postmodernist cannot wish to remove one version of the truth and replace it with the 'correct' one. All notions of truth must be viewed with suspicion. Clearly, this refutation of grand narratives, then, makes it difficult for some religious people to reconcile their belief in textual wisdom and sacred moral principles with postmodernism. Another key argument against postmodernism, which relates again to people's discomfort with Baudrillard's 'anti-truth' position, is that the alternative to a belief in truth is relativism – whereby 'anything goes', leading to moral chaos and ethical anarchy – if truth is absent, then how do we deal with matters of justice?

Hyperreality

Returning to the more basic idea that there is no longer a distinction between reality and its representing image, or simulacrum, Baudrillard introduced the idea of hyperreality, claiming that Disneyland is the best example for understanding how our reality works in the postmodern world – a place which is at the same time a real, physical space, but also clearly a fictional, representational world. You will by now be familiar with basic semiotic ideas – that signs represent ideas, people or places. For Baudrillard, there is now only surface meaning; there is no longer any 'original' thing for a sign to represent – the sign is the meaning. We inhabit a society made up wholly of simulacra – simulations of reality which replace any 'pure' reality. 'Pure' reality is thus replaced by the hyperreal where any boundary between the real and the imaginary is eroded. Baudrillard's work is an attempt to expose the 'open secret' that this is how we live and make sense of the world in postmodern times. As you can imagine, he is considered a pretty controversial philosopher.

JEAN-FRANÇOIS
LYOTARD
LE POSTMODERNE
EXPLIQUÉ
AUX ENFANTS

Figure 4.6.1 Jean-François Lyotard's *Postmodernism Explained to Children* – simple ideas really, hence the title

Examples of postmodern media

Baudrillard and the media: news, 9/11 and *The Matrix*

It is ironic, fittingly, to 'use' Baudrillard's ideas on a media studies course, as he famously declared: 'There is no theory of the media' (1971: 164). But despite this resistance, Baudrillard's work is of great help in making sense of postmodern media. There is a very useful book by William Merrin (2005) dedicated to this, but here we will pick out some key applications of Baudrillard's ideas to media texts and products. Baudrillard's idea that we are immersed beyond our control in a world of simulation makes his position different to the 'active audience' theories, which take a more optimistic view of media consumption. So while on the one hand he is seen as an antipolitical postmodernist, on the other he could be interpreted as quite a traditional analyst of how media exercises power over our lives, as Merrin (2005: 25) suggests here, with reference to the relatively new development of interactive television news, where viewers are invited to blog, email, telephone or vote in response to news items.

The media do not reflect and represent the reality of the public but instead produce it, employing this simulation to justify their own continuing existence. Thus news feedback functions to confirm to itself, and to convince us, that someone is watching, that the news is important, and that the public are politically interested and mobilised. Desperately needing this confirmation, news programmes tailor questions, debates and features to provoke it, encouraging viewers to follow and contribute towards the arguments or the fluctuating percentage results of the selected vote of the day.

Baudrillard's most controversial claim was that the Gulf War never happened. Or rather, that the Gulf War and the World Trade Center attacks that came later can only be understood as media events. He sees the events of 9/11 in terms of image – this is what we recall when it is mentioned: the endless television repeats of the live pictures – and sees the US/British 'war on terror' response as a symbolic war primarily. So terrorism and military invasion are seen here as semiotic and symbolic as much as physical. Here is Merrin's (2005: 102) explanation of Baudrillard's argument.

Baudrillard describes the 9/11 attacks as 'the absolute event'. Instantly passing into and imploding with its electronic transmission, this was a global media event, accelerating us into a state of hyperreality and of feedback, interference and uncertainty. Despite the audience's extension into the heart of the event – the real-time montage of close-ups, long shots, multiple angles and ground images, edited and replayed and mixed with commentary, speculation, political reaction, and the apprehension and adrenalin of the live moment – no event was 'happening' for them. Their electronic experience simultaneously actualised and hyperrealised the real, and de-actualised and deterred it, in its semiotic transformation and presentation as televisual spectacle for domestic consumption in the comfort and security of the sign.

This is 'deep' material, and you may be surprised that an A2 textbook is expecting you to get your head round such intense philosophical ideas. Without doubt, some publishers and teachers would probably prefer it if we left Baudrillard to one side here, thinking that this kind of theory is more suitable to degree-level study, and a bit too hard for A level. But to think along those lines is to mistakenly think that theory is 'levelled', when really it is just a case of exploring the ideas in the appropriate language. So we just need to translate Baudrillard a bit, like this (Baudrillard 2002: 228).

At the same time as they have radicalised the world situation, the events in New York can be said to have radicalized the relation of the image to reality. Among the other weapons of the system which they turned round against it, the terrorists exploited the 'real time' of images, their instantaneous worldwide transmission, just as they exploited stock-market speculation, electronic information and air traffic. The image consumes the event, in the sense that it absorbs it and offers it for consumption. Admittedly, it gives it unprecedented impact, but impact as image-event. The collapse of the World Trade Center towers is unimaginable, but that is not enough to make it a real event. An excess of violence is not enough to open on to reality. For reality is a principle, and it is this principle that is lost.

This is Baudrillard's clearest contribution to the theory of postmodern media. He is arguing that the events of 9/11 are as much televisual as 'real', that we cannot distinguish the representation of the events on television from the actual events, so the events are hyperreal, neither real nor 'just' media, but both in combination, impossible to separate. If we accept this, it does not mean we no longer believe in reality, but that the idea of 'pure reality', untainted by media representation, is no longer any use. So the attacks on New York cannot be seen to exist as 'pure' event, before or away from the televised images we are so used to.

Next we can look at *The Matrix* films as further examples of Baudrillard's view of the postmodern. Given that the main character, Neo, can be seen reading one of Baudrillard's books during the film (*Simulation and Simulacra*), we can probably assume some influence on the directors, but what is of more relevance is that the film has been interpreted by many as a cinematic portrayal of Baudrillard's notion of postmodern simulation as a controlling force, keeping the masses enslaved. In the film, a few 'chosen' individuals wake up to the unhappy realisation that the human race is plugged into a network of machines (the matrix) and that their existence is virtual, masking a much less savoury 'reality' – the machines have taken over and plugged us into their virtual world. Not only is the subject matter postmodern in theme, but the style of film-making employed by the Wachowski directors is self-referential, which means that its resemblance to video games, other films and graphic novels, rather than to 'reality', is deliberate, as is the use of 'bullet time' as a hyperreal filmic approach. Merrin (2005: 131) describes how the film immerses us in its postmodern simulations.

The Matrix has us. Our consumption of the films, the merchandise, and the world and myth the Wachowskis sell us, and our collective orgasm over the effects and phones, guns, shades and leather, represent our integration into the virtuality it promotes. *The Matrix* became a viral meme spreading through and being mimetically absorbed into popular culture, extending our virtualisation. Just as the film offered the stark choice of being inside or outside the matrix so you were either in or outside the zeitgeist. To paraphrase Morpheus: The Matrix is everywhere. As Baudrillard makes clear, however, its fans and public are caught in a similarly invisible matrix that is far greater than that depicted in the film, and that the film itself is part of and extends.

'Like tears in rain' – *Blade Runner* as postmodern cinema

Blade Runner is a film which did not do terribly well at the box office when first released, but since the original release in 1982 it has become a huge critical success – a cult, now heralded as a 'classic' piece of dystopian science fiction, the subject of a Director's Cut release (with the famous voice-over removed) and, more recently, a Final Cut edition. *Blade Runner* is the subject of a wealth of books and websites – Google it and you will see (at the time of writing) that there are 10,500,000 links to try! And, most importantly for us, *Blade Runner* is very often discussed as a postmodern film. It ticks all our boxes because the film can be viewed as postmodern in style, in its reception and in its subject matter.

Style

Blade Runner is said to have a postmodern aesthetic, mixing textual references and images. The film-noir voice-over of the original release is juxtaposed with the futuristic, dystopian images (time is manipulated, as a 1950s film convention is displaced into the future), but at the same time the shadows and constant rain fit with the film-noir style – resulting in a 'neo-noir' visual style and thematic range. The city depicted – Los Angeles in the future – is in itself a pastiche of our ideas of the East, the West and the future. The images we see give us a *mise-en-scène* of decay and decline, of things coming to an end for humanity as we know it, and the story is to do with replicants (people who feel human but are synthetic) striving for an extension to their lifespan.

Reception

The questions that the film poses are to do with the meaning of humanity in the postmodern age, when the distinction between the human and the machine is unclear. Can emotions be programmed? Can humanity be manufactured? These are the same questions asked by the postmodern philosophers about the hyperreal, and how we cope with a world where the image overrides the individual. The Los Angeles of *Blade Runner* has been discussed as a vision of the postmodern city – huge advertising images promoting an off-world colony and the idea that everyone who can has fled the 'real world' for a more attractive virtual equivalent.

Subject matter

The film is about time and our lack of it. One of the replicants is a young man, but his body is ageing. We are never sure whether the main character, played by Harrison Ford, is human or not – this remains an enigma, more so in the Director's Cut. A dying replicant in the final scene delivers the line, 'all these moments will be lost in time, like tears in rain', and as in most postmodern films, we are forced to confront the way in which the 'modern' world is constructed through a set of binary oppositions – truth/lies, reality/fiction, human/machine, life/death and good/bad. One reading of *Blade Runner* is that it deals with racism – the extermination of replicants – and, like all science fiction, therefore, it places 'real-world' concerns in a fantasy setting. But the postmodern reading of the film focuses more on the way that the classic oppositions that have defined our philosophy are undermined, or at least exposed as vulnerable.

Postmodern auteurs: Michael Winterbottom, the Coens and Wong Kar-wai

Cinema is an area where there is a tradition of labelling films and directors as postmodern. Here we deal with three examples of film-makers whose collective work has been evaluated in this way.

Michael Winterbottom's films could also be studied for the Media and Collective Identity theme, since they are interesting in terms of how they represent a changing Britain. *In this World* portrays the hazardous journey made by two refugees en route to London, while *The Road to Guantanamo* fictionalises the real aftermath of 9/11 and the British/US response – the 'war on terror'. *24 Hour Party People* – its name taken from a song by the Manchester band the Happy Mondays – offers another fictionalised version of 'real life', in this case the rise and fall of Factory Records in the 'Madchester' music scene in the 1980s and early 1990s. The less conventional *9 Songs* and the playful *A Cock and Bull Story* might seem to share little with the more straightforwardly docudrama examples we have listed here, but what they certainly share is an interest in blurring the boundaries between real events and fiction, which is, as we know by now, a defining principle of postmodern media. A key example is the beginning of *24 Hour Party People*, when Steve Coogan, playing the part of Factory Records and Granada TV frontman Tony Wilson, turns to the camera, thus breaking the first rule of 'realism' and says: 'You're going to be seeing a lot more of that sort of thing in the film. Although that did actually happen, obviously it's symbolic – it works on both levels'. Winterbottom is to some extent mocking the idea of postmodernism here, by having a character so explicitly discussing to camera the film he is appearing in. But at the same time, this mocking approach is entirely in keeping with postmodernism, since a disregard for realist conventions and a playful approach to the construction of the text itself, whereby the audience is 'in on the joke', is really the whole point.

Winterbottom's films all deliberately mess around with the boundary between suspending disbelief, reality and the obviously artificial. In some films this is lighthearted, and in others it is anything but, given the subject matter – *Road to Guantanamo* is an obvious example. *A Cock and Bull Story* is another great example. The film adapts a 'classic' novel by Laurence Sterne, but at the same time provides a 'making of' documentary of the construction of the adaptation. While you might think that all DVDs are now postmodern in the sense that we can choose to watch a director's commentary or a behind-the-scenes film as well as the theatrical release, it is still unconventional to put both together in the film itself. *A Cock and Bull Story* takes the idea even further, by deliberately playing with the star image of Steve Coogan, so it is really hard to work out when he is being himself, when he is playing up to the image of Steve Coogan that has been disseminated as a media commodity during his career, when he is rehearsing to be his character and when he is actually playing the character. While *In this World* might appear to be very different – a much more 'serious' film about Afghan refugees – similar techniques are used to 'deconstruct' the film as a text. The actors are real refugees and the film mixes 'real' footage of their journey with scripted scenes. Similarly, *Road to Guantanamo* is a hybrid of documentary and drama, but unlike a conventional docudrama, the rhythm of the film constantly reminds the audience that this remixing of real events is taking place. No attempt is made in any of Winterbottom's films to disguise the mixing of styles and the deliberate lack of any one, stable version of 'the real'.

Activity

To be sufficiently familiar with the work of this director to enable you to make your own judgement about the idea presented here that we can think of his collective work as postmodern, you need to have seen at least three of these films, but preferably all of them:

- *24 Hour Party People* (2002)
- *In this World* (2002)
- *9 Songs* (2004)
- *A Cock and Bull Story* (2005)
- *The Road to Guantanamo* (2006).

For each film, choose one micro example – a scene, a technique, a moment – which you think helps show how Winterbottom is postmodern at the macro level.

Figure 4.6.2 *24 Hour Party People* deliberately reveals the 'remixing' of reality

The Coen brothers are also film-makers who have been labelled 'postmodern auteurs'. The term 'auteur', as you might expect, suggests that we think of films as the products of individual creators, and this is problematic in the context of postmodernism as it is quite an old-fashioned way of thinking about texts. Nevertheless, like Winterbottom, the Coens are described by critics and academics as having created a body of work that consistently demonstrates postmodern techniques. In films such as *Fargo, The Big Lebowski, The Man Who Wasn't There* and *Miller's Crossing* (and there are many more to choose from), the importance of intertextuality to our reading of the films is what gives them this postmodern flavour. The Coens are so famous for intertextuality that one critic argues that 'The Coens are clever directors who know too much about movies and too little about real life' (Levy 1999, in Coughlin 2003: 3).

Intertextuality describes the way that our knowledge of other media texts cannot be 'unknown' when we respond to a film, so we are either deliberately referred to other texts and the meaning on the screen is dependent on this cultural know-how, or there is an option to pick up on invited intertextual cues. For example, in *Fargo*, the Coens create a pastiche of the film-noir genre, but displace this idea by surrounding the characters with snow – whereas in film noir they are half-lit in shadows and live nocturnally. At the same time, the title of the film itself refers to a range of western films which lends a hybrid element, or at least might deliberately confuse expectations. The characters are often seen watching TV shows. Perhaps most obviously postmodern, though, is the claim at the start of the film that this is a true story, which is unsupported anywhere in historical record and is never evidenced in the film itself. Levan (2000: 18) offers the following helpful summary of how the labelling of *Fargo* and other Coen products as postmodern has happened over time.

> The term postmodern is often used to describe the work of the Coen brothers. This is a term which has no easy definition. Their telling of stories which comment on the nature of stories and of storytelling, their reaction against classic genres, their turning over and examination of genre stereotypes and conventions from within their films, are all part of what is being referred to when they are said to be postmodern.

In two other Coen films that have been assessed as postmodern, *The Hudsucker Proxy* and *Barton Fink*, references to popular culture (intertextuality again) override any sense of 'pure reality'. Irony is used constantly, and existing material and ideas are remixed and played with – the effect is cinema eating, or at least recycling itself. Many postmodern media texts enjoy a love/hate relationship with the audience. Those that are disturbed by this playfulness criticise the Coens for lacking originality or authenticity. This, they argue, leads to the creation of one-dimensional characters with no depth, since the characters are merely reworked constructions of other characters – which resonates with Baudrillard's work on the dominance of simulation. The other criticism is that a postmodern approach is a cynical, mocking treatment of human beings, and therefore that postmodern directors are guilty of being aloof, or of thinking they are superior to the constructed characters they set up for humour. But fans of the Coens will celebrate the same things – seeing wit and skill in the use of intertextuality, pastiche and dialogue which can be interpreted on a number of different levels. The Coens' consistent style seems to be the development of a 'rhetorical reality' in which images of the past from media texts are invoked, described here by Coughlin (2003: 3).

> The role of memory, reception and intertextuality are crucial to the design in the Coen brothers' films. By engaging the texts of the past the directors are able to challenge and critique history through the agency of parody, irony and self-reflexivity. This confrontation with history's textual construction enables an exploration and interpretation of ideologies of the past. Despite all the criticism of their work—their films are merely about other films, their work smugly proposes the emptiness at the core of art, they hide behind style to avoid moral and ethical issues—the Coen brothers nevertheless set up a connection to history through their pithy investigation into the texts that represent the past. With their keen approach to historical periods and texts of bygone eras, and their reliance on irony and parody, the Coen brothers not only engage with history but they question and challenge the ideologies by which it is constructed.

Activity

To be sufficiently familiar with the work of the Coen brothers so that you can make your own judgement about whether their postmodern techniques are cleverly ironic or cruel and mocking, you need to have seen at least five of the following films:

- *Blood Simple* (1984)
- *Miller's Crossing* (1989)
- *Barton Fink* (1991)
- *The Hudsucker Proxy* (1994)
- *Fargo* (1996)
- *The Big Lebowski* (1998)
- *Brother, Where Art Thou?* (2000)
- *The Man Who Wasn't There* (2001)
- *Intolerable Cruelty* (2003)
- *The Ladykillers* (2004).

For each film, choose one micro example of pastiche – where existing filmic conventions from a particular genre are exaggerated, displaced or brought to life during the film by intertextual references. These should be examples of the use of intertextual filmic reality instead of 'pure' reality that exists outside of, or before, its representation in cinema.

Wong Kar-wai's films are also given the label 'postmodern', but in this case the situation is slightly different, because some might argue that the location of his films, Hong Kong, is itself a postmodern space. This is because the island is seen as being perpetually caught between the past and the present, and between the East and the West, due to its changing status and recent independence. Add to that the visual, architectural merging of old and new styles and aesthetics, and you get pretty close to a physical manifestation of postmodernism.

Wong Kar-wai's films, such as *Chungking Express, In the Mood for Love* and *Days of Being Wild* – the key three films for our focus here – deal with the ways that these contexts impact on people's lives in Hong Kong; and in particular he pays attention to time, memory and space, between people and between times – more postmodern themes. His characters are often lonely, despite living in an overpopulated, frenetic high-rise cityscape, and a key convention of his style is the way he makes characters' lives intersect. He manipulates space and time in unusual ways, and this is what leads to his being ascribed the status of a postmodern film-maker. Key micro examples are these. In *Chungking Express*, the main male character is referred to only by his police number, and the female lead is often accompanied by a sound motif – 'California dreaming' by the Mamas and Papas. Sometimes she dances along to this song as a **diegetic** soundtrack; sometimes it plays in the background non-diegetically; and sometimes it is not clear which it is – and this confusion is deliberate, an explicit revelation of the constructed nature of the text, another postmodern motif.

Figure 4.6.3 'California dreaming' – *Chungking Express* depicts postmodern Hong Kong as a hybrid of East and West

In the Mood for Love is set in an earlier Hong Kong, before independence, and features an establishing statement at the start: *It is a restless moment. Hong Kong 1962.* The film mixes the historical context with contemporary thematics, and explores isolation and the difficulty of pinning down time. Again, both space and time are thus played around with, and the viewer is invited to reflect on this remixing of chronology. *Days of Being Wild*, like the two films already discussed here, makes liberal use of popular culture references and music to create a rich layer of intertextual meaning, whereby the isolated nature of the characters (often 'anchored' by voice-over) is contrasted with both the location (bustling Hong Kong) and the music (love songs). Irony thus pervades.

Hong Kong's unique identity, with its fusion of Chinese and western culture and complex history, provides a culturally diverse space in which technology and tradition coexist in various forms. Wong's avant-garde filmic aesthetic is composed of elliptical storytelling through the use of slow motion, jumpcuts and fragmented images. Wright (2002: 3) offers a summary of the postmodern depiction of Hong Kong that recurs throughout Wong Kar-wai's work.

Spectators must suspend their beliefs in chronology, time and in many cases, their memories too, in order to fully experience the depth of Wong's evocative filmic creations. Wong's story is continual and the narrative as dependent on the context of the present as of the past. Through Wong's *oeuvre*, Hong Kong becomes a metaphor for the characters and their varied existence. It represents an urban pastiche in which individuals struggle to come to terms with a sense of detachment and loneliness despite the territory's high-density population. Wong's endless array of *possible scenarios and the navigation of his protagonists' internal and external journeys in turn constitute an unravelling and reconfiguring of spatio-temporal constrictions.*

But it is important in this theme for us to remember that for every act of postmodern labelling, there will be resistance. This is the site of much disagreement, and in fact most artists, film directors, musicians and media producers of all kinds dislike being categorised as postmodern, as they worry that this makes them sound superficial – fashionable but disposable, lacking depth and substance. In interviews, Wong Kar-wai has expressed annoyance at being given the label, insisting that his films are concerned with 'real' emotions and situations, rather than the second-hand imitation, or pastiche, of them. Then again, he might seem to accidentally reinforce Baudrillard's denial of reality and origin when he says, in an interview with *Sight and Sound* magazine: 'Too many people are doing Wong Kar-wai these days, so I have to do something else' (Rayns 2008: 33). This comment was made in regard to his latest film, *My Blueberry Nights*, which on the one hand looks like something of a departure from his previous work as it is set in the USA and is in English, but at the same time sticks with the themes of relationships, time and isolation. And another leaning to the postmodern (whereby nothing new can be done, everything is a remix of what has gone before) is suggested by the establishing voice-over provided this time – 'the stories have all been told'.

Activity

Watch all three of the following films:

- *Days of Being Wild* (1991)
- *Chungking Express* (1994)
- *In the Mood for Love* (2000).

For each film, choose one micro example of Wong Kar-wai's treatment of time – as slow/fast/both; one micro example of how he portrays Hong Kong as caught between East and West; and one micro example of how his characters are located in space – how they come together, or miss each other. Then connect these nine micro examples (and those of your fellow students if you can work together) to form a picture of Wong Kar-wai as a postmodern film-maker. How far do you agree with this label? And if these films are postmodern, is it the film-making style or the subject matter that makes them so?

DJ Shadow – *Endtroducing*

Released by Mo Wax Records in 1996, DJ Shadow's first studio album made history by being the first album to be produced entirely from pre-existing sampled music. As such, it is an essential example in a study of postmodern media. The title itself, mirroring the irony of the word postmodern, *Endtroducing* by DJ Shadow is a media text that is almost always referred to as postmodern in reviews, articles and fan discussions. There are a number of reasons why it gets this label. First, it includes so many different recognisable but mixed-up styles of music that it is not useful in any way to try to apply genre to the collection. Second, this is one album that many critics have celebrated for producing 'art' out of sampling (we could have a longer debate here about what counts as art). And then there is the cross-media experimentation of Shadow as a DJ, film composer, musician – so more boundary blurring. The track 'Stem/long stem' is a case study in itself, blending classical sounds with Nirvana to make something new, possibly as close as we are likely to get to a textbook example of what is meant by postmodern. His own description of the album – 'a lifetime of vinyl culture' – is also helpful as an illustration of the remix concept. DJ Shadow has made a new musical contribution out of what was already there. Whether you celebrate this as postmodern art or deride it for lacking originality is entirely up to you, but it will force you to a judgement call on postmodern media either way.

Synoptic Link

For the AS TV Drama theme area, you may have engaged with *Life on Mars* and *Doctor Who* as postmodern texts. Here are amended extracts from **OCR Media Studies for AS** as a recap.

Life on Mars can be described as a postmodern police/crime drama, but also a period drama. The representational meanings of the programme at the macro level are entirely dependent on the audience recognising the distinction between the viewing times (2007) and the story times (1970s). The idea of a female PM being strange, the treatment of Irish men, the exotic nature of Asian clothing and the collision between Hunt's no-nonsense style of policing and Tyler's sensitivity are all reliant on the audience bringing a great deal of cultural knowledge to the drama.

Doctor Who certainly appeals to a wide audience (around 8 million on average), with its pleasures being derived on many levels. First broadcast in 1963, taken off the air in 1989, and returning in 2005, it is now viewed by a young audience for the first time, and also by original viewers, now adults. Because of this multilayered context, at times the programme takes a 'postmodern' approach, parodying itself and referring back to previous versions. We are in the Tardis, looking up at the Doctor and Rose, who appear to be on the ceiling laughing manically. As the camera cuts to their level, we realise we were above them as they completed their time-travel journey, landing with a bump. The *mise-en-scène* inside the Tardis is familiar to viewers, and under normal circumstances might be described as futuristic, but really there is a kind of 'retro-futurism' to it, compared to the more high-tech imagery of contemporary science fiction. This is a postmodern element – we are given a nostalgic form of futurism! In the episode where the Doctor and his assistant meet Queen Victoria, at the macro level the representation is entirely postmodern. Jeremy Points (2007: 82) calls this 'conspicuous constructedness'. Time is placed on its side – we are in the past with a stereotype from history, playing up to her future image and the main characters playfully responding. Rose is an empowered female, yet there is subtle flirtation with the Doctor. The treatment of history is on one level educational – hence the centrality of the series to a renewal of the BBC's public service remit. In the accidental arrival in 1879 instead of 1979, the science-fiction convention of time travel is treated lightheartedly, and the way the programme uses intertextual elements, such as the *Balamory* reference, can be described as a form of postmodern pastiche.

Postmodern TV: *The Mighty Boosh*, Ricky Gervais and *The Wire*

These are just three examples from a cast of thousands. As television gets older, the distinction between reality, ordinary people and TV personalities blurs; writers and producers seek new ways of being creative within successful formats; and television converges with the internet through catch-up websites – television starts to feel a bit like Hong Kong, an 'already postmodern' medium. Let us explore these three examples to get a sense of how specific TV programmes can be distinguished in this way.

The Mighty Boosh was the subject of a highly illuminating analysis by Richard Smith (2008), which I make no apologies for passing on here. Smith identifies nine elements of postmodern media which we can locate in *The Mighty Boosh*. These features are an eclectic mix of conventions, influences and genre traits which makes it impossible to situate the product in any one style. This amounts to a predominance of intertextual references (to other TV shows) and a liberal dose of parody – the humorous imitation of other media products the audience will recognise – establishing a 'knowing' humour for the viewer to share. Smith uses the term **bricolage** to describe the remixing of existing formulas, explaining how the show demands a more active audience response – decoding a 'media puzzle' on a number of levels; and sees the programme as hyperreal in as much as it exposes and plays around with the conditions of its own possibility (my words) – meaning it deliberately messes about with its own status as a television programme, rather than striving to create the illusion that what we are seeing is 'real'. Smith's (2008: 9) summary is helpful.

> *The Mighty Boosh* provides us with an effective framework for postmodern **deconstruction** and is bursting with its characteristics from the music, costumes, characters, design, *mise-en-scène* and dialogue. It provides its active audience with a contemporary variety show that is all knowing, highly aware and above all, a celebration of the medium of television.

Ricky Gervais's two most popular TV series, *The Office* and *Extras*, can both easily be given the postmodern tag for their knowing, self-reflective approach and, crucially, the way they parody the conventions of genre. *The Office* is a situation comedy using and subverting docusoap conventions; the character of David Brent works because of its pathos – the mixture of pleasure and pain we feel when he performs in the role of an office manager. Without our cultural awareness of this genre – documentary series in which ordinary people behave in such ways that they take on characteristics beyond their daily work – the humour would not work.

Extras can be seen as postmodern in the way that it deconstructs itself – a situation comedy about an extra who becomes a situation-comedy writer deliberately confuses, for comic and satirical effect, the line between Gervais the sitcom writer and comedian and his on-screen character. The famous Christmas special episode, in which he rejects the vacuous trappings of celebrity from the *Big Brother* house, is one of the best micro examples of a postmodern pastiche of television itself that you could find, and all the more powerful because it was achieved within the format of a highly successful format show itself – this is what we mean by self-reflective, hyperreal media. But beyond this one example, the way that Gervais persuaded real celebrities to appear 'as themselves' within the show was radical – most amusingly David Bowie's musical humiliation of Gervais's character in the VIP area of a nightclub ('fat man blows his stupid brains out'). The audience is forced to respond to a deliberate decontextualisation: what is Bowie doing – is he acting, is he 'being himself'? As Bowie and the other celebrities lending their services – Les Dennis, Ross Kemp, Kate Winslett – are themselves media texts, we see here a really direct, visible and unusual example of intertextuality: is this their real character, or are they playing a role?

The Wire has acquired a cult status in the UK, despite never being broadcast on a UK terrestrial channel, which is a great example of how TV is increasingly watched by a fragmented audience – most of the viral marketers of this show (people who love it and 'sell' it to their friends) are watching it on catch-up or on-demand TV, through the internet (Torrent offers a host of streaming options, but these are not legal, so be warned) and through the discount DVD box-set option. This is another TV

Figure 4.6.4 *Extras*: postmodern intertextuality, parody, pastiche and polemic

product which is seemingly intended to be postmodern, and unlike the films of Wong Kar-wai, where the director pays lip service to the idea but is uncomfortable with the label, this quote from *The Wire*'s writer, David Simon (in Hornby 2007: 1), is explicit in its acceptance of postmodernity as a context for the drama.

> *The Wire* is a Greek tragedy in which the postmodern institutions are the Olympian forces. It's the police department, or the drug economy, or the political structures, or the school administration, or the macroeconomic forces that are throwing the lightning bolts and hitting people in the ass for no reason. In much of television, and in a good deal of our stage drama, individuals are often portrayed as rising above institutions to achieve **catharsis**. In this drama, the institutions always prove larger, and those characters with hubris enough to challenge the postmodern construct of American empire are invariably mocked, marginalised, or crushed. Greek tragedy for the new millennium, so to speak.

So we have a very different example of postmodern media here. This TV show is not postmodern in style or aesthetics (or at least not explicitly so). But it takes as its subject matter postmodern society, in which, according to the creator, the individual human being's life is increasingly meaningless in relation to the huge corporations and institutions that dominate the world in the capitalist system. This takes us back to Baudrillard's work on the power of the system over the human, and here we can think of *The Matrix* as a series of films that deal with similar themes but in a less 'real' context. The world as represented in *The Wire* is a matrix of power-holding institutions immersed in a capitalist system which has its own force. Here is another explanation from the writer (quoted in O'Rourke 2006: 1).

> Thematically, it's about the very simple idea that, in this postmodern world of ours, human beings – all of us – are worth less. We're worth less every day, despite the fact that some of us are achieving more and more. It's the triumph of capitalism. Whether you're a corner boy in West Baltimore, or a cop who knows his beat, or an Eastern European brought here for sex, your life is worth less. It's the triumph of capitalism over human value.

But what is the story? *The Wire* has so far been five series long. Each series has a different theme, but in each case it explores the network of corruption and exploitation across institutions and organisations, to the extent where this dominates daily life for the everyday human being. The first series represented a family of drug dealers and the police officers attempting to bring to justice the organised crime fraternity. The next series featured the murder of a group of sex workers and the way that these crimes were 'sanctioned' by the corrupt system. Series three took a more political theme, and the most recent series took the viewer into the

Figure 4.6.5 *The Wire* depicts a postmodern world in which human life is worth less each day

US school system to look at the life chances afforded to inner-city youth during a political election. If season five is, as is suggested (at the time of writing), about the media, then this will be the best example yet for your studies of postmodern media.

Postmodern soap opera: *Echo Beach/ Moving Wallpaper*

The web page (http://www.itv.com/Drama/contemporary/ EchoBeach/default.html) is a great example of a postmodern TV show that is anything but subversive or countercultural, and it shows us how mainstream postmodernism has become – or how postmodern the mainstream has become! Here we have two TV shows which relate to one another so that the viewer is always explicitly aware of the constructed nature of the soap opera, because a parallel show portrays this construction simultaneously. And you will notice from the website that the blurring of reality with media reality is set up by the opportunity to 'visit the real store that was used for the surf shop on location'. At first glance, a mainstream ITV show like this might seem a million miles away from the 'high theory' offered by French philosophers like Jean Baudrillard. But actually, here we have the hyperreal in all its postmodern glory. And this is not a new idea. Did you know that there has been a 24-hour webcam pointing at *EastEnders'* Albert Square for years? Soap opera has always been a postmodern media form. The way that the fiction of the soap leads to a state of hyperreality is nothing new. Tabloid papers treat the characters as real. Members of the public send birthday cards to the characters.

Figure 4.6.6 *Echo Beach/Moving Wallpaper* – postmodern television goes mainstream

Magazines and websites offer 'extra-textual' information about the characters and storylines, and in the case of *Coronation Street*, we can visit the set, and even have a pint in The Rovers – a pub which, therefore, is real and not real at the same time. Hyperreal.

The Cadbury gorilla

We need balance in this section, and it is crucial to remember that there are probably more critics of the postmodern idea than there are advocates. As well as the political concerns about relativism and the denial of truth, which many see as dangerous and immoral, there is the simpler argument that the postmodern media just is not very clever, certainly does not count as art and often amounts to little more than an anything-goes attitude that rips off the consumer. An article from *Spiked* (see http://www.spiked-online.com/index.php?/site/article/4088) is a good example of this perspective. Here Patrick West begins with an attack on the Cadbury advert that features a gorilla playing drums to a song by Phil Collins (with no apparent connection to chocolate), and then extends the criticism to a broader range of postmodern adverts.

But while West's argument is well made, other industry commentators are less convinced that the Cadbury ad represents such a departure from advertising the product itself. In an interview in 2008, Stephen Bromberg, marketing and communications manager at the Science Museum and an expert in contemporary advertising strategy, suggests that the advert strips back the unspoken pleasure of eating chocolate, and thus the man in the animal suit playing the drums to a Phil Collins track actually offers a direct connection to the appeal of the product – as a secret, guilty pleasure and even a basic desire, a primal instinct despite cultural pressure to eat more healthy food. We can even make a link here to Maslow's hierarchy of needs. Bromberg views the Cadbury campaign as a very clever, low-spend strategy to connect the postmodern viral web 2.0 zeitgeist to the most old-fashioned of advertising ideas – the unique selling point – and to prove this he reminds us that the advert signs off, as all Cadbury ads have done, with the 'glass and a half of milk' motif, taking us back to the Cilla Black adverts for the same brand in the 1980s. So, Bromberg (2008) suggests:

> The viral release on YouTube led to many imitations, as people made a subconscious connection to the advert. The less obvious promotion of the product is nevertheless a focus on the key ingredient and the pleasure of consumption, and so despite the appearance of a postmodern advert with no connection to the product, the reality is very different – we are reminded of the things that Cadbury want us to see as distinct elements that mark out their chocolate from the competition – quality and taste.

Magazines and postmodernism: the pick-and-mix reader

The section on Media and Collective Identity includes a detailed discussion of the ways in which magazines construct a sense of belonging for their readership. As that part of the book explains, media theorists have argued that this idea of belonging to a collective group, a 'club' of readers, is actually a misrecognition, and that we can best analyse this by adopting a triangular approach to the representations at work – how does a magazine represent its 'own' gender to the reader? how does it represent its 'own' gender to the other gender? and how does it represent the other gender to its reader? So we have to consider female readings of *Nuts* and male readings of *Sugar*, as this duality of representation serves to reinforce ideas of the other. Next, we can consider the unintended 'secondary reader' – such as the gay male reader of *Elle*, or the female reader of *Men's Health* – and we move towards another example of postmodern media. But this one is fundamentally different to the films of the Coen Brothers or the music of DJ Shadow, because we are not looking at the magazines as deliberately constructed in a way that we might call postmodern. Instead, we are considering whether a secondary audience might create postmodern readings of these media products. There is an idea that in these postmodern times, we increasingly 'pick and mix' our media, and we similarly select in more or less regular ways how we form our identities in relation to media. Kendall researched young people's reading habits and, predictably, magazines featured heavily. Kendall was concerned with readers' notions of themselves as particular kinds of readers – after all, young people today are demonised for their lack of literacy in conventional terms. She found that male readers adopted a less critical stance than their female counterparts (Kendall 2008: 126).

> The magazines functioned, as for female readers, to offer prompts and possibilities for representing self through negotiation of symbolic codes. However, the male readers were characteristically less critical and more acquiescent to the identities inscribed through the modalities of their 'hobby' magazines.

Gauntlett (2002: 180), through sustained audience research, describes readers' active negotiations in response to both women's and men's magazines.

> I have argued against the view that men's lifestyle magazines represent a reassertion of old-fashioned masculine values, or a 'back-lash' against feminism. Whilst certain pieces in the magazines might support such an argument, this is not their primary purpose or selling point. Instead, their existence and popularity shows men rather insecurely trying to find their place in the modern world, seeking help regarding how to behave in their relationships and advice on how to earn the attention, love and respect of women and the friendship of other men. In post-traditional cultures, where identities are not 'given' but need to be constructed and negotiated, and where an individual has to establish their personal ethics and mode of living, the magazines offer some reassurance to men who are wondering 'Is this right?' and 'Am I doing this OK?', enabling a more confident management of the narrative of the self.

Gauntlett's idea – that identity is fluid and gender and sexuality are 'performative' – is one that we can relate to postmodernism, even though this is not a term he attaches to his work himself. And it takes us to the heart of the debate over relativism, an important concept for discussing the potential danger in a postmodern culture. A relativist position is value-free, meaning that we have to accept that people will make their own meaning out of the range of cultural products on offer, and it is therefore pointless trying to ascribe value to media, to say that one media text is worth more than another. From this perspective, there is no harm to be identified in gender-based magazines. We have to give the readership more credit, to pick and mix the bits they want to use in the construction of their identities, and we cannot assume that people are simply 'influenced'. But a feminist perspective, seeking to draw attention to the ways that women's magazines and men's magazines both represent the female gender as objects, as decorative and as subordinate, might view the relaxed position of the postmodernist with some serious concerns.

Grand Theft Auto IV

Unlike 'older' media forms, where we can distinguish between postmodern texts and others, video games might be considered postmodern in themselves. This is because they subvert our traditional ideas about the distinction between reality and simulation or image. An online experience like *Second Life* takes this even further, offering the participant the opportunity to purchase *virtual* land with *real* money. Slavoj Zizek, a theorist often associated with postmodernism, makes this observation about the different levels of reality (in Easthope and McGowan 2005: 231).

Virtual reality simply generalises the procedure of offering a product deprived of its substance, of the hard resistant kernel of the Real – just as decaffeinated coffee smells and tastes like real coffee without being real coffee, Virtual Reality is experienced as reality without being so. What happens at the end of this process of virtualisation, however, is that we begin to experience 'real reality' itself as a virtual entity.

Two concepts which help us to understand video games as postmodern are **flow** and **immersion**. Immersion describes how the gamer invests imagination in the game and is subsequently absorbed into the gameworld. The first concept, flow, is described by Csikszentmihalyi (1997: 113) as a state whereby an activity demands incrementally harder, but increasingly pleasurable and achievable challenges, while providing regular feedback (a 'loop') on degrees of success.

It is easy to recognise the conditions of flow. These include having a clear goal or problem to solve, ability to discern how well one is doing, struggling forward in the face of challenges until the creative process begins to hum and one is lost in the task, and enjoying the activity for its own sake.

Within flow, immersion (a pleasurable loss of reality) becomes difficult and challenging, while also feeling creative and pleasurable, so the feeling of being 'lost' in the gameworld leads to an enhanced state of 'happy hyperreality'.

Grand Theft Auto IV is probably the most discussed video game of all time. This is a media product that made roughly $500 million in its first week, eclipsing even Hollywood blockbuster releases with that scale of distribution and demand. As the section on Contemporary Media Regulation explores, this game has polarised the public – there are not many people who are in between the two conflicting opinions: the game is a masterpiece versus the game should be banned. But what both sides of the argument do seem to agree on, whether they use the term or not, is that *GTA IV* is postmodern – that it immerses the player in a convincing, intricate and believable world, but that the reality it represents is the stuff of films and other media. Like Disneyland, *The Matrix* and the Gulf War, to take on the character of Niko Belic and live in Liberty City is a profoundly hyperreal experience. The emotive debate is about the extent to which intense experiences of violence, sex, crime and vice in the hyperreal situation translate into effects in our real society, and, of course, a postmodern position on this has to be that there is no discussion to be had, as the separation of the two 'states' is meaningless. But as the postmodern theorists tend to see contemporary media experience in terms of play and picking and mixing aspects of identity and meaning, the idea of effects is also off-limits.

Much of the discussion of *Grand Theft Auto IV* as a media product with the potential for harmful effects focuses on the content, which is undoubtedly 'seedy' in many ways, but ignores crucial contextual factors, the most important of which is what we call 'situated literacy practices'. This means, simply, that we need to explore how players of the game 'read' it, and whether playing this game is very different to reading a book or watching a film. Until we know this, we will not be able to make very informed judgements about what is going on in people's heads when they fight innocent members of the public or visit prostitutes in Liberty City. So what we are saying here is that it is not so much a question of whether the content of *Grand Theft Auto* is postmodern – as far as the working definition we are using goes, it probably is – but rather it is a matter of whether the playing experience is postmodern, whether the player/reader of the text/game is immersed in a set of practices that cannot be understood using the 'old' concepts – representation, narrative, audience.

The player in *GTA IV* has so many options that we cannot list them all here – not just options within the single-player game (which are, if not infinite, then at least countless), but also the chance to play in multiplayer mode, within which there are several 'mini-games', such as 'Cops and crooks', 'Hangman's noose' and 'Mafiya workout'. Equally, when first playing the new product in this long-running franchise, many players will be comparing the game to its previous incarnations. Certainly, a great deal of the 360-degree media coverage of the fourth game in the series has obsessively made these intertextual observations.

Even if we are thinking of video games as 'always-already' postmodern as a media form more broadly, considering the whole *GTA* series for a moment, we can identify the experience provided by the product as being 'more' postmodern than other games because of the 'sandbox' principle and the choices offered to the player, as this extract from *Play* (2007: 9) magazine's *Unofficial History* agrees.

It was in the gameplay itself where *Grand Theft Auto* managed to break the mould in many ways. *Grand Theft Auto* contained free-form 'go anywhere you please' gameplay that saw you tied to an over-arching plot that contained various missions to complete but also left you free to explore the huge world in your own time, finding hidden packages and rampage icons, exploring the world and doing what you wanted.

(a) A long night in Liberty City, it seems for Nico Bellic and his cousin Roman. After the mass bloodbath, which we created in last night's wild antics at the Splitsides comedy club in central Liberty City, before the face-off with police. As I bring Nico out of the police station, my character is greeted with a phone call from Roman asking me to collect him from the hospital. After collecting him, I then took my eastern European cousin for a drink in Blarneys Irish pub, before a game of darts, where I participated in a sensation, which I have never discovered before on a video game, my character being drunk. Whilst walking around the beer garden of the pub I found another feature which makes GTA a favourite of mine, not just due to the revolutionary aspects of gameplay, but the humour, as I chuckled to myself while reading an umbrella on one of the tables with a sign for a mock German beer, Pißwasser, GTA never ceases to amaze me, or to make me laugh. Next up a quick trip out again with my beloved cousin Roman, we hit the comedy club and low and behold, something else I can connect with, a brat is performing, short, stupid beard, starting to lose his hair. No it's not Rafa Benitez, it's Ricky Gervais. Quickly watch his comedy set about charities for diseases (particularly cancer and AIDS). Offensive explicit and outrageously funny, I leave the club after 10 minutes (the end of his set) feeling happy and more importantly bloodthirsty. But before the killing spree, I've seen the docks, the sea and it's tempting me. This when combined with the game telling me to take Roman home, I cannot resist taking him the long way, through the water! At this point I realised I do not want to swim around so whip out my in-game phone to tap in the cheat code (oh cummon no one plays this game completely legitimately do they?). No sooner have I tapped in the code and the boat is spawned into the water. I jump in quickly followed by my fellow comrade and the journey through the water begins.

(b) Starting the game from scratch isn't easy. Your first task is to drive an associate round Liberty City – driving is an absolute nightmare! First few plays is simply consumed with trying to sort out how to drive the car – kept writing the car off and thereby terminating the mission. Not being terribly experienced with driving games, found this tough at first. Anyway, in between trying to sort this, this being a GTA game, I decide to take a walk down the street and fight some random passers-by. Got beaten up by a girl at one point – couldn't learn how to fight fast enough. Once I master the art of street fighting, its back to driving the car round Liberty City. By now, about 40 mins into playing I'm starting to pick up the thread a bit – I can drive, I can fight and this starts to impress the ladies! A girl tells me she 'likes' me but my clothes are no good – I guess this is a cue for material self-improvement. An hour into playing and I'm starting to get into the swing of it – what to do, how to do and just as importantly how it's similar and different to previous GTAs. An hour and a bit into the game, feeling like I've made a decent start but also knowing it'll take me some time to master this version of Liberty City.

As part of a research project called 'Just gaming: on being differently literate' (McDougall and Kendall 2008), a range of *GTA IV* players posted 'playblogs', summarising one-hour sessions in Liberty City, which were analysed, along with follow-up interviews, in relation to the ways the bloggers/players chose to switch between the metalanguage of the gamer (to do with controlling the action, navigation, missions and rules) and the first-person narrative of the **avatar**/character. Above are two of the postings, with the most obviously 'postmodern' references in bold type, and a full analysis of second blog (b).

We can get a lot of insight about *GTA IV* as a postmodern experience from these postings, but we will focus on the last one here. The blogger's description of his first encounters with the new game illustrate a number of complex interactions. Most

Activity

This activity is only for students aged 18 or over. The author and publisher do not encourage or take responsibility for students aged 17 or under playing *Grand Theft Auto*.

This activity sounds crazy, but it will take you to a really good example of how postmodernism breaks boundaries and remixes culture.

- Read the quote from *Play* above again, and focus on the idea of free-form play within a structure that imposes certain limits.
- Then go to Wikipedia and search for 'free-form jazz'. Read what you find, follow some links and see where they take you.
- Play *GTA* (any version) and make as many free-form decisions as you can.
- Listen to at least three of the free-form jazz examples you find during your research.
- Set up a blog on blogger.com with a few of your fellow students called '*Grand Theft Auto* – jazz gaming', and discuss the idea that *GTA* and free-form jazz are doing the same thing. If it works, this is the postmodern in practice, and if enough readers of this book do this, you could end up with one huge blog and a new theoretical idea could be born – you read it here first.

straightforwardly, he describes getting to grips with the technical aspects of playing the game, coping with the first task when he is not experienced with driving games, and learning how to 'fight fast enough'. After 40 minutes his confidence increases and he describes this competence in terms of his ability to fight 'random passers-by'. But on another level we can see how his response to the game is profoundly intertextual. His decision (moral or otherwise) to wander around enacting acts of violence on pedestrians for no strategic purpose is made on the basis of prior experience – 'this being a *GTA* game'. So the writer is trying to learn the skills he will need to progress, but is also demonstrating a metalanguage about ways of being in the game. It is difficult to imagine such a multilayered 'reader response' being so easily articulated in relation to films, TV or print media. While we will all make intertextual and critically reflective decisions as we watch films or read books, it is fair to say that this will be less conscious and visible/tangible.

It is not possible to 'read' *GTA IV* in a linear fashion. The second blog is the most immediately 'useful' if we are looking for evidence of the postmodern condition. We get a clear explicit identification of the intertextual nature of his reading of the game – 'previous GTAs'. And on another level, we witness him encountering and evaluating the values and conditions of Liberty City – 'this is a cue for material self-improvement'. This is metadiscourse – when the savvy player can critically assess the ideological premise of what is being experienced. Just as research (McDougall 2006) has shown that students playing and studying *Medal of Honor* can be offended by the version of history being represented (or at least be aware of how this might be offensive – a different position to take) but still enjoy the game, so players of *GTA IV* can be perfectly aware of how the verisimilitude of the gameworld relies entirely on an unpleasant 'deficit model' of human behaviour in an advanced capitalist society where people are incrementally worth less as the capitalist machine's relentless expansion continues, at the same time as taking great pleasure from the game. This relates to the comments made by the writer of *The Wire* (summarised earlier in this section) and also Gauntlett's notion of the pick-and-mix reader (also discussed in this book). In all these cases, the postmodern nature of the reading experience is crucial and complex. Our game blogger knows that the need for him to improve his appearance and learn how to fight better, in both cases to 'impress the ladies', is morally dubious, but this is not going to stop him enjoying the challenge in the gameworld.

Notice also how he switches between player and character – detail about competences is articulated simultaneously in terms of 'making a decent start' (playing, learning, mastering technical tasks) and 'a girl tells me she likes me' (story, characters, narrative). This takes us smoothly into a discussion of **ludology** and **narratology**.

Story or game?

There is a debate among games academics over the ideal starting point for serious analysis of video games. Some games critics insist that games are games rather than stories, arguing that adapting narrative theory to this new form of text does not work. Aarseth (1997) suggests that the narrative elements of games are certainly there for us to identify (particularly in games like *Harry Potter*, where the player takes on an existing character from the fictional world of a film, novel or both), but that these are not especially significant to the game, and actually the player may not take much notice of them. Instead, writers like Aarseth adhere to an approach called ludology, which studies the act of play. In this approach, the practice of 'reading' games pays particular attention to the structure of play, and the degree to which games share structures. Whereas academics who want to adapt narrative theories traditionally used to study literature and film believe that games share structural storytelling principles with these older media forms, ludologists argue that this misses the point that the game player is doing something fundamentally different to the film viewer or novel reader, as s/he is actively influencing the flow of game time. Dovey and Kennedy (2006: 102) summarise some of these textual differences here.

Meaning generated by play is different to meaning generated by reading. To read is to create meaning cognitively in the encounter with the text. To play is to generate meaning, to express it through play. Play allows us to actively express meaning (to be part of your clan, to be a stealth assassin or princess rescuing plumber). By playing out these roles we are temporarily inhabiting an avatar that functions as part of the gameplay and offers consumers a point of entry in to the game world. Because we know we are going to be using our characters and their world for purposes other than pure interpretive pleasure, we have far less investment or interest in the meanings generated by the worlds we inhabit. This is not to argue that representation and meaning are not in play. Players clearly have interpretive responses to game worlds, and computer games in their wider circulation are clearly meaningful. However, the importance of players' interpretive pleasure is less than it would be in a novel or film.

While Dovey and Kennedy do not use the term, we can assess their summary here as a postmodern intervention, because they are arguing that the experience of temporary identity-play is central to gaming. Playing with or shifting identity, contextualised by a 'blurring' of text and 'reader' are, as we know by now, central to the postmodern condition.

Production Tip

The thing about postmodernism that sometimes leads to its status as a serious theoretical idea being undermined is that if we look at media texts from a certain angle, it is almost always possible to find postmodern elements. And of course, if we take the view that postmodernism is a state that pervades the way we use media, then all media is postmodern. But here are some specific examples for a few of the A2 production briefs that should be useful in planning, evaluating and theorising your outcomes.

- Music promotion – in what ways do your promotional materials make intertextual references to other music or other media/culture that the audience will recognise?
- Film – in what ways does the film you are making, or the promotional materials for the film, use postmodern techniques to make intertextual references, play with the boundaries between film and reality or subvert traditional approaches to narrative?
- Websites – we can argue that websites are hyperreal in the sense that links and tags take the user outside of conventional narrative and textual boundaries. Relate this idea to your work.

- Video games – whether working on a game level, or the promotion of a new game, you will be working with a form that many see as postmodern because of the way that games relate to other media forms (intertextuality), blur the boundary between media and reality, player and reader (hyper-reality) and do not follow linear narrative structures. Think about your own game in these contexts.
- Soap opera – the promotion of your soap will be intertextual, because you will be using a magazine as well as a website to promote this television product. Soaps, despite being an 'older' media form, have always blurred the boundaries between fiction and reality, when other media (newspapers, magazines, other TV shows) deliberately confuse the actors with the characters, and when the physical space the soap is set in is represented as a real location (e.g. the webcam on Albert Square or the Rovers Return as a tourist attraction). How will you use postmodern, cross-media techniques to construct your physical soap world and the characters as 'real'?

Case Study

Fan production

If a defining feature of postmodern media is the breaking down of traditional boundaries between producer and audience, then the proliferation of fan-generated material in response to video games is a great example of this. Video games – those with more traditional narratives that relate to other media products in an intertextual relationship and franchises that do not relate to any pre-existing media product (so we can include *Harry Potter* and *Final Fantasy* games) – have led to the creation of a broad range of fan-produced material, which includes the following forms:

- Alternative scripting
- Fan art
- Game walkthroughs
- Level editing
- Machinima
- Modding
- Player-developed cheat guides and patches.

Choose a game that you know has a large fan-base and, with Google as your starting point, research the above fan-produced materials. Once again, web 2.0 is the facilitating development here, so you will be interested in how these user-generated creative offerings are exchanged in the public sphere via the internet. Pay particular attention to machinima, an animation format that allows fans to upload their own moving-image material in response to games, usually via YouTube. See these two websites for more on machinima: www.machinima.com and www.mprem.com (accessed August 2008).

Second Life

We create avatars to leave our bodies behind, yet take the body with us in the form of codes and assumptions about what does and does not constitute a legitimate interface with reality – virtual or otherwise.

(Rehak, in Wolf and Perron 2003: 123)

Second Life is postmodern, without question. It is almost as though a group of postmodern theorists had got together to design something that would make all their ideas make sense, and came up with Linden Island. In *Second Life*, you log in, create an avatar and then move around the island, talking to other avatars connected to real people who are at their screens doing the same thing as you. *Second Life* has taken off to the extent where business, entertainment and education are all clamouring to develop more and more virtual land and spaces to do more virtual activities. The benefits in terms of cost, efficiency and time are obvious. You can trade real money for Linden Dollars and then buy and sell in *Second Life*. At The Serious Games Institute in Coventry, businesses are supported in running elements of their work in this virtual world, so here we have an example of a video game template being the starting point for serious commerce. For media studies, our interest is in the 'everyday' part of *Second Life*, rather than the business end. And in terms of postmodern media, we want to know what is going on when someone takes on this virtual identity, in relation to the quote from Rehak above. The postmodern label is very easy to tag onto *Second Life* because of the duality and boundary-blurring Rehak describes – physical and virtual at the same time. There is much debate over whether *Second Life* really counts as a massively multiplayer online role-playing game (**MMORPG**) in the same way as *World of Warcraft*, because it is not actually a game. But if we look at it in the same way – a large group of people online sharing virtual experiences – we can say that it challenges traditional media studies concepts to say the least, in the same way as it challenges 'traditional' gamers. Here Bennett (2007: 6) describes this discomfort.

> With all video games there is a defined 'objective' and for video games as opposed to multi-user online games a narrative as well. A user must 'do' within this environment and has specific goals to achieve at all stages (kill this dragon and find this treasure) and receives feedback and rewards when each goal is achieved. These users often feel initially disenfranchised when they enter the *Second Life* world because they are not immediately greeted with a narrative and set a goal or task. They find the concept that they can simply 'be' in this environment rather than 'do' alien and sometimes intimidating.

However, since Bennett offered this view, *GTA IV*, as we considered above, has offered players a similar opportunity to just 'be' rather than 'do'. This might lead us to the view that postmodern video games always involve an interplay of tasks/goals and non-strategic hanging around in virtual space, but that *Second Life* may be influential in moving game designers away from narratives (already there is some discussion over the value of cut scenes which interrupt the flow of play in favour of an intertextual cinematic feel) towards free-form gameplay, where the space is provided but the objective is defined by the players.

Also analysing MMORPGs, Filiciak (2004) writes about postmodern 'hyperidentities', taking Baudrillard's theory of hyperreality and internalising this for the mediated individual. Filiciak observes that in postmodern culture we are able to design our 'selves' in ways that are fluid and temporary; we get to change our identity through media and technology in ways that previous generations could not. The argument that a 'second life' is a virtual substitute or an escape is turned around here, and Filiciak instead suggests that technologies allow us simply to extend expressions of ourselves beyond physical limitations. These statements are a perfect way to end this chapter, and subsequently this book, as they neatly summarise the impact media 2.0 might have on the whole of our social realities, our cultures and our ways of making sense of being alive (Filiciak, in Wolf and Perron 2003: 101).

> The dissemination of new ways of thinking which make the real and the virtual equal is only a matter of time. Videogames, and

Exam-Style Question

What is postmodern media? Refer to two areas of the media in your response.

especially networked games, are one of the most accurate metaphors of contemporary life. Games are the medium that most perfectly describe our existence and express the way the human 'self' functions in the contemporary world. It is on the screen that we can compose our hyper-identity in the most imposing way. Having a free hand when creating our own images is a commonly-accepted convention in Internet, but not in the offline world; or rather, not yet, because the future belongs to interactive media and hyperidentity.

Examiner's Tip

Perhaps postmodern media is the theme where this is least likely to be a problem, but this tip is applicable across all the Critical Perspectives themes. You may be aware that some people think that media studies A level is easier than 'hard science' subjects like physics. Media teachers usually get very upset about this, as you might expect. But if we replace the word 'easier' with 'more accessible', then it is probably true that you have more of a fighting chance with a media essay than you do writing about the speed of light, just by being immersed in your own media culture. But this is not necessarily good news, because you have to work harder to distance your writing from everyday knowledge and opinion. You have to *theorise* at all times. So, a basic tip to help with this: – pick someone you know – a relative or friend – who is highly immersed in media culture and knows a lot about media from the perspective of a producer, consumer, fan or all of these, but is not a media student. Keep that person in your head, and when you are writing your exam answer, keep reading over your writing and ask yourself – could they have written this? If the answer is yes, then you are not doing your job.

5
Preparing for a media degree

One of the defining features of the OCR Media Studies A level specification that you are studying – and, given that you are reading this section, that you have probably more or less got to the end of – is that it is designed for progression to undergraduate study in media. In the past, university lecturers used to think (wrongly, in the main) that A level media studies was a bit old-fashioned and a bit too text-based – a bit too much like English. But the OCR units – with their emphasis on production, online media, reflective writing and a range of highly contemporary theoretical themes that take a 'cultural analysis' approach to how people make sense of media in situated contexts – are quite similar to the content of degree courses in media.

Just as we considered the assessment objectives for OCR's A2 Media Studies early on in this book, now it is well worth glancing at the higher education equivalent – the Higher Education Academy Subject Benchmarks for Media Studies (QAA Subject Benchmark Statements for Communication, Media, Film and Cultural Studies, from www.qaa.ac.uk/academicinfrastructure/benchmark/statements/CMF08.asp#p4 – accessed August 2008). These statements are important because they frame what you will be doing at university.

As fields of study, communication, media, film and cultural studies are distinguished by their focus on cultural and communicative activities as central forces in shaping everyday social and psychological life, as well as senses of identity in the organisation of economic and political activity; in the construction of public culture; in the creation of new expressive forms; and as the basis for a range of professional practices.

Degree programmes within communication, media, film and cultural studies share the aim of producing graduates who have an informed, critical and creative approach both to understanding media, culture and communications in contemporary society, and to their own forms of media, communicative and expressive practice.

While these programmes are committed to enabling students to meet the challenges of employment (including self-employment) in a society in which the cultural and communications industries play an increasingly central role, they emphasise that the fostering of employability requires the development of students' creative, intellectual, analytical and research skills.

But we need to distinguish here between the different kinds of courses on offer. There are many academic courses – Media Studies, Media and Communication, Media and Film Studies, Media and Cultural Studies, Screen Studies, Media and Culture, to name just a few. Then there are broad production courses which include a range of media, usually called Media Production or Media Arts. And there are the more specialist production courses, ranging from Film and Television Production to Animation or Games Design.

In selecting the kind of course that is right for you, as well as the geographical and financial considerations, you need to do your research. And once again, the internet opens doors for you. As a rule of thumb, if you are interested in a more academic route, you want to be searching for the staff who teach on the course and find out what they have published, what research they are conducting and what conferences they are speaking at. These are the people who are going to be teaching you and helping you learn about the media at a higher level, so they ought to be influencing the field in some way. If you are more interested in production, then you want to know about links with employers and what recent graduates are doing for a living now. And when you visit universities and take your showreel or e-portfolio, you need to be asking questions as well as answering them – it is *your* future at stake. In addition, for production-orientated courses, equipment and space are key, but this might be small and portable rather than studio-based, depending on the course.

In addition to full-time media courses, another route which A level media studies students are increasingly keen on is a combined honours degree, which allows you to take media as 50 per cent of your degree, with another subject, like English, art or drama; or as a minor degree where the other subject takes up 75 per cent of the degree. This is a good option for students who are concerned that a full degree in media might not be taken seriously by employers, or for students who think they might want to teach in the future and are aware that media is not a National Curriculum subject, so they combine it with a subject that is. At some universities media students only work in combinations – Media is a minor or joint degree, or there is the option to take Media within Creative Arts, where Drama and Media are joined by either Art or Music; as the media sectors converge, this course is increasingly popular with employers who are seeking graduates with a broader range of connected creative skills.

One thing you need to be aware of, whichever course you opt for, is the much higher level of independent study you will need to be comfortable with. For every hour of lecture, seminar or workshop time with staff, they expect three hours of independent study – production, research, discussion with other students and, most often – even in these postmodern web 2.0 times – reading (*lots* of reading!).

So, if you are not put off by that, what next? Your media studies teachers will guide you through this, but you will need to apply through UCAS and you will need two things– a showreel or e-portfolio of your work and a personal statement that stands out from the others. You should avoid general statements about

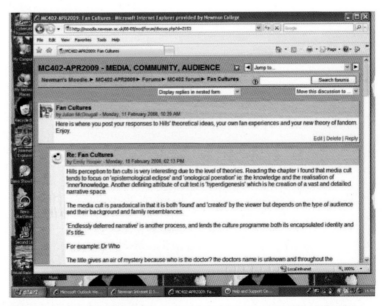

Figure 5.1 A university media module – independent study is expected in higher education

enthusiasm and passion (everyone says those things) and concentrate on the micro detail – what production work you have done and what technical skills you have developed. The Critical Perspectives exam will help you greatly with this, as OCR has already asked you to critically reflect on your skills development. How can you make links between your creative outcomes and media theory? Again, if you did okay in Critical Perspectives, then 'job done' there. And how have you disseminated your creative output through web 2.0 platforms? One other crucial element for this 'presentation of self' is teamwork. The media is, generally speaking, a collaborative world. You have probably worked in a number of groups during coursework assignments. How did you manage the collaborative creative process? How did you overcome group problems? What are the most important elements in successful group activities? Your university lecturers will want to see that you can do well in collective projects in higher education as well. Finally, you need to include extracurricular experience as well, and this advice from Andrew Ireland at Bournemouth Media School, a centre of excellence for Media Education, is well worth reading (McDougall and Ireland 2006: 38).

> Have you done any work experience? Have you made any films yourself? Do you write music maybe? Have you been involved in the process of producing media in any way, or just consuming it? Been at any workshops, one or two day courses, talks by media figures? This kind of information helps us see how committed you are, and we can then picture you on our course, extending your awareness and involvement.

Glossary

academic: The development of new forms of knowledge and theoretical ideas of ways of thinking. An academic approach to media is one that attempts to develop a conceptual framework to describe the various ways that media products are shared and understood.

aesthetic: Visual appearance, related to taste.

audience: A collective group of people reading any media text. Digital technology has led to increasing uncertainty over how we define an audience, with general agreement that the notion of a large group of people, brought together by time, responding to a single text, is outdated and that audiences now are 'fragmented'.

avatar: An on-screen representation of a player in a video game.

BBFC: British Board of Film Classification.

binary: Thinking in opposites. In digital coding, binary describes the coding of digits as noughts and ones. In media analysis, we often find that meaning is constructed around binary opposites which are simplistic.

Bollywood: Popular Indian cinema, originating in Mumbai (Bombay).

bricolage: The construction of meaning through remixing a combination of elements to make a new style. Ranges from surrealist work, where things are deliberately put out of context, to postmodern media where there is no sense of 'original' material to worry about, as everything new is made up of a bricolage of the old – what was already there.

broadband: High-speed, thicker cable, transmitting a powerful digital signal that can deal with complex data such as moving images, music and games.

catharsis: To purify or cleanse yourself by releasing emotions or feelings. In relation to video games, the question is whether playing a violent game releases pent-up anger and frustration, which in turn makes a person less likely to be violent or angry in the 'real world'.

censorship: The practice of 'cutting' or preventing access to media material.

classification: Restricting access to media material on the grounds of age.

commodity: A thing that has value when sold.

compression: Transferring data into less space and sending it from one place to another, through encoding data using fewer units in digital coding.

connotations: The cultural meanings brought to a sign or symbol by the person/people interpreting it.

conventions: The expected ingredients in a particular type of media text – usually associated with genre.

convergence: Hardware and software coming together across media, and companies coming together across similar boundaries, making the distinction between different types of media and different media industries increasingly dubious. In this book, the critical perspectives themes also converge.

copyright: The ownership of ideas as creative or intellectual property.

cut scene: The parts of a video game which require the player to be passive and over which one has no control; these are viewing/listening/reading experiences, often filmic in nature.

DAB: Digital radio.

data: Original information acquired through research, or just information to be processed – as in digital data.

deconstruction: A theoretical investigation of a cultural product or cultural actions, to see how they are put together and how they can only be understood in relation to other texts or cultural products or meanings.

democracy: Society founded on equality, in which the decision-making powers are elected and are thus representative and accountable.

demographic: Measuring people and characterising them according to characteristics such as age, gender, ethnicity, occupation, income and socio-economic status.

diegesis/diegetic: Describes what is present in the world of a text, as opposed to extra material added for the audience, which is extra-diegetic or non-diegetic.

digital: Information broken down into noughts and ones.

discourse: A way of speaking, thinking and understanding that becomes powerful and appears 'natural'. The ways in which we come to understand the world through talking, thinking and writing that become dominant. Taking a step back to explore how we come to say what we do, believing it to be common sense, is called discourse analysis. A key thinker in this area is Michel Foucault.

download: The practice of selecting and receiving digital information from an online source on a computer, as opposed to sending it by upload.

effects: The idea that the media have influence over people and can play a role in changing behaviour. The suggestion that people's behaviour is influenced or altered as a result of exposure to media – direct or indirect, significant to others or relatively unimportant – is described in terms of 'media effects'.

ethnography: Detailed research with a particular social group in its situated contexts.

feminism: The belief that we should oppose media texts that represent women as unequal to men, or as mere unthinking objects for male scrutiny.

flow: A state of mind which happens when someone is involved in activity which is challenging but pleasurable and incrementally more difficult over time, with staggered rewards and feedback.

form: The basic shape or structure of a text or product.

gatekeeping: The role played by editors, producers, owners and regulators in opening and closing, to greater and lesser extents, the flow of media information, through selecting which information to provide and which to deny people access to.

globalisation: The shift in media distribution from local or national to international and to the whole world at once. Culturally, describes the process of 'sameness' around the world, typified by the availability of McDonald's in most nations.

hybrid: A fusion of more than one media form, or a mixing of global and local, or a mixing of identities.

hyperreality: A state in which images, and simulations, take on more reality than the state they represent, so that the distinction between reality and representation is no longer sustainable. A key thinker in this area is Jean Baudrillard.

iconic: A sign which resembles directly what it represents.

identity: The complex way that one has a representative sense of oneself. David Gauntlett is a key thinker in this area.

ideology: A dominant set of ideas presenting itself as common sense or truth. Power relations are reinforced through ideology. Karl Marx and Louis Althusser are key thinkers in this area.

immersion: Used in analysis of video games in two ways: first, perceptual (the senses are dominated by the experience of the game), and second, psychological (the player is drawn into the game in their imagination).

interactive: Media texts which offer audiences the opportunity to choose, respond to or shape the text in some way.

internet protocol television: Television distributed through a computer network instead of a broadcast or cable route. Answer to activity on p. 97 = advertisers.

interpellation: Althusser's idea that media products lead us to a false recognition of ourselves so that we get lost in an ideal image of ourselves that will never be possible.

intertextual (or intermedial): The chain of signification in which texts make references to one another. When one text refers to another it is called 'intertextual', while 'intermedial' describes a media form which relies on understanding and experience of other media (e.g. film and music) to make meaning.

linear: In a clear, logical order, moving in one direction.

literacy: A way of communicating, usually understood as the ability to read and write. Media literacy extends this to include all forms of writing (e.g. taking photographs) and all forms of reading (e.g. listening to music), and activities which may combine them (e.g. playing a computer game). With this extended definition, such forms of communication as video gaming, blogging, social networking, film-making and viewing, and a range of other newer media practices are included as forms of language to be learned and used. Being 'media-literate' is now seen by the regulatory body Ofcom as a key aspect of citizenship.

long tail: Chris Anderson's idea that the large amount of niche markets are now worth as much as the smaller amount of big markets.

ludology: The study of play.

macro: Big, broad themes. The sum of lots of micro things added up.

male gaze: From Laura Mulvey (1975), an analysis of media images which suggests that the camera represents a male perspective, and as such casts men as subjects and women as objects.

market forces: This idea likens the 'natural' flow of competition leading to consumer choice and selection, and hence the survival of the fittest, to the laws of nature.

Marxist: All theory derived from the works of Marx, founded on a belief that the ruling classes at any time and place maintain their economic and systematic power through controlling not only the means of production, but also culture and ideology, including the media.

media access: Describes the degree of ease with which citizens can be seen and/or heard in the media, and can respond to the media and be provided with a dialogue with institutions, and the amount of opportunities evident for people to produce media texts themselves and for them to be distributed.

media language: An umbrella term to describe the ways in which audiences read media texts through understanding formal and conventional structures (e.g. the grammar of film editing). Media literacy describes our ability to read and write in this extended sense of language.

mediasphere: John Hartley describes a 360-degree environment for media consumption in 2009, the mediasphere, and says that this fundamentally changes how we need to think about media audiences.

media studies 2.0: A response to web 2.0, proposed by Gauntlett (2007b), in which the role of online user-generated content and sharing is seen as fundamental to how we understand media audiences. This makes it mandatory for media studies to change how it operates, which impacts greatly on media students.

meme: An idea or creative item that is passed on virally from person to person, to the point where lots of people know about it and are talking about it.

metalanguage: When we are able to step outside of language to analyse meaning rather than just using language to make meaning, we have a metalanguage. This is an advanced form of literacy.

micro: A small, specific example.

micropolitics: The way that small, seemingly insignificant decisions and interactions amount to outcomes that have an impact on people's lives.

mise-en-scène: Everything that is put into the frame (essentially, considering the paused moving image as a still image). Includes set design, location, costume, actors, make up, non-verbal communication, colour and contrast, lighting and filter.

MMORPG: Massively multiplayer online role-playing game (e.g. *World of Warcraft, Second Life, Club Penguin* or *Counterstrike*).

mode of address: How a text, in any media, speaks to its audience.

moral panic: Exaggerated media response to the behaviour of a social group. A phrase coined by Stanley Cohen in 1972, this refers to overstated reactions to seemingly deviant aspects of popular culture, usually mobilised by the mass media. Clearly, certain video games have been the subject of widespread moral panics, and they are often blamed for declining moral standards in general, as well as specific cases of violent behaviour and tragedy.

multimedia: Fairly self-explanatory, a cultural product produced using a variety of media.

myth: The key thinker in this area is Roland Barthes, who analysed the way that dominant ideas in a culture take on the status of myth, so they appear natural and neutral. In semiotics, signs and symbols when added together amount to a system of myths.

narrative: The way information is ordered, or a story is told.

narratology: The study of video games as stories – usually seen as in conflict with ludology, but it is possible to combine both theoretical approaches.

news values: The idea that editors select and construct news within a framework influenced by political, corporate, cultural and commercial objectives.

Ofcom: Regulator of UK broadcasting and telecommunications industries.

online video: Television watched online through the world wide web.

paraphrase: When you make use of someone else's ideas but do not quote them directly.

parody: A text which does not simply imitate the style of another (pastiche), but instead is transformative in that it either mocks or shifts in some way the original text's conventions.

PCC: Press Complaints Commission.

peer to peer: The sharing of media material between two parties in an equal relationship.

piracy: Distribution of media material that infringes copyright law.

pleasure: All forms of engagement with media texts.

podcast: Uploading an MP3 file over the internet for others to access through subscription.

politics/political: Politics is simply to do with people making decisions that have impact on other people's lives.

polysemy: Plural meaning, as opposed to fixed, singular meaning.

popular culture: Texts which are consumed by a wide range of people – as opposed to a smaller group, seen as an elite – tend to be described as 'popular', and this implies a lesser cultural status or value.

postmodern: Describes an approach to culture which sees all texts as being intertextual, and meaning as mediated rather than representative of a state of original reality. Postmodernists believe that it is no longer sensible to describe media texts in terms of how they represent real life or events, and that instead we should see reality as increasingly mediated, so the boundaries between reality and media-reality are blurred. The most famous postmodern philosophers are both French – Jean François Lyotard, who described 'the postmodern condition', and Jean Baudrillard, who said Disneyland was a good example of this blurring of reality and simulation, which he called 'hyperreality'.

promotion: An aspect of distribution, creating audience interest in a media product.

psychological: The academic/scientific study of the workings of the mind, including perception, emotion, behaviour, personality and interpersonal communication.

public service: Founded on principles of democracy as opposed to profit. Funded through public taxation (e.g. the television licence fee).

realism: The degree and the variety of ways in which media texts represent and fit with ideas about reality.

reference: Making an explicit mention of a writer or other source in your work and correctly identifying the year of publication, so that someone using your material can follow up this source easily.

reflective: Being reflective is very difficult – it is to do with analysing yourself, your ways of understanding the world, your actions and the way you think.

regulation: The monitoring of and intervention in media production and consumption.

remix: Describes how people are able to combine and reformulate a range of information from different sources, reworking media content.

representation: Students of media are taught that media texts do not present a neutral, transparent view of reality, but offer instead a mediated re-presentation of it. The processes by which audience members come to understand media texts in terms of how they seem to relate to people, ideas, events, themes and places. This is a very complex idea, as the reader of a media text will play an active role in constructing these meanings him/herself. At its most simple, it is how media texts are understandable.

scheduling: The strategic positioning of media texts within broadcasting time. Digital television is increasingly disrupting this approach, since viewers can choose more easily than before when to watch.

semiotics: The science of signs and symbols, from Saussure's linguistics (1974), and Barthes' structuralism (1973). The study of the sign, in terms of its connotations within cultural myth systems.

simulation: The deliberate artificial imitation of an experience or a process with the intention of making the imitation as close as possible to the 'real thing'. Baudrillard is a key thinker in this area.

sociocultural: Describes considerations of how our social experiences and cultural choices combine, and how meanings are constructed by audiences through experience as much as through any fixed, intended, preferred messages from producers' points of view.

sociological: The study of society and social interaction. Different from psychology, which analyses the individual human mind. Sociology is concerned with studying what humans do together or between each other.

stereotype: A blunt, overstated representation of a type of person. Usually negative.

structuralism: The study of language and meaning as a system – a network of meaning.

symbolic: When an image or sign stands for something it does not directly resemble.

synergy: Interconnected marketing and distribution of media products across a range of platforms and sectors.

synoptic: Bringing a range of things together. For a media student at A2 level, it is about connecting all the different units of study, coursework and case studies.

terrestrial: Analogue broadcasts from land-based transmitters as opposed to cable or satellite digital transmissions.

text: All media products are texts. But we can extend this term to include people, ourselves and others – anything that is made up of a range of signs that are decoded and interpreted by people.

theory/theorise: Often described as the opposite of practice, or practical, theory is actually the understanding of how things work.

Just as a plumber needs to know how water pressure works in order to fix a tap, so a film-maker needs to understand how people make meaning. To theorise media, we need a systematic way of thinking about how culture works.

transgressive: A practice which transcends conventional approaches, and either subverts these existing ways of working, or challenges their value. Pushing boundaries, forcing change, breaking rules, going against accepted practices or social norms, causing shock and outrage. Often threatening the established 'order of things'.

upload: Transferring information or material from a computer to an online network.

verisimilitude: The logical, seemingly authentic world of a text. Not the same as 'realist', because every text has a logical, sensible world constructed through continuity, detail and recognition.

viral: Describes the spread of ideas from person to person, just like germs spread illness.

virtual: A simulation of reality or experience.

we media: See Gillmor (2004). Ordinary people deciding that they want to create media, through easily accessible technologies such as blogging, digital video, podcasting and v-logging, wikis, YouTube and *Second Life*.

web 2.0: The second phase of the internet, where the focus shifts from people receiving information and services to people creating and sharing material. It is argued that the second phase of the world wide web starts to take on the appearance of what Tim Berners-Lee originally envisaged. Defined by collaboration, social networking and the democratic development and distribution of content by ordinary people. Examples are MySpace, YouTube and Wikipedia. The term web 2.0 is accredited to Tim O'Reilly.

wiki: Web-based, shared authored communication between people to build a set of ideas or a knowledge base.

wikinomics: A term invented by Tapscott and Williams (2006) to describe the impact of web 2.0 on economics as well as media.

Study resources

All the books, articles and websites mentioned in this book are listed here. There is also a range of others that will be of general value to the A2 Media Studies student (and one or two that teachers might make use of). You are encouraged to follow up as many of these as you can to add value to your studies.

(All websites listed were accessed in August 2008.)

Books and articles

Aarseth, E., 1997, *Cybertext: Perspectives on Ergodic Literature*, Baltimore: Johns Hopkins University Press.

Al-Jenaibi, B., 2007, 'Al-Jazeera and media pressure', in *Global Media Journal* 6, no.10.

Althusser, L., 1971, 'Ideology and ideological state apparatuses', in *Lenin and Philosophy, and Other Essays*, London: New Left Books.

Anderson, C., 2006, *The Long Tail*, London: Random House.

Appignanesi, R. and Garratt, C., 2004, *Introducing Postmodernism*, Cambridge: Icon.

Barham, N., 2004, *Disconnected: Why Our Kids Are Turning their Backs on Everything We Know*, London: Ebury Press.

Barker, M. and Petley, J. (eds), 1998, *Ill Effects: The Media/Violence Debate*, London: Routledge.

Barthes, R., 1973, *Mythologies*, London: Paladin.

Barton, L., 2004, 'It's all gone tits up', in *The Guardian*, 17 January.

Baudrillard, J., 1971, 'Requiem pour les media', in *Utopie* 4.

—, 1988, *Selected Writings*, M. Poster (ed.), Cambridge: Polity.

—, 2002, Extract from 'The spirit of terrorism', in Easthope, A. and McGowan, K. (eds), 2005, *A Critical and Cultural Theory Reader*, Maidenhead: Open University Press.

Bauman, Z., 1998, *Globalisation: The Human Consequences*, London: Polity.

Bennett, J., 2007, 'Teaching and learning in a MUVE. A social constructivist and game-based model for learning in a 3D virtual learning environment', paper presented to IMCL conference.

Berger, J., 1990, *Ways of Seeing*, London: Penguin.

Blake, R., 2008, Speech at Ofcom Media Literacy Research Seminar, London, May.

Boyd-Barrett, O. and Rantenen, T. (eds), 1999, *The Globalisation of News*, London: Sage.

Brabazon, T., 2007, *The University of Google*, Aldershot: Ashgate Publishing.

Brook, S., 2008, 'The heat is on', interview with Julian Linley, in *The Guardian*, 30 June.

Brooker, C., 2008, 'Review of GTA IV', in *The Guardian*, 12 May (www.guardian.co.uk/commentisfree/2008/may/12/games).

Brown, M., 1997, 'Yesterday, the world', in *The Guardian*, 16 June.

—, 2008, 'Is self-regulation of the press working?', in *The Guardian (Media Guardian)*, 19 May.

Buckingham, D., 2000, *After the Death of Childhood: Growing Up in the Age of Electronic Media*, London: Polity.

—, 2007, *Beyond Technology: Children's Learning in the Age of Digital Culture*, London: Polity.

— (ed.), 2008, *Youth, Identity and Digital Media*, Cambridge, MA: MIT Press.

—, with contributions from Whiteman, N., Willet, T. and Burn, A., 2008. *Literature Review for the Byron Report*, London: Department for Children, Schools and Families.

Burn, A. and Parker, D., 2003, *Analysing Media Texts*, London: Continuum.

Burn, A. and Durran, J., 2007, *Media Literacy in Schools: Practice, Production and Progression*, London: Paul Chapman.

Byron, T., 2008, *Safer Children in a Digital World: The Report of the Byron Review*, London: Department for Children, Schools and Familes.

Card, N. and Herd, M. (eds), 2007, *The Guardian Guide to Photography*, London: www.guardian.co.uk/buyguides

— (eds), 2008, *The Guardian Guide to Making Video*, London: www.guardian.co.uk/buyguides

Carr, D., Buckingham, D., Burn, A. and Schott, G., 2006, *Computer Games: Text, Narrative and Play*, London: Polity.

Carson, N., 2008, *Digital Media in the West Midlands*, Birmingham: Advantage West Midlands.

Cohen, S., 1972, *Folk Devils and Moral Panics*, Oxford: Martin Robertson.

Conrad, P., 2008, 'Fresh guns for hire', in *The Observer*, 4 May.

Coughlin, P., 2003, 'Joel and Ethan Coen', in *Senses of Cinema*, at www.sensesofcinema.com/contents/directors/03/coens.html

Csikszentmihalyi, M., 1997, *Creativity: Flow and the Psychology of Discovery and Intervention*, New York: HarperPerennial.

Davey, O., 2005, 'Pleasure and pain: why we need violence in the movies', in *Media Magazine* 12, London: English and Media Centre.

Dawkins, R., 2006, *The Selfish Gene*, Oxford: Oxford University Press.

Dixon, S., 2008, *Meme, Myself and I*, Birmingham: Rodney Lockwood Press.

Dovey, J. and Kennedy, H., 2006, *Game Cultures: Computer Games as New Media*, Maidenhead: Open University Press.

Dudek, D., 2005, '*Edukators* offers lesson in beliefs', in *Journal Sentinel*, 22 September.

Durham, M., 2004, 'Constructing the new ethnicities: media, sexuality and diaspora identity in the lives of South American immigrant girls', in *Critical Studies in Mass Communication* 2.

Easthope, A. and McGowan, K., 2005, *A Critical and Cultural Theory Reader*, Milton Keynes: Open University Press.

English and Media Centre, 2008, *Doing Ads Study Pack*, London: English and Media Centre.

Faludi, S., 2003, *Backlash: The Undeclared War Against Women*, London: Vintage.

Filiciak, M., 2004, 'Hyperidentities: postmodern identity patterns in massive multiplayer online role-playing games', in Wolf, M. and Perron, B. (eds), *The Video Game Theory Reader*, London: Routledge.

Foucault, M., 1975, *Discipline and Punish: The Birth of the Prison*, London: Penguin.

—, 1980, *Power/Knowledge: Selected Interviews and Other Writings 1972–1977*, C. Gordon (ed.), London: Harvester.

—, 1988, *Technologies of the Self: A Seminar with Michel Foucault*, L. Martin, H. Gutman and P. Hutton (eds), Amherst, MA: University of Massachusetts Press.

Fraser, P., 2007a, 'Editing music promos: interview with Suzy Davis', in *Media Magazine* 20, London: English and Media Centre.

—, 2007b, 'Ten tips for making your own music video', in *Media Magazine* 19, London: English and Media Centre.

Freire, P., 1972, *Pedagogy of the Oppressed*, London: Penguin.

Gauntlett, D., 2002, *Media, Gender, Identity*, London: Routledge.

—, 2007a, *Creative Explorations: New Approaches to Identities and Audiences*, London: Routledge.

—, 2007b, 'Media Studies 2.0', at www.theory.org.uk/ mediastudies2.htm

Gee, J., 2007, *Social Linguistics and Literacies: Ideology in Discourses*, London: Taylor and Francis.

Gentile, D., Lynch, P., Linder, J. and Walsh, D., 2004, 'The effects of violent videogame habits on adolescent hostility, aggressive behaviours and school performance', in *Journal of Adolescence* 27, pp. 5–22.

Gibson, J. (ed.), 2008, *Media 08*, London: Guardian Newspapers.

Gillmor, D., 2004, *We, The Media*, California: O'Reilly.

Goffman, E., 1990, *The Presentation of Self in Everyday Life*, London: Penguin.

Goldkorn, J., 2006, 'Al Jazeera: global change in the media environment', at www.danwei.org/tv/global_change_in_the_media_env.php

Green, H. and Hannon, C., 2007, *Their Space: Education for a Digital Generation*, at www.demos.co.uk/files/Their%20space%20-%20web.pdf

Hall, S., 1980, *Culture, Media, Language*, Birmingham: Unwin Hyman.

Hartley, J., 2008, *Television Truths*, Oxford: Blackwell.

Hendry, S., 2008, 'Cloverfield: a monster of a marketing campaign', in *Media Magazine* 24, London: English and Media Centre.

Hills, M., 2002, *Fan Cultures*, London: Routledge.

Hornby, N., 2007, Interview with David Simon, creator of *The Wire*, in *The Believer*, August.

Humm, M. (ed.), 1992, *Feminisms: A Reader*, London: Harvester Wheatsheaf.

Irvine, S., 2006, 'Globalisation and media education', in *in the picture* 54, Keighley: itp publications.

Jenks, C., 2005, *Culture*, London: Routledge.

Johnson, S., 2005, *Everything Bad Is Good for You*, London: Penguin.

Kendall, A., 2008, 'Playing and resisting: rethinking young people's reading cultures', in *Literacy* 42, no. 3, pp. 123–30.

Kermode, M., 2001, *Introduction to C4 screening of* Bad Lieutenant, London: C4.

Kung, L., Picard, R. and Towse, R., 2008, *The Internet and Mass Media*, London: Sage.

Lacey, N., 2000, *Narrative and Genre: Key Concepts in Media Studies*, London: Macmillan.

Lankshear, C. and Knobel, M., 2006, *New Literacies: Everyday Practices and Classroom Learning*, Maidenhead: Open University Press.

Leadbetter, C., 2008, 'People power transforms the web in next online revolution', in *The Observer*, 9 March.

Lemish, D., 2006, *Children and Television: A Global Perspective*, London: Blackwell.

Levan, S., 2000, York Film Notes: *Fargo*, Harlow: Longman.

Levy, E., 1999, *Cinema of Outsiders: The Rise of American Independent Film*, New York: New York University Press.

Lilley, A., 2008, 'This review builds consensus – now let's act on it', in *The Guardian*, 31 March.

Livingstone, S., 1999, *Young People, New Media Report*, London: LSE.

Lull, J., 2006, *Media, Communication, Culture: A Global Approach*, Cambridge: Polity.

Lyotard, J., 1984, *The Postmodern Condition*, Manchester: Manchester University Press.

Marsh, J. and Millard, E., 2000, *Literacy and Popular Culture: Using Children's Culture in the Classroom*, London: Paul Chapman.

Martinez, D., 1997, 'Chasing the metaphysical express', in Lalanne, J., Martinez, D., Abbas, A. and Ngai, J. (eds), *Wong Kar-wai*, Paris: DisVoir.

Mazierska, E. and Rascaroli, L., 2000, 'Trapped in the present: time in the films of Wong Kar-wai', in *Film Criticism* 25, no.2.

McDougall, J., 2006, *The Media Teacher's Book*, London: Hodder Arnold.

—, 2007, 'What do we learn in Smethwick Village', in *Learning, Media, Technology* 32, no.2.

—, 2008, *AS Media Studies for OCR*, London: Hodder Arnold.

— and Ireland, A., 2006, 'Moving on up: media in HE', in *Media Magazine* 17, London: English and Media Centre.

— and Kendall, A., 2008, 'Just gaming: on being differently literate', paper presented at *Future and Reality of Gaming* conference, Vienna, 17 October.

— and O'Brien, W., 2008, *Studying Videogames*, Leighton-Buzzard: Auteur.

McLuhan, M., 1994, *Understanding Media: The Extensions of Man*, London: MIT Press.

— and Carpenter, E. (eds), 1960, *Explorations in Communication*, Boston, MA: Beacon Press.

McMillin, D., 2007, *International Media Studies*, London: Blackwell.

Merrin, W., 2005, *Baudrillard and the Media*, Cambridge: Polity.

Miller, T., 2006, *A Companion to Cultural Studies*, London: Blackwell.

Moores, S., 2005, *Media/Theory*, London: Routledge.

Mulvey, L., 1975, 'Visual pleasure and narrative cinema', in *Screen* 16, no.3.

Murphy, P. and Kraidy, M. (eds), 2005, *Global Media Studies*, London: Routledge.

Murray, R., 2008, 'The new social realism', in *Splice: Studying Contemporary Cinema* 2, no.2.

Naughton, J., 2006, 'Blogging and the emerging media ecosystem', at http://reutersinstitute.politics.ox.ac.uk/fileadmin/documents/ discussion/blogging.pdf

Newman, J., 2004, *Videogames*, London: Routledge.

— and Oram, B., 2006, *Teaching Videogames*, London: BFI.

O'Rourke, M., 2006, 'Behind *The Wire*', at www.slate.com/id/ 2154694/pagenum/all

Play magazine, 2008, *Grand Theft Auto: Unofficial History*, London: Fusion Publishing.

Plunkett, J., 2008, 'Let's get digital', in *The Guardian (Media Guardian 100)*, 14 July.

Points, J., 2007, *Teaching Television Drama*, London: BFI.

Quy, S., 2006, 'Getting your short film seen', in *Media Magazine* 16, London: English and Media Centre.

—, 2008, 'Making a short film', in *Media Magazine* 19, London: English and Media Centre.

Rayns, T., 2008, 'The American Way – interview with Wong Kar-wai', in *Sight and Sound* 18, no.3, London: BFI.

Rehak, B., 2003, 'Playing at being: psychoanalysis and the avatar', in Wolf, M. and Perron, B. (eds), *The Video Game Theory Reader*, London: Routledge.

Reid, M., 2001, 'Teaching genre', workshop at BFI Media Conference, London.

Robertson, R., 1994, *Globalization: Social Theory and Global Culture*, London: Sage.

Roddick, N., 1999, 'Show me the culture', in *Sight and Sound*, 8, no.12, London: BFI.

Ruddock, A., 2007, *Investigating Audiences*, London: Sage.

Saussure, F., 1974, *Course in General Linguistics*, London: Fontana.

Sexton, J. (ed.), 2008, *Music, Sound and Multimedia*, Edinburgh: Edinburgh University Press.

Smith, R., 2008, 'Postmodernism on television: *The Mighty Boosh*', in *Media Magazine* 23. London: English and Media Centre.

Stafford, R., 1997, 'Sex and drugs and rock 'n' roll: innoculate, regulate or celebrate?', in *in the picture* 31, Keighley: itp publications.

—, 2001, *Representation: An Introduction*, London and Keighley: BFI and itp publications.

—, 2002, *British Cinema*, Keighley: itp publications.

—, 2003a, *Audiences: An Introduction*, London and Keighley: BFI and itp publications.

—, 2003b, 'Nowhere to run to? Nowhere to hide for asylum?', in *in the picture* 46, Keighley: itp publications.

—, 2007, 'Global cinema', in *Media Magazine* 21, London: English and Media Centre.

— and Branston, G., 2006, *The Media Student's Book*, 4th edn, London: Routledge.

Strinati, D., 1995, *An Introduction to Theories of Popular Culture*, London: Routledge.

Sweeney, M., 2008, 'TV for the iPod generation', in *The Guardian (Online TV supplement)*, 30 June.

Tagg, J., 1988, *The Burden of Representation*, Basingstoke: Palgrave Macmillan.

Tapscott, D. and Williams, A., 2006, *Wikinomics: How Mass Collaboration Changes Everything*, London: Atlantic Books.

Vint Cerf, V., 2004, 'Vint Cerf, aka the godfather of the net, predicts the end of TV as we know it', interview in *The Guardian*, at www.guardian.co.uk/technology/2007/aug/27/news.google

Wainwright, M., 2008, 'Local heroes', in *The Guardian (Media Guardian)*, 3 March.

Waters, M., 1995, *Globalisation*, London: Routledge.

Watson, J. and Hill, A., 2003, *Dictionary of Media and Communication Studies*, London: Hodder Arnold.

Willis, P., 1990, *Common Culture*, Buckingham: Open University Press.

Winship, J., 1987, *Inside Women's Magazines*, London: River Oram.

Wolf, J. and Perron, B., 2003, *The Video Game Theory Reader*, London: Routledge.

Wright, E., 2002, 'Wong Kar-wai', in *Senses of Cinema*, at www.sensesofcinema.com/contents/directors/02/wong.html

Zizek, S., 2002, 'Welcome to the desert of the real', in Easthope, A. and McGowan, K. (eds), *A Critical and Cultural Theory Reader*, Maidenhead: Open University Press.

Web resources

(All websites listed were accessed in August 2008.)

Apple Tutorials: www.apple.com/ilife/tutorials
Self-explanatory and invaluable for production work.

Audit Bureau of Circulation: www.abc.org.uk
Offers updated circulation figures – essential for institutions and audiences.

BBC iPlayer: www.bbc.co.uk/iplayer
You no longer need to record programmes to help you with television analysis.

BBC online: www.bbc.co.uk
Archives and daily news, an essential site for media research.

BFI Education: www.bfi.org.uk/education
The British Film Institute's education resources are wide-ranging and very useful for moving-image analysis.

Big Film Shorts: www.bigfilmshorts.com
A short film festival.

Bill Thompson: www.andfinally.com
The website and blog of the technology critic – really useful for all things media studies 2.0.

Blogger.com: www.blogger.com
You can create your own blog for free in minutes here.

Brief Encounters: www.brief-encounters.org.uk
Short film festival.

British Board of Film Classification: www.bbfc.co.uk
Regulatory body for UK film, DVD and games.

Campaign for Press and Broadcasting Freedom:
www.cpbf.org.uk
Very useful for research on newspapers.

DepicT!: www.depict.org
Short film audience participation project.

Ehow: www.ehow.com
Photography tutorials.

Emusu: www.emusu.com
West Midlands based digital music distribution website.

English & Media Centre: www.englishandmedia.co.uk
This organisation offers a range of high-quality resources and
INSET events, as well as the wonderful *Media Magazine* and the
MoreMediaMag website, which students can subscribe to through
school or college. They also publish A level media studies student
work, and pay for it!

Facebook: www.facebook.com
Essential social networking site.

Film Birmingham: http://community.filmbirmingham.co.uk
Useful information and funding source.

Film Education: www.filmeducation.org
Excellent film study resources.

First Light Movies: www.firstlightmovies.com
Useful website for short film work.

Flickr: www.flickr.com/photos/cogdog/269039506/
Essential photo-sharing platform, with much more available. This
URL is a guide to annotating images in Flickr.

Game-Culture online journal: www.game-culture.com
Academic journal offering a range of perspectives on video
games.

GameSpot: www.gamespot.com
Offers downloads of video game sequences and a range of other
information about video games.

***Grand Theft Auto* fan site:** www.gta4.net/news/index.php
Excellent resource for a case study on GTA.

Hitwise: www.hitwise.co.uk
Searchable internet usage statistics.

in the picture: www.itpmag.demon.co.uk
A range of very good study materials are available from this site. in
the picture also runs student events in the North of England.

Indymedia UK: www.indymedia.org.uk/
Excellent for research on media access.

Internet Movie Database: www.imdb.com
Find details about any film here.

iTunes U: www.itunesu.com
Shared, free, searchable educational content.

Long Road Sixth Form College media site:
www.longroadmedia.com
Be inspired by some great media students' production work here,
and make full use of the resources that the staff have put up for
general availability.

Machinima for Dummies: www.machinimafordummies.com
Website/blog supporting this introductory book on machinima.

Machinima Premiere: www.mprem.com/e107/news.php
Website devoted to promoting this form of 'fanimation'.

Machinima.com: www.machinima.com
A useful website for machinima.

Making Movies (C4): www.channel4.com/film/makingmovies
Channel 4 online film-making site.

Media and Communications Studies Site:
www.aber.ac.uk/media
Useful academic site.

Media College: www.mediacollege.com
Helpful tutorials for production work.

Media Guardian: www.guardian.co.uk/media
Online version of the Monday supplement. Essential for
institutions and audiences.

Media HE guide: www.he.courses-careers.com/media.htm
Information about careers and degree courses in media.

Media Magazine: www.mediamagazine.org.uk
See English and Media Centre.

Media Week: www.mediaweek.co.uk
Website of trade magazine for general media.

Media UK: www.mediauk.com
Useful for any media research related to UK institutions.

Moviestorm: www.moviestorm.co.uk
Software that you can use for a variety of media studies 2.0
production outcomes.

National Readership Survey: www.nrs.co.uk
Readership figures broken down demographically.

New Media: www.newmediastudies.com
Useful for up-to-date facts and figures, such as global internet
usage statistics.

Newman University College Media Department:
www.newman.ac.uk/CreativeArts/?pg=978
Information about a specific media degree.

Ofcom: www.ofcom.org.uk
The regulatory body for broadcast media and telecommunications.
A very useful Ofcom report on social networking can be found at

www.ofcom.org.uk/advice/media_literacy/medlitpub/medlitpubrss/
socialnetworking

onedotzero: www.onedotzero.com
Arts Council funded computer-generated short films.

Screen International: www.screendaily.com
Website of international trade magazine for the film industry.

September 12th: www.newsgaming.com/games/index12.htm
A counter-cultural political video game simulation.

Serious Games Institute: www.seriousgamesinstitute.co.uk
Very interesting site for virtual worlds.

Skillset: www.skillset.org
The National Training Organisation for broadcasting media. Useful
for employment details.

The Movies: www.lionhead.com/themovies
'We media' film-sharing site, including machinima.

Theory.org: www.theory.org.uk
David Gauntlett's excellent cultural studies and research website.
Check out the media studies 2.0 section.

**Thurston Community College Contemporary British Cinema
blog:** http://tccbritishcinema.blogspot.com
Student blog – very useful for studying British cinema for media
and collective identity.

UCAS website (Media Studies): www.ucas.com
Searchable UCAS site – this is the Media list.

UK Film Council: www.ukfilmcouncil.org.uk
Essential for industry stats, funding and the Digital Shorts project.

UK Press Gazette: www.pressgazette.co.uk
Website of press trade magazine.

VideoJug: www.videojug.com
web 2.0 DIY tutorials.

WeGame: www.wegame.com
A video-capturing application, popular with machinima creators.

Wikimedia: http://en.wikipedia.org/wiki/Wikimedia
The original 'we media' resource.

Word Press: http://wordpress.org/
Alternative to blogger.

YouTube: www.youtube.com
Essential. Needs no explanation.

Index